WRITING THEMES
About
LITERATURE

THIRD EDITION

WRITING THEMES
About
LITERATURE

Edgar V. Roberts

Herbert H. Lehman College,
The City University of New York

PRENTICE-HALL, INC., *Englewood Cliffs, New Jersey*

Library of Congress Cataloging in Publication Data

ROBERTS, EDGAR V
    Writing themes about literature.

    Includes bibliographical references.
    1. English language—Rhetoric. 2. Literature—
Study and teaching. I. Title.
PE1408.R593 1973   801'.95   72-8508
ISBN 0-13-970731-X
ISBN 0-13-970723-9 (pbk.)

PE1408
R593
1973

PRENTICE-HALL INTERNATIONAL, INC., *London*
PRENTICE-HALL OF AUSTRALIA, PTY. LTD., *Sydney*
PRENTICE-HALL OF CANADA, LTD., *Toronto*
PRENTICE-HALL OF INDIA PRIVATE LIMITED, *New Delhi*
PRENTICE-HALL OF JAPAN, INC., *Tokyo*

for Nanette

Acknowledgments

I present the third edition of *Writing Themes About Literature* with continued gratitude to those instructors and students who have used the second and first editions. The confidence shown by the acceptance of these earlier editions leaves me with a sense of awe and responsibility; I hope the present edition will continue to justify that confidence. The changes made in this edition are based on my own experience and thought—my personal copy of the second edition, for instance, is filled with marginal notations made over the years. I have also applied the experience and wisdom of a number of instructors throughout the United States, to all of whom I should like to extend my thanks. I appreciate in particular the comments and suggestions of Professors Randall Brune, Syracuse University; Donald E. Keesey, San Jose State College; and John Robert Keller, University of Portland, Oregon. Also I should like to extend my thanks to William Oliver of Prentice-Hall for his continued interest and good advice. Of the extent of his influence toward the improvement of the third edition, perhaps only I can be aware. A special word of thanks is due Hilda Tauber of Prentice-Hall, whose knowledge of design and spatial arrangement has made the physical appearance of the third edition so gratifying.

Edgar V. Roberts

Contents

To the Instructor

This book provides a tested but fresh approach to writing themes on literary topics. Each assignment is about a phase of literary study that is usually considered in literature and composition courses. The book is different from handbooks, rhetorics, textbooks on poetry and prose, and collections of critical essays because it concentrates on literary problems *as* they bear on writing themes. I have tried to keep in focus the needs of the student with a difficult assignment on a work of literature, and I have emphasized how the assignment may be treated within the confines of a theme. This approach has worked; it has the virtue of making the theoretical discussion of a technique of literary criticism immediately vital to the student. If he can see a literary problem in the light of his necessity to write about it, he is more likely to learn his lesson well. This book might be called a rhetoric of practical criticism for students.

Students need guidance before they write a theme about literature. It is a common complaint among teachers that papers on literary topics written by their students are not really to the point. The reason is simple: the majority of students asked to "analyze the structure of X play, or Y poem, or Z short story" do not really understand what structure is or how to go about analyzing it. Students asked to discuss "point of view in X literary work" are similarly handicapped, and so on through most themes they write about literature. Under these conditions, instructors either waste valuable time explaining theme assignments or else continue to receive inadequate student writing about literature. This book is offered as a solution. Its aim is to free instructors from the drudgery and lost time of making assignments and to help students by explaining and illustrating many approaches to literary technique in order to provide a sound basis for analysis. The practical aim of the book is to aid students in improving their reading and writing skills.

It has been many years since the first edition of *Writing Themes About Literature* was published in 1964. During the interval a number of books on the same general topic have appeared, and their appearance may be interpreted as evidence of a widening use of literature in the composition class, and also as evidence that professional literary criticism does not offer practical guidance for students who are about to write on literary topics. It no longer seems necessary, therefore, to justify the need for the approach found in *Writing Themes About Literature.*

Nevertheless, I should like to re-assert that each of the assignments in this book has been worked out in the classroom and has demonstrably helped students improve their themes about literature. Even though the assignments can stand alone, they may be used as bases for discussions before assignments are due or as supplements to the discussions. Of course, the assignments may be modified if you desire. Flexibility should be the guiding principle in using the book. In their present form, however, the chapters can assist you immeasurably in assigning themes. Too frequently, when assignments are made orally, students lose important directions; many a slip occurs between your words and the student's mind, or notebook. This book is therefore designed to make assignments clear and unequivocal so that no questions should arise late on the night before an assignment is due.

Each chapter is devoted to the consideration of a separate literary approach that creates a problem in composition. The method is to go from precept to example, in the belief that both will benefit a student more than each can separately. The first part of each chapter is thus a discussion of the problems raised by a particular assignment, and is followed by a sample theme that illustrates a way of handling the problems in a theme-length form. The discussions are always focused on critical techniques as they bear on writing assigned to students. The sample themes show how the student himself might handle the various assignments. Although some students will follow the patterns closely, others will wish to adapt the discussions and samples to their own needs. The result in either case should be superior student writing about literature.

The samples have been conceived and written in the belief that the word *imitation* does not need to be preceded by words like *slavish* or *mere.* Much poor composition results from uncertainty about what is expected in the way of imitation. While the student seeks a *form* in which to express himself, he dissipates his energies and does not devote enough attention to a careful study of the literary text that has been assigned. If the student can learn from the discussion of a technical problem and can compare this discussion with a sample theme, he will set his mind working in the right channels and produce superior themes.

For illustrative purposes, the sample themes are slightly long, yet they are within the approximate lengths of many undergraduate themes. Although the various lengths cannot always coincide with the word-limits set by individual instructors, the organization and method of the sample themes should be, and have been demonstrated to be, helpful. These samples should be regarded both as goals toward which the fresh-man can work and as guides for more advanced students.

An additional word seems necessary about the completeness of the various themes, for it has been suggested that an in-class impromptu theme cannot come anywhere near the scope and detail of the samples. The themes are guides, and as such they represent a full treatment, not a minimal treatment, of each of the various topics. If a student is pre-paring his theme outside of class, he can readily approximate the scope of the sample. Even though the samples usually treat an average of three aspects of particular topics, there is nothing to prevent the assign-ing of only one, either for an impromptu theme or for an outside-class theme. If the subject is tone, for example, a student may be asked to discuss only how the tone is shown through selected diction in the work assigned. Similarly, in considering point of view a student might be asked to limit himself only to the influence of point of view on the way characterization is presented in a story, and so on. If the sample themes are taken in this way, as materials to be used in a flexible system of assignments rather than as hard-and-fixed goals from which there can be no variation, then their purpose will have been realized.

In this edition of *Writing Themes About Literature,* the short anthology included in the second edition has been abandoned. The consensus was that the sample themes were sufficiently illustrative with-out the full stories and poems on which they were based, and also that many instructors could find the works readily available elsewhere when needed. However, the present edition still does include those passages from works on which there are analytical and stylistic sample themes, for a close textual study necessitates the availability of the subject of the study.

In several important areas the present edition has been expanded. The Introduction has been revised to include more detail on writing themes, from early note-taking stages, to outlining, to the final draft. It also includes other ideas on the stance of writing that have proved helpful to students. In response to many requests I have restored the "book report" as a separate chapter. As a concluding chapter I have included a discussion on writing about film, after many suggestions that I do so and after extensive deliberation about the wisdom of including, in a book about literature, a chapter on technically non-literary matters such as art and motion-picture photography. The chapter is there for the use of the increasing number of instructors who include film as a part of their courses. Those who do not regard themselves among that number may easily "turne over the leef, and chese another tale." In Appendix C, I have included a section on research themes, emphasizing primarily those aspects of research that differ from the problems of writing posed by the other assignments. In addition, there are a number of other changes that I have made in many other chapters. All these changes embody ideas that have developed during the years I have been teaching theme writing with the second edition of the book, and they also reflect the helpful thoughts of many interested commentators on the book, whom I have thanked in the Acknowledgments.

There are, of course, frequent references throughout the book to many literary works, and it is unlikely that any student will yet have encountered all. Because references cannot be justified unless they clarify, I have tried to make each one self-explanatory and have included enough details to achieve this end. Lack of familiarity with the particular work being discussed therefore should not deter a student from understanding the point of the reference. In addition, I have tried to refer to works that a college student is likely to encounter, if not in freshman English, then in survey or other upper-level courses, or even, let us hope, in his own independent reading. Thus, there are many references to Shakespeare's plays and sonnets, to Joyce's *Portrait of the Artist,* and also to Dreiser's *Sister Carrie.*

The chapters have been arranged in an order of increasing difficulty and technicality. Although a full-year course could be devoted to the progression of themes from beginning to end, you may wish to assign the same type of theme on different works of literature until the students show mastery of that particular type. As has been suggested in reference to the sample themes, you might also base theme assignments on single aspects of any one chapter. In whatever way the assignments are used, they offer a thematic unity to an entire year's course in composition—namely, writing themes about literature. In addition, I believe that the student beyond the freshman year will continue to find the book useful, because the advanced assignments here are as difficult and technical as those for upper-division courses.

The book offers a practical solution to a very real problem in many composition courses. Composition is frequently regarded as a service, for it teaches writing techniques essential in all college work. This need has forced the content in composition to cover too wide a range of subject matter. There can be little unity when students write themes on topics derived from many unrelated fields. All this material is usually taught by instructors who have been prepared by years of literary study. Here is the rub: although you yourself may want to teach literature as a discipline and as a pleasure, you know that your students must have intense work in composition for all their other college work. One purpose of this book is to reconcile this conflict by unifying the course and making it challenging to you as well as to the student. Using the assignments here, you can satisfy the needs of your course by teaching composition while you satisfy your own discipline by teaching literature and literary techniques. Although these assignments attempt to integrate the teaching of literature and composition, many have a residual effect on other courses. For example, the lesson learned from the comparison-contrast theme can be applied to the heredity-environment controversy in a psychology or sociology class; or the themes on tone and point of view will benefit the student of political science who must read and analyze speeches.

An almost foolproof solution to another difficulty in teaching composition—plagiarism—is offered. During the semester, for example, you might assign a theme about the main idea in "The Garden Party," whereas during the next you might assign a theme about the main idea in *Macbeth,* and so on. In colleges and universities where a common syllabus is used in all freshman courses, the same procedure could be followed uniformly. This plan, whereby the form of each theme is preserved while the subject material is changed, could render extinct the traditional fraternity-house theme barrel. The possibilities for varied assignments are virtually endless.

Most important of all, however, is that the book is aimed at the appreciation of good literature. Literature is the property of all; its appeal is to all. But literature, as an art, employs techniques and offers problems that can be understood only through analysis, and analysis means work. The immediate aim is to help the student in this work, but the primary object of the book is to promote the pleasurable study and, finally, the love of literature.

WRITING THEMES
About
LITERATURE

INTRODUCTION

The chapters in this book are theme assignments based on a number of analytical approaches important to the study of literature. The assignments are presented in the hope of fulfilling two goals of English courses: (1) to write good themes, and (2) to assimilate great works of literature into the imagination. Negatively, the book aims to avoid your writing themes that are no more than synopses of a work, vague statements of like or dislike, or biographies of an author. Positively, the book aims to raise your standards of judging literature—and therefore your ability to appreciate good literature—by requiring you to apply, in well-prepared themes, the techniques of good reading.

No educational process is complete until you have applied what you have studied. That is, you have not really learned something until you can talk or write intelligently about it, or until you can apply it to some question or problem. The need for application forces you to recognize where your learning is complete or incomplete, so that you may strengthen your knowledge and supplement your deficiencies. Thus, it is very easy for you to read the chapter in this book on *point of view*, and it is presumably easy for you to read, say, Thomas Mann's story "Mario and the Magician." But your grasp of point of view as a concept will not be complete—nor will your appreciation of at least one aspect of the technical artistry of Mann's story be complete—until you have written about point of view in the story. As you write, you may suddenly discover that you need to go back to the work, to study your notes on it, and to compare them with what you understand about the problem itself. In writing, you must verify facts, grasp their relationship to your topic, develop insights into the value and artistry of the work, and express your understanding in a well-organized and well-developed theme.

After you have finished a number of such themes, you should be able to approach other literary works with more certainty and skill. The more you know and the more you can apply, the more expert and demanding will be your critical taste.

Reading Habits to Develop

It is to be hoped, too, that the need to apply principles of literary study in writing themes will have a positive influence on your reading and study habits. The essential principle of being a good reader is to derive from the reading process a factual basis for emotional responses and intelligent interpretation. Each person goes about reading in his own way, but it stands to reason that a casual reader may often read so superficially that his reactions to a work may be uncertain and unreliable. Preparing to write a theme on a work, however, should create the need for improved reading habits. Accordingly, here are some habits that you should develop and always pursue:

1. Study each reading assignment carefully. Look up all words that you do not know.

2. Make notes on interesting characterizations, events, and ideas. If you like a character, say so, and try to describe what you like about him. If you dislike an idea, say so, and try to describe what you dislike about it.

3. Try to see patterns developing. Make an outline of the story or main idea. What are the conflicts in the story? How are these resolved? Is one force, or side, triumphant? Why? Or is the conflict unresolved? Why?

4. With specific reference to your assignment, take notes on features of style and organization that seem to have an immediate bearing on your topic. If, as you read, you get ideas about how the topic can be handled, write a little paragraph for later use or adaptation. Sometimes you may get good ideas as you are reading. Do not forget them.

5. Do you see anything in the story that you do not understand? Do not forget the difficulty; write a note about it and ask your instructor in class.

6. For further study, underline what seem to be key passages. Write some of these passages on cards, and carry the cards with you. Then, when you are riding or walking to class, or at other times, try to memorize key phrases and sentences and lines of poetry.

What Is Literary Analysis?

Analysis attempts to find truth. The process of analysis is to divide a problem into various parts, for although a whole object is difficult to comprehend at one glance, the parts may be examined more easily, and their natures, functions, and interrelationships may be more fully understood when they are examined one by one. For example, if you have the problem in chemical qualitative analysis of discovering the elements in a chemical solution, you can make only one test on the solution at a time, because if you tried to make all your tests at once you would not be able to control or distinguish your results.

The analysis of literature is based on the same truth. Although the work you have read is an entirety, you must make separate inquiries in order to discover its full meaning and to appreciate it fully. You could not talk about everything in *Paradise Lost* at once, for example, without being guilty of the greatest superficiality. It is better, in your discussion, to narrow the scope of your topic by talking about the diction, epic conventions, theology, or dramatic action. An attempt to discuss everything at once would inevitably distort some things and omit others; results of this sort of investigation are usually wrong or misleading. Truth, however, can emerge only if all possibilities are considered. So your problem in making an analysis is to make the subject small enough so that you can go deeply into it. In other words, you can write a good theme about a relatively restricted part or aspect of the work you have read; but you would find it impossible to discuss everything unless your analysis grew to the length of a book.

A serious objection sometimes arises about literary analysis. Although scientific analysis is necessary, it is said that too much literary analysis "spoils" appreciation of a work, or that in making an analysis, you "murder" literature as you "dissect" it. This objection is not valid, for the purpose of analysis is not to cut up literature like a frog and leave it in pieces. No matter how completely you analyze a work, the work will remain healthy and untouched. For example, the fourth voyage of Swift's *Gulliver's Travels* has not been changed by all the critical essays that have been written about it. But what has changed is what people *see* in the fourth voyage. It used to be that critics saw evidence in the work that Swift hated mankind. More recent analyses of the work have disclosed evidence that Swift was a humanitarian urging men to change their behavior by steering a course between emotion and pure reason. Other analyses have seen the work as an appeal to follow religion. The effect of these and other analyses has been to uncover the work's rich complexity and its basic affirmation of life, and ultimately to raise it in critical esteem. Such is the real business of literary analysis. By pointing out the author's insights into problems of life, and by describing various aspects of his skill, literary analysis aims at the appreciation of literary excellence.

It is therefore important for you to keep literary analysis in perspective: analyzing a work is a *means* toward appreciation and evaluation, not an end in itself. It is an honest attempt by you, the reader, to discover the truth about a work and to base your appreciation on your own thought and discovery, not on a vaguely aesthetic reaction. If you analyze the work to know it better and to like it better, you have really dismissed the entire objection.

Another way to think of literary analysis is that it is a way of fulfilling the objectives of good reading. If you had a choice, you would no doubt prefer to be a good reader rather than a bad reader. But once you have finished the composition and literature classes you are now taking, you may never again have to write a literary analysis. Invariably, however, you will continue reading and also talking about what you have read. You can choose. If you establish good reading habits now, reinforced by the exactness of mind required for writing, then your future discussions will be forever improved. The themes you write today will have a residual impact on your reading habits tomorrow.

As you think about what to put into your theme, remember that literary analysis is a way of getting at the heart of the work. To this end, there are four broad areas that literary analysis explores: (1) meaning, (2) structure, (3) style, and (4) background and influences. There is usually overlapping among these; for example, in writing about point of view, you would emphasize its impact on both meaning and style. In discussing background and influences, you might emphasize how things seemingly extraneous to the work enable a fuller comprehension of meaning, structure, and style. It is always wise, in fact, to emphasize that your particular topic has a relation to the entire work. In this way you are really demonstrating the relationship of literary analysis to literary appreciation, which is the goal implied in all intelligent discourse about literature and in all themes about literature.

WHAT IS A THEME?

As you begin any of the following assignments, you should consider the following ideas about the nature of themes. A theme should be a short, accurate, and forceful presentation of ideas or descriptions, well contrived as a totality or unity. A theme should not ramble in any way, but should be clearly united around a dominating thought or *central idea*. A theme is a brief "mind's full" on any particular subject; that is, it presents and considers the subject in several of its various aspects. The theme cannot cover all aspects, as might a book or a long essay.

There are two basic needs that you must always remember: the first is for a *central idea* or *point*, and the second is for a *clearly ascertainable organization*.

The Central Idea or Point

Themes are so named because throughout the composition called a theme there runs a basic or central idea—a theme—that unifies the paper into a logical whole. On every subject you encounter there should be some dominating idea or mood that will suggest itself to you or one that you will derive from your own intensive concentration. For example, when you look at a room, you might feel that it is cheerful; when you listen to the latest news, you might decide that it is depressing. Were you to write a theme describing the room or another discussing the news, you would have to keep your central idea foremost in your reader's mind *throughout* your theme, or else you would not have a theme.

Whenever you are to write a theme, one of your first objectives should be to decide on a central idea for it. Usually you are working on an assignment that has been given to you by your instructor. With this problem or topic in front of you, your task will be to formulate a central idea that will in effect be your solution to the problem raised by the assignment. As always, study the work carefully and take notes describing the major actions and statements. If the author has stated an idea that he develops in the work, make a note of that. Then, consider your notes with care and try to work up a central idea on the basis of your observations and conclusions.

Let us assume, for the moment, that your assignment has been a "specific problem" theme, the question being: "In Katherine Mansfield's story 'Miss Brill,' is Miss Brill worth your sympathy?" The following material represents a collection of notes and observations that are typical of what you yourself might write when reading the same story in responding to the same assignment. Notice that page numbers are given, so that you could easily go back to the story to refresh your memory of any particular details when you start sketching out your theme.

p. 14   Miss Brill is introduced. She loves her fox fur, and lives alone. She is observant. Goes to the park often. Is familiar with the park and the band there.

p. 15   She eavesdrops, but not with a bad intention. She lives in others, not herself. She recalls a dull conversation of the week before.

p. 16   Many people are in the park, some seeming to be like Miss Brill. She is quiet and harmless, with no more aggression than a bag of popcorn. She is observant. Life seems to have passed her by, and therefore she enjoys looking at the people in the park. She seems to have some sympathy for the lady in the "ermine toque."

pp. 16–17   She discovers a way to identify herself with life in the park: she is an actress, with a part to play. She almost expects that everyone will join the band in singing. She would be a part of the choir.

p. 17   A boy and a girl come. They insult Miss Brill so that she can hear them.

pp. 17–18   She goes home to her small, dark room. She cries. Her emotions have gone from calm, to excitement, to being terribly hurt, to being just about heartbroken. She is like a hurt bird, a helpless victim. She is a nobody, but a nobody I feel sorry for. Her real sorrow results from the fact that the insults make her aware of just how insignificant she is. The only joy she knew is taken away from her. What more would she have? Not much.

In response to the initial question, this set of notes leads naturally to the following central idea: "Miss Brill is worth my sympathy." The conclusion is not startling in any way, and a reader might just as easily have arrived at it without the system of notes. The virtue of the notes, however, is that they will provide a factual basis for developing the theme.

Once you have established the central idea, you should concentrate on the use you can make of it. All the ideas you now bring out about the work you have read will be related to the central idea. When you finally write your theme you should bring out the idea in your introduction, for you should leave your reader in no doubt about what you wish to assert. Also, throughout your theme, you should think about reminding your reader that references to the story or poem, and all conclusions you are drawing, are relevant to the central idea. Anything not related to this point will not belong in your theme.

The need for a central idea will also make you aware of the need for paragraph transitions, because you are proving or showing *one* central idea, not a *number* of ideas. Transitions form bridges to connect one part of the theme with another; having a central idea always in mind makes continuity between paragraphs both essential and natural.

Organizing Your Theme around the Central Idea

The next job is to establish a clearly ascertainable organization for your theme. You should look carefully again at your notes and at any ideas they suggest. It may be that some ideas have already come to you, for quite often a person decides even before he has finished reading the assigned work that he would like to write on such or such a point. Get these ideas down on paper, for when you can see them in front of you, you can work with them. If you try to keep them only in your mind, you may forget them. Here are some raw thoughts on the subject of the story we have been examining, "Miss Brill." They represent a stage beyond the first stage of note taking. Each one of the topics could make separate parts of a possible theme:

1. Miss Brill has little human contact except what she imagines.
2. She is lonely and vulnerable.
3. She doesn't have much insight into her life until the end of the story, or else she is self-indulgent.
4. She is no threat to anyone in the park. Therefore the young people who insult her must be at least somewhat unkind if not vicious.
5. The author views Miss Brill with apparent understanding and kindness, but she underplays the ending.
6. If Miss Brill can keep people at a distance, she seems to function fairly well. When they get close, they hurt her.

These are six thoughts on the story. There might be more, or fewer. Working with these thoughts, however, together with others that may occur as he goes along, the writer should create topics that will serve as the basis for developing the entire theme. Let us say that he chooses number 4 as a topic, then number 2, and then number 5. These topics may be entitled: (4) harmlessness, (2) loneliness and vulnerability, and (5) artistic treatment. If he changes these numbers to an order 1, 2, and 3, he now has the topics for a potential thesis sentence and an outline.

THE THESIS SENTENCE

A thesis sentence is like an itinerary of a journey, a plan of action. Just as few people would ever think of taking a trip before planning a route, so no one should start to write before he has a clear notion of the topics he will consider. The thesis sentence does just that; it connects the central idea and the plan of topics for them. The first thing to do, then, is to put the central idea together with the topics, in order to plan the form of the thesis sentence. Again, let us suppose that our writer uses the materials that have been developed thus far:

CENTRAL IDEA	TOPICS
Miss Brill is worth my sympathy.	1. harmlessness
	2. loneliness and vulnerability
	3. artistic treatment

From this arrangement he can now write the following thesis sentence:

> My feeling of her worthiness results from her harmlessness, from her loneliness and vulnerability, and from Katherine Mansfield's skillful treatment of her plight.

THE TOPIC SENTENCE

Just as the entire theme is to be organized around the thesis sentence, each of the paragraphs should be organized around a *topic sentence*. The topic sentences are derived, grammatically speaking, from the topics in the predicate of the thesis sentence. Thus, the first topic will be Miss Brill's harmlessness. But something more must be done than just announcing the topic; the topic must be shown to have a bearing on the central idea. Let us suppose that the original raw thought can be brought back into consideration here, so that our writer can create the following topic sentence:

> Her harmlessness [topic] makes the hurt done to her seem unjustified and unnecessarily cruel [connecting topic to central idea].

Notice that the words "unjustified" and "unnecessarily" indicate a judgment by the writer which is related to his conclusion that Miss Brill is worthy of his sympathy. With such a judgment the writer could go ahead to develop a paragraph in which he might develop an argument like this one: "Unjustified and unnecessary hurt done to anyone makes me defensive and sympathetic to the person receiving the hurt." In such a way the topic sentence eventually enables the writer to expand upon the central idea, and at the same time it channels his thoughts into a development related to the central idea.

The writer should follow the same process in forming his other topic sentences, so that when he finishes them he can put them together in the form of an outline. The particular type of outline that we have been developing here is the "analytical sentence outline." This type requires (1) that the central idea is modified so that it can be used in the grammatical subject of the thesis sentence, (2) that the topics in the predicate of the thesis sentence become the subjects of the topic sentences, and (3) that the predicates of the topic sentences will have a clear bearing on the central idea. Such a plan will ensure that the writer always is thinking within a clear, definite pattern of organization.

As an optional final part of the outline, there may be a concluding or summarizing sentence, which should generally govern the conclusion of your paper. Because this sentence is not derived from the predicate of the thesis sentence, it is technically independent of the material to be included in the body of your theme. But it is a part of the thematic organization, and hence should bear a close relationship to the central idea. It may represent a summary of some of the leading ideas; it may suggest an evaluation or a criticism of some of these ideas; it may also suggest further avenues of exploration that you did not examine in the body of the theme.

As you plan your outline, and start to write, bear in mind that writing is in many ways a process of discovery. New ideas often come as you write. If these ideas do not conform to your original plan, change the plan to accommodate them.

When completed, the analytical sentence outline should have the following appearance. Again, we use as material the subject of Miss Brill.

THEME: *Miss Brill as a Sympathetic Character*

Paragraph 1   INTRODUCTION containing CENTRAL IDEA and THESIS SENTENCE

CENTRAL IDEA: Miss Brill is worth my sympathy.

THESIS SENTENCE: My feeling of her worthiness results from her harmlessness, from her loneliness and vulnerability, and from Katherine Mansfield's skillful treatment of her plight.

BODY containing three TOPIC SENTENCES

Paragraph 2   TOPIC SENTENCE: Her harmlessness makes the hurt done to her seem unjustified and unnecessarily cruel.

Paragraph 3   TOPIC SENTENCE: Her loneliness and vulnerability make her pitiable.

Paragraph 4   TOPIC SENTENCE: Katherine Mansfield's skillful treatment of Miss Brill's plight encourages the right proportion of sympathy.

CONCLUSION

Paragraph 5   TOPIC SENTENCE: Sympathy for Miss Brill is the dominant effect of the story.

By the time you have created an outline like this one, or any outline, you will have been thinking and organizing for a considerable time, and you should be well prepared to write your theme. The outline should now be put into operation. In your introduction you should include both the central idea and the thesis sentence. The various topic sentences will belong at the beginnings of the paragraphs in the body of your theme. You may, of course, use the sentences just as they are, or you may, as you become more experienced as a writer, wish to modify them in order to make them seem less obvious.* "It is the purpose of art," said one very wise person, " to hide art." If the machinery of your themes is creaky at first, your experience and development may eventually oil it and allow it to run smoothly and noiselessly.

The Sample Theme

So that you may see more clearly the relationship of the outline and the theme, the following theme is based on the material we have been discussing thus far. It is drawn mainly from the ideas contained in the notes, and is wholly dependent for its structure on the analytical sentence outline.

Miss Brill as a Sympathetic Character

To raise the question of whether Miss Brill, of Katherine Mansfield's story "Miss Brill," is sympathetic is to imply that there are reasons for which a reader may be put off by her. I can see a number of reasons. Objectively, Miss Brill is an odd person, one of the many scarecrows sitting on the park benches. She is not communicative; she does not lead an exciting or interesting life; she is simple and almost verges on stupidity; and finally, she is self-indulgent to the point of being almost unconnected with reality. Despite these bad qualities, I believe that she is worth my sympathy.

My feeling results from her harmless character, from her loneliness and vulnerability, and from Miss Mansfield's skillful treatment of her plight.   **THESIS SENTENCE**

Miss Brill's harmlessness makes the hurt done to her by the young couple seem unjustified and unnecessarily cruel. Her manner, her   **TOPIC SENTENCE**
thoughts, and her activities all make a person feel that she is to be let alone and tolerated, but never to be harmed. If she eavesdrops on people in the park, the simple solution would be for the offended people to move to another bench, perhaps with a glare on their

---

* In the sample themes of Chapters 1–4, the central ideas and the thesis and topic sentences are italicized to help you identify them.

faces but with no other expression of anger toward her. She does not mistreat anyone, or lure any small children to their destruction. Nor could she do so. In view of these facts, the hurt done her by the young couple is far beyond anything she deserves. It seems almost calculated to hurt her in the worst possible way. Even if one did not like Miss Brill, his heart would have to go out to her as a result of the insults. Mine does.

She is, then, no threat to anyone, and she is made to seem even more pitiable because of her loneliness and vulnerability. The thought of **TOPIC SENTENCE** this lone creature imagining herself part of the park scene, and almost believing that everyone in the park will join the band in singing, makes one realize just how solitary she is. She has almost nothing. The best one could claim for her, even by stretching the imagination, is that she is a nobody. She has no one, and no one cares. All of her joy, pathetic as it is, hangs from the very thin thread of her imagination. With only that she is defenseless and alone, like a hurt bird. There can be no delight, but only sorrow, when the defenseless are destroyed.

This is not to say that the story is a sentimental one, for Katherine Mansfield's skillful treatment of Miss Brill's plight encourages exactly the right proportion of sympathy. Particularly crucial in this **TOPIC SENTENCE** regard is the treatment of Miss Brill when she returns home after the insults. She does not buy her honeycake, but rushes home. As she puts away her fur she is crying, but Katherine Mansfield does not overdo her tears. Instead she makes the reader figure out what is happening. This brief moment, when the reader ponders just whom Miss Brill hears crying, is enough to keep everything from going overboard. Also, the story ends abruptly at this point, with the reader being left to imagine the life that Miss Brill will have afterward, with no more of the joys she had experienced before the insults. There is no indulgence, but there is great sympathy here.

Sympathy, rather than deep sorrow, is the major effect of the story. Miss Brill is shown realistically as a person of solitude and harmlessness. Her faults are at worst those of an eccentric, and her happiness is marginal and fleeting. If a person has many things and loses one of them, the loss causes little sympathy or grief. But if he has only one thing, and that is taken from him, as joy is stolen from Miss Brill, then that person has nothing. Is Miss Brill worthy of my sympathy? She most certainly is.

The Main Problem in Writing

Once you have understood and applied the principles of thematic development and thesis-sentence organization, you will still be faced with the problem of how to write well. There is little difficulty in recognizing superior examples of student writing when you see them, but there is usually much difficulty in understanding precisely what constitutes the superiority. For this reason the most difficult and perplexing questions you will ask as you write are these: (1) "How can I improve my writing?" or (2) "If I got a *C* on my last paper, why wasn't the grade a *B* or an *A*? How can I improve my grades?" These questions are really both the same, with a different emphasis. Your concern is with improvement.

As an undergraduate, you should not be offended if you are told that you probably have not yet acquired a great deal of knowledge and understanding of literature. Your mind is growing, and it still has many facts to assimilate and digest. As you accumulate these facts and develop your understanding, you will find that ease of expression will also develop. But at the moment your thoughts about literature might be expressed thus: "When I first read a work, I have a hard time following it. Yet when my instructor explains it, my understanding is greatly increased. I would like to develop the ability to understand the work without my instructor's help. How can I succeed in this aim? How can I become an independent reader?"

In answer, you started trying to overcome the problem the day you enrolled in college. This action testifies to your desire to improve. Bear in mind also that education is a process, and that what baffled you as a freshman may seem child's play when you are a junior or senior. But in the meantime you want to know how to assist growth. There is no magic answer, no shortcut to knowledge. You must work constantly to develop the habits of the good reader described earlier.

The second major obstacle to writing well is inexperience. As a result, when you start you may be tempted simply to write a synopsis or précis of the story or argument. A synopsis of a work is inadequate for your themes, mainly because a synopsis does not indicate real understanding.

Your education is aimed first at acquiring knowledge and second at digesting and using knowledge. A synopsis indicates only that you have read the material. Therefore if you wish to show your understanding, you must do something more—you must show that you can put what you have read into a meaningful pattern.

The theme assignments in this book are designed to help you do just that. As you work out each assignment, you will be dealing with particular methods of assimilating and using knowledge. In only one assignment are you asked to provide a synopsis or précis: this is the *summary theme*, but even here, the synopsis is relevant only if it can be related to your central idea. The summary theme (Chapter 1) therefore represents more thought and organization than does a synopsis. In all the other assignments in this book you are asked to concentrate on a particular point raised in the study of literature. In every case it is important that you read and follow the work, but it is more important that you show you understand the work.

There are a number of ways in which you may set up patterns of development that can assist you in showing your understanding. One way is to make a deliberate point of referring to events or statements in the work in a reverse order. Talk about the conclusion first before you refer to anything that went before it. Or you may wish to refer to something in the middle of the work first. But rarely if ever refer first to the opening of the work. Invariably, beginning your discussion with references to parts of the work other than the beginning will almost force you to discuss your understanding of the work rather than to summarize events, and thus you will have broken the grip of being just a story re-teller. If you look back at the second paragraph of the sample theme on "Miss Brill," you will see that this technique has been used. One of the last events in the story, an occasion in which Miss Brill is insulted by a young couple, is the main reference material of that paragraph, yet the paragraph is the first in the body of the theme. You can see that the technique, if you were to adopt it, would permit you to impose your own organization on your theme and would free you from the organization of the work being analyzed.

Another important method is to consider the reader for whom you are writing your theme. Imagine that you are writing to *another student like yourself, a student who has read the assigned work but who has not thought very much about it.* You can immediately see what you would write for such a mythical reader. He knows the events or has followed the thread of the argument. He knows who says what and when it is said. As a result, you do not need to tell this reader about everything that goes on, but should regard your role as that of an explainer or interpreter. Tell him what things mean, but *do not tell him the things that happen.*

To look at the situation in still another way, you may have read stories and novels about Sherlock Holmes and Dr. Watson. Holmes always points out to Watson that all the facts are available to both of them, but that, though Watson sees, he does not observe. Your role is like that of Holmes, explaining and interpreting facts, and drawing conclusions that Dr. Watson has been unable to draw for himself. Once again, if you look back at the sample theme on "Miss Brill," you will notice that everywhere *the assumption has been made that the reader has read the story already*. References to the story are thus made primarily to remind the reader of something he already knows, but *the principal emphasis of the theme is to draw conclusions and develop arguments.*

USING LITERARY MATERIAL AS EVIDENCE

The analogy with Sherlock Holmes should remind you that whenever you write, on any topic, you are in a position much like that of a detective using clues as evidence for building up a case, and also like that of a lawyer using evidence as support for arguments. If you argue in favor of securing a greater voice for students in college government, for example, you would introduce evidence in support of your claims, such as past successes with student government, increased maturity of modern-day students, the constitutional amendment granting 18-year-olds the right to vote, and so on. Writing about literature requires evidence just like any other kind of writing. *For practical purposes only,* when you are writing a theme, you may conveniently regard the work assigned as evidence for your arguments. You should make references to the work not for their own sakes but as a part of the logical development of your own discourse. Your objective is to persuade your reader of your own knowledge and reasonableness, just as the lawyer attempts to persuade a jury of the reasonableness of his arguments.

The whole question of the use of evidence is a far-reaching one. Students of law spend years studying proper uses of evidence. Logicians have devised the system of syllogisms and inductive reasoning to regulate the use of evidence. It would not be logical, for example, to conclude from Shakespeare's play *Macbeth* that Macbeth behaves like a true friend and great king. His murders, his rages, and his pangs of guilty conscience form evidence that makes this conclusion absurd. A more difficult problem in evidence concerns Hamlet, one of the most universally admired of Shakespeare's characters. At the end of the play, after Hamlet has died, it is claimed that he would have made a great king had he inherited the throne of Denmark. But even here there is evidence that has been used as a counter-claim: some critics have asserted that Hamlet is too introspective, too hesitant, to have carried out the action necessary for being a great king. But other critics have pointed out specific instances in which Hamlet does act, and have cited other evidence to explain why he hesitates. How should the apparently contradictory evidence be reconciled? As yet, there is no consensus on this question.

To see how evidence may be used as part of a theme, let us refer once again to the sample theme on "Miss Brill." The fourth paragraph is about how Katherine Mansfield's artistic skill keeps a balance in the reader's sympathy for Miss Brill. The writer uses the conclusion of the story as the main evidence in his argument. The event at the conclusion is this: Miss Brill returns to her room and thinks she hears "something crying," but the reader immediately perceives that Miss Brill herself is the one crying. Notice again how the paragraph from the sample theme uses this rather simple and brief episode as evidence. It is clear that the writer's argument is more important to him than a description of the episode. In this sense, the literary work has become evidence for argument.

It is vital to use evidence properly if you wish your reader to follow your ideas. Let us look briefly at two examples to see how writing can be made better if the writer truly considers the needs of his reader. These examples are from themes analyzing Thomas Hardy's story "The Three Strangers."

1	2
After a short lapse of time, the second stranger enters to seek shelter from the rain. He is a rather full-fleshed man dressed in gray, with signs on his face of drinking too much. He tells the guests that he is en route to Casterbridge. He likes to drink, exhausting the large mug full of mead that is offered to him, and quickly demanding more, which makes Shepherd Fennel's wife extremely angry. With the mead going to his head and making him drunk, he relates his occupation by singing a song in the form of a riddle. This second stranger is a hangman who is supposed to hang a man in Casterbridge for stealing a sheep. As he reveals his occupation, stanza by stanza, an increasing air of dismay is cast over the guests. They are horrified by the hangman's description of his job, but he makes a big joke about all the grim details, such as making a mark on the necks of his "customers" and sending them to a "far countree."	Hardy uses the second stranger—the hangman—to produce sympathy for the shepherds and distrust of the law. By giving the hangman a selfish thirst for mead, which drains some of the Fennels's meager supply, Hardy justifies Mrs. Fennel's anger and anxiety. An even greater cause for anxiety than this personal arrogance is the harsh legal oppression that the hangman represents to the shepherds. Indeed, the shepherds were already sympathetic to the plight of Summers, the first stranger (whose crime seems rewardable, not punishable), but the domineering manner of the hangman clearly makes them go beyond just sympathy. They silently decide to oppose the law by hiding Summers. Hardy thus makes their obstructionism during the later manhunt seem right and reasonable. Perhaps he has stacked the deck against the law here, but he does so to make the reader admire the shepherd folk. In this plan, the hangman's obnoxiousness is essential.

Although the first example has more words than the second (174 words in column 1, 151 in column 2), it is not adequate, for it shows that the writer felt only the obligation to re-tell the story. The paragraph is cluttered with details and it contains no conclusions and no observations. If you had read the story, the paragraph would not provide you with a single piece of new information, and absolutely no help at all in understanding the story. The writer did not have to think much in order to write the paragraph. On the other hand, the second column is responsive to the reader's needs, and it required a good deal of thought to write. Phrases like "Hardy thus makes" and "In this plan" show that the writer of the second theme has assumed that the reader knows the details of the story and now wants help in interpretation. Column 2 therefore leads the reader into a pattern of thought that may not have occurred to him when he was reading the story. In effect, column 2 brings evidence to bear on a point and excludes all irrelevant details; column 1 provides nothing more than raw, undirected evidence.

The answer to that difficult question about how to turn *C* writing into *A* writing is to be found in the comparison of the two columns. Besides using English correctly, the superior writer always allows his mind to play upon the materials. He always tries to give his reader the results of his thoughts. He dares to trust his responses and is not afraid to make judgments about the literary work he is considering. His principal aim in referring to events in a work is to develop his own thematic pattern. Observe this quality again by comparing two sentences which deal with the same details from the story:

1	2
He likes to drink, exhausting the large mug full of mead that is offered to him, and quickly demanding more, which makes Shepherd Fennel's wife extremely angry.	By giving the hangman a selfish thirst for mead, which drains some of the Fennels's meager supply, Hardy justifies Mrs. Fennel's anger and anxiety.

Sentence 1 is detailed but no more. Sentence 2 links the details as a pattern of cause and effect within the author's artistic purpose. Notice the words "By giving" and "Hardy justifies." These indicate the writer's *use* of the facts to which he is referring. There are many qualities in good writing, but perhaps the most important is the way in which the writer uses known facts as evidence in a pattern of thought that is new and original. Always try to achieve this quality in all your writing about literature.

KEEPING TO YOUR POINT

Whenever you write a theme about literature, then, you must pay great attention to the proper organization and to the proper use of references to the work assigned. As you write, you should try constantly to keep your material unified, for should you go off on a tangent, you are following the material rather than leading it. The easiest thing in the world to do is to start with your point, but then to wander off into a re-telling of events or ideas. Once again, resist the tendency to be a narrator rather than an interpreter. If you can stick to your point, you will be master and not slave.

Let us look at another example. The following paragraph is taken from a theme on the "Idea of Personal Responsibility in Homer's *The Odyssey*." This is the third paragraph; the writer has stated his thematic purposes in the first paragraph, and in the second has shown that various characters in *The Odyssey* believe that men are responsible for their actions and must bear the consequences. In the third paragraph he writes:

> More forcefully significant than these statements of the idea is the way it is demonstrated in the actions of the characters in the epic. Odysseus, the hero, is the prime example. Entrapped by Polyphemus (the son of Poseidon the Earth-Shaker by the nymph Thoosa) and threatened with death, Odysseus in desperation puts out the eye of his captor, who then begs his father Poseidon for vengeance. Answering his son's anguished curse, Poseidon frustrates Odysseus at every turn in the voyage back to Ithaca, and forces him to wander for ten years before reaching home.

This paragraph shows how easily a person may be diverted from his objective in writing. The first sentence adequately states that the idea is to be demonstrated in the actions of the epic. That the remainder of the paragraph concentrates on Odysseus is no flaw, because the writer concentrates on other characters in following paragraphs. The flaw is that the material about Odysseus does not go beyond mere synopsis; it does not come to grips with the announced topic of personal responsibility; it does not indicate understanding. The material may be relevant to the topic, but the writer does not point out its relevance. The writer began well, but he did not show how the material illustrates his point, and thus the paragraph is bad. Remember always that in expository writing you should not rely on making your meaning clear simply by implication; you must make all relationships explicitly clear.

Let us see how this problem can be solved. If the ideal paragraph could be schematized with line drawings, we might say that the paragraph's topic should be a straight line, moving toward and reaching a specific goal (explicit meaning), with an exemplifying line moving away from the straight line briefly in order to bring in evidence, but returning to the line after each new fact in order to demonstrate the relevance of this fact. Thus, the ideal scheme would look like this:

Notice that the exemplifying line, or the example or the documenting line, always returns to the topic line. A scheme for the paragraph on *The Odyssey*, however, would look like this:

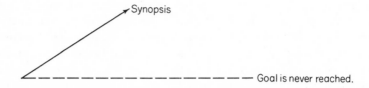

How might this paragraph be improved? The best way is to reintroduce the topic again and again throughout the paragraph in order to keep reminding the reader of the relevance of the exemplifying material. Each time you mention the topic you are bringing yourself back to the line or back to the point, and this practice should prevail no matter what the topic. If you are analyzing *tone*, for example, you should keep pointing out the relevance of your material to the tone of the work, and the same applies to *structure* or whatever aspect of literature you are studying. According to this principle, we might revise the paragraph on *The Odyssey* as follows, keeping as much of the original wording as we can. (Parts of sentences stressing the relationship of the examples to the topic of the paragraph are italicized.)

> More forcefully significant than these statements of the idea is the way it is demonstrated in the actions of the characters in the epic. Odysseus, the hero, is the prime example. When he is entrapped and threatened with death by Polyphemus (the son of Poseidon the Earth-Shaker by the nymph Thoosa), Odysseus in desperation puts out the eye of his captor. Though his action is justifiable on grounds of self-preservation *he must, according to the main idea, suffer the consequences.* Polyphemus begs his father Poseidon for vengeance. Poseidon hears, *and accordingly this god becomes the means of enforcing Odysseus' punishment,* since Odysseus, in injuring the god's son, has insulted the god. The Ithacan king's ten years of frustration and exile are therefore not caused by whimsy; *they are punishment for his own action. Here the idea of personal responsibility is shown with a vengeance;* despite the extenuating circumstances, *the epic makes clear that characters must answer for their acts.*

The paragraph has been lengthened and improved. You might object that if all your paragraphs were lengthened in this way your theme would grow too long. The answer to this objection is that it is better to develop a few topics fully than many scantily. Such revision might require you to throw away some of your topics or else to incorporate them as subpoints in the topics you keep. This process can only improve your theme. But the result of greater length here is that the exemplifying detail points toward the topic, and the paragraph reaches its goal.

The same need for sticking to your point is true of your entire theme, for you will not be successful unless you have thoroughly convinced your reader that your central idea is valid or true. The two following themes should illustrate this truth. The theme on the left is only rudimentary. The writer suggests at the outset that he will explore the harm the parents cause their children in the two plays being compared. Although occasionally he gets back to this point, the theme rarely gets above the level of synopsis. The theme in the right-hand column is superior because the writer announces his central idea and pursues it throughout. As in the earlier paragraph, those parts of the following themes that emphasize the central idea will be italicized. The type of theme is *comparison-contrast* (Chapter 9), and the assignment was made specifically on Arthur Miller's *All My Sons* and Tennessee Williams's *The Glass Menagerie*.

THEME 1	THEME 2
A Comparison of Two Plays	*The Destruction of Children by Parents in Two Plays*

Miller's *All My Sons* and Williams's *The Glass Menagerie* are the two plays being compared. Both plays have the family as the center around which the characters revolve. In both families, *the parents hurt the children*. Miller writes of a well-off, factory-owning family; Williams of a low-class family.

In both Miller's *All My Sons* and Williams's *The Glass Menagerie*, the family is the center of the action. Miller's family is well off; Williams's is lower class. This difference is not material in view of the fact that both dramatists demonstrate the *destructive effects of parents upon children*, regardless of class. It is true that these parents were once children themselves, and that presumably they were recipients of *equally destructive effects from their parents*. This element gives both plays direct, universal appeal: that is, both plays dramatize the process by which our society is *generally hurt by what*, to the dramatists, *are outmoded economic and social values, transmitted by parents to children*. The fathers, mothers, and children will be discussed in that order.

The comparison of the families may start with the fathers. Joe Keller, of *All My Sons*, is an ambitious, conniving, and good businessman. He allows a defective shipment to go through because, as he says, he could not let forty years' work go down the drain. He also says to Chris that he did what he did because he wanted Chris to have something for his fu-

The fathers in both plays seem to be the ones *first to do hurt*, because they both lack responsibility and social conscience. Joe Keller is shown as ambitious and conniving—qualities which in America go to form the good businessman. The Wingfield father, never seen except in portrait but only described, is a drifter and worthless drunkard. *Both are irre-*

ture, a business. Not much is mentioned of the father in *The Glass Menagerie*, but from what is given the reader, we picture him as a worthless drunkard. He had no purpose in life and consequently was a poor provider for his family. One should not condone Keller for what he did, but at least Keller had some initiative and foresight whereas the Wingfield father had nothing. *Both fathers hurt their children.*

Next we can compare the mothers in the two works. In Miller's play the mother is a sensitive, unyielding, and loving person. It is she who stands firm in her belief that Larry is still living. By doing this she prevents her other son Chris from marrying Ann. In a sense, she is looking out for her son's interest because if Larry was ever to return, chaos would result. Amanda, the mother of *The Glass Menagerie*, is a very sociable person. Her daughter is unbelievably shy. The mother attempts to help her daughter. She does, also, what she thinks will be in the interests of her daughter. Therefore she concludes that marriage is the answer to Laura's problems. We can see how two different mothers with the same goals— happiness for their children—*achieve the opposite results because they fail to attend to the needs and desires of their children.*

sponsible. Joe's unscrupulousness causes the death of twenty-one boys who flew in airplanes made defective by his deliberate negligence. The Wingfield father simply *abandons his family.* The trouble is that both characters are simply pawns in a game much larger than themselves. Joe's defense of his action, for example, makes good sense. *His motives are not bad* from a short-term point of view. He really did not want to let forty years of work go down the drain, and he really did want to give Chris (and Larry) a thriving business. His means, however, *were selfish and hurtful—primarily economic rather than human and loving*—just as the Wingfield father causes his family *untold damage* by abandoning them for a life that to many might seem very pleasant.

While less *creators of hurt* than *agents of it,* the mothers in both families also *cause much damage.* Kate Keller, while sensitive and unyielding, is nevertheless loving. Her firm belief that her son Larry is still alive is caused, we ultimately learn, by a defense against her awareness of *Joe's great crime,* but *the end result is the unhappiness of her son Chris.* Her love is mixed with a *deliberately unreal outlook.* While superficially different from Kate, *Amanda is similarly destructive.* Attempting to look out for the interests of her daughter, she tries to make a carbon copy of herself, even though her background is dead as far as her daughter is concerned. Her failure is that she does not see her daughter as an individual with separate and distinct needs. Laura's reaction to her mother's manipulation is *withdrawal,* but Amanda cannot see any *harmful effect.* Both mothers, desiring to make their children happy, *produce the same unhappy results.*

THEME 1

Lastly, the children will be compared. Chris is both an idealistic as well as realistic person. He tries to think the best of people, as he does with his father. When he finds out otherwise, he is *terribly shocked and disappointed.* Much the same thing happens when Laura finds out that Jim is going to get married; her reaction is one of *disappointment and withdrawal.* Just when she has finally gotten socially involved with someone, he leaves. So we see how both children have to put up with *disappointments;* one finds out his father is a murderer, while the other loses the first person she ever loved.

Through comparing and contrasting the members of each family we have been able to see how these families are different and how they are similar. In both *families, however, the children are hurt by well-intentioned* but foolish parents.

THEME 2

The full effects of *these destructive parents are felt by the children.* Larry, we learn, *has killed himself because of shame for his father's deed.* Chris, we see demonstrated, *is shocked, angered, and embittered by it. Laura is disappointed,* ostensibly by hearing that Jim is going to marry another, but ultimately by having been brought up *without a father and with her mentally disjointed mother.* Tom simply leaves, but he remembers his mother objectively and his father condescendingly. *While a bang marks the destruction* in *All My Sons,* one might say that a sigh— or a whimper—marks it in *The Glass Menagerie.* But the effects of the parents on the children, and beyond that of the society on its members, are the same—*destruction and decay.*

Comparing and contrasting the two families in this way finally brings out their basic similarities. The parents in both families are interesting and not particularly abnormal. In both groups of parents there are strongly contrasting values which contend to *the destruction of children.* In the Kellers it is *money against humanity.* In the Wingfields it is *social position against individuality.* In both families *everyone really loses,* because neither family is clearly enough committed to the idea of humanity and individuality. Though the relevance of this theme to society at large has been only mentioned, the implication in both plays is that our society must make a commitment to human and individual values if it is to survive. If people do not make this commitment, *the destructive patterns in the Keller and Wingfield families will continue.*

There is another reason for the superiority of the theme on the right. In addition to sticking to the point, the writer in a number of spots suggests that the harmful influences of the parents are related to impractical or unjust economic values. At the end, the writer interprets his central idea by stating that society at large needs to commit itself to human values. In short, *the writer has made his idea grow.* He has not simply exemplified it but has tried to delve into some of its implications. You should be trying, always, to develop your central ideas in a similar way. Admittedly, in a short theme you will be able to move only a short distance with an idea, but you should never be satisfied to leave an idea exactly where you find it. Nurture it and make it grow. Constantly adhere to your topic and constantly develop it.

ACCURATE AND FORCEFUL LANGUAGE

It would be premature to conclude a section on good writing without stating that the best writing has a quality of accuracy, force, and insight. Quite often the first products of our minds are rather weak, and they need to be re-thought, re-cast, and re-worded. Sometimes this process cannot be carried out immediately, for it may take days or even weeks for us to gain objectivity about what we say. As a student you usually do not have that kind of time, and thus you must acquire the habit of challenging your own statements almost as soon as you write them. Ask yourself whether they really mean what you want, or if you can make a stronger statement than you have.

As an example, consider the following statement, a central idea about E. M. Forster's short story "The Machine Stops," an allegory about a future world in which people are dependent completely on machinery but perish when the machinery breaks down:

> The central idea of this story is that because of the machine and its marvelous powers, the people place their total dependence on it.

This central idea could not carry you very far if you were writing a theme based on it. But try to re-state and to strengthen the essential material in the sentence. Two possibilities are as follows:

1. Forster shows that man, by accepting the machine and by becoming hostile to Nature, has alienated himself from his environment and is therefore responsible for his own destruction.
2. Forster shows that the pursuit of ideas and technology to the exclusion of Nature has led man to destroy himself.

Either of these two sentences would be more helpful as a statement of a central idea than the first example.

It is also true that sometimes, in seeking to say something, we wind up saying nothing. Here are two sentences from themes about Robert Frost's "Stopping by Woods on a Snowy Evening."

1. It seems as though the author's anticipation of meeting with death causes him to respond as he does in the poem.

2. This incident, although it may seem trivial or unimportant, has substantial significance in the creation of his poem; by this I mean the incident which occurred is essentially what the poem is all about.

The vagueness of sentences like these must be resisted. A sentence should go somewhere, and not end up in limbo the way these do. The first sentence is satisfactory enough up to the verb, but then it falls apart completely. If Frost has created a response for the speaker in the poem, it is best to describe *what* that response is rather than to state simply that there *is* a response. A more forceful restatement of the first sentence may thus be, "It seems as though the author's anticipation of meeting with death causes him to think about the need to meet his present responsibilities." With this revision, the writer could go on to a consideration of the meaning of Frost's final stanza and could relate the ideas there to the events and ideas described in the first part of the poem. Without the revision, it is not clear where the writer would go.

The second sentence is so vague that it is virtually hopeless. It belongs in that category of statement that confuses rather than informs. Essentially, such sentences hint at an idea and claim importance for it, but they never directly define what that idea is. If we adopt the principle that it is always better to name the specific things we are talking about, however, perhaps the second sentence could be revised as follows:

Although stopping by the woods to watch the snow fall may seem trivial or insignificant, the incident causes the poet to meditate on beauty and responsibility; the important thoughts in the poem thus grow from the simplest of events.

When you write your own sentences, you might test them in a similar way. Are you referring to an idea? State the idea directly. Are you mentioning a response or impression? Do not say simply, "The poem left me with a definite impression," but describe the impression, such as, "The poem left me with an impression of sympathy," or "of understanding of the hard lot of the migrant farmer," or of whatever the impression was. Similarly, do not rest with a statement like "I found this story interesting," but try to describe what was interesting and why it was interesting. If you always confront your impressions and responses by trying to name them and to pin them down, your sentences should take on exactness and force. Naturally, your instructor will probably tell you whatever you have accomplished or failed to accomplish. Good writing habits that you develop from his criticisms of your work, and from your discussions with him, will help you to write more forcefully and accurately.

Whenever you write a theme, then, keep these ideas in mind. Keep returning to the point you wish to make; regard the material of the work you have read as evidence to substantiate your arguments, not as material to be described as a synopsis or précis. Keep demonstrating that all exemplifying detail is relevant to your main point. Keep trying to develop your topic; make it bigger than it was when you began writing. Constantly keep trying to make your statements accurate and forceful. If you observe these precepts, you should be well on the way toward handling any of the following theme assignments successfully.

THE SUMMARY THEME

CHAPTER

1

The summary theme presents a number of important objectives for you as you begin writing themes about literature. First, you should show in the theme that you are able to follow intelligently and to understand the actions and dialogue in a literary work. Second, you should demonstrate your awareness that in literature, as in life, some actions and statements are more significant than others. Third, you should attempt to show that the events in the work do not occur haphazardly but take place as part of a pattern or form. If you can achieve the first objective in your theme, you have reached a plane, a platform, of understanding. If you can achieve the second and third objectives, you will demonstrate that you possess the insight and alertness needed for putting things together, for creating the new awarenesses that characterize the best thinking and writing.

The summary theme therefore represents a building block for the other kinds of themes to follow. Before you write a theme about the structure of a poem or a novel, for example, you must be sure that you understand the story and the main idea behind it and also that you can describe the relation of one part of the work to the others. If you cannot perform these basic tasks of the disciplined reader, everything you say about structure will be inaccurate or misleading. In short, writing a summary theme anticipates all the other writing about literature that you will do.

The first requirement for writing a summary theme is to read the assigned work carefully: be sure to take notes on the important events or ideas; be sure to look up all words that you do not know; be sure that you are able to understand the special context of the work. Without a knowledge of the context, you can get into difficulty. For example, a student once interpreted Wordsworth's poem "The Solitary Reaper" as Wordsworth's celebration of the advent of the industrial age, since this student thought all the descriptions referred to the McCormick reaper! If he had provided himself with a wider context by reading even a few of Wordsworth's other poems, and also by checking the date of the invention of the reaper, he could have avoided this absurdity.

What Do You Summarize?

Once you have collected your notes on the work, you face the fundamental problem of exactly what to summarize. This problem may seem simple at first glance, but the experience of many students has shown otherwise. Most defects in summary themes result from an apparently imperfect idea of what is needed. You can solve the problem—and produce a good summary theme—if you keep the following in mind; in the literary work that you will be asked to summarize, there are two major elements that you should consider. The English novelist E. M. Forster has conveniently classified these elements.[1] The first is the *story,* or the main events, details, or happenings in the work as they appear in chronological order. The second is the *plot,* or the reasons or logic underlying the story and causing that story to take the *form* it does. The essence of plot is the existence of a *conflict* between opposing forces—either man against man singly or in groups, man against himself, or man against some natural or supernatural force. The conflict produces those actions and interactions that culminate in a *climax* or *dénouement.* In other words, attention to plot requires you to formulate some idea of the *why* and the *how* of the story, not just the *what.*

There is little question, of course, about what happens in the story, since all the events are before you and can easily be verified. But there is more room for interpretation and subjectivity about the plot, because the reasons why characters do things are not always clear, even to the characters themselves, and also because a particular work of literature may mean many things at once, all equally deducible from the story.

To show that the plot may be described in different ways, the short story summarized in the sample theme, F. Scott Fitzgerald's "Babylon Revisited," may be illuminating. The story relates the unsuccessful attempts of a man to regain custody of his nine-year-old daughter from his in-laws, who took the child when he was confined to a sanitarium for alcoholism. The plot, however, is not as easily described, and discussion of the story might bring out the following ideas about what the plot is:

1 *Aspects of the Novel* (New York: Harcourt, Brace & World, Inc., 1927), p. 130.

(1) the past constantly influences the present, (2) moral stability and strength can be acquired only at great cost, (3) wealth destroys human values and perspectives, (4) thoughtless or frivolous action produces unforeseeable consequences, and (5) men must answer for their actions even though they are driven by forces that they cannot control. Each one of these statements, taken singly or collectively, would serve as a satisfactory description of the plot. They do not cancel themselves out but complement and enrich one another.

Regardless of the work you have read, to write a good summary *theme* you must not only summarize the story but also must convey to your reader an explanation of why the story is as it is—in short, you must treat the plot as a part of your summary in order to convey an idea of the organization of the story. All these elements must be included in your summary theme.

The Summary Theme and the Précis

A distinction should be made between a summary theme and a précis. Commonly, the two are regarded as identical, particularly if we use the word *summary* without the word *theme*. A précis is an abridgment, a brief re-telling of events, with no attempt to be responsible for anything but the events in the order in which they appear in the original work. But in a summary theme there is need to provide a central idea, a thesis sentence, and topic sentences that impose the writer's own organization on the events. Writing a summary theme should help you to see the logic of time, not just the sequence of events. That is, if you have read a story that ends with the marriage of the girl and the boy, writing a précis would require only that you state that they got married. The summary theme would require you to embody that fact in a pattern such as, "The author's aim is to show that the determination of young lovers is stronger than all the obstacles in their path." Your reference to the marriage would then come as the final statement in support of this central idea. In short, the summary theme makes you analyze the logic of sequential events—the plot—and requires you to include details only as they bear on your analysis. In fiction, as in life, events do not simply happen in time, but are caused. The summary theme requires you to get at this causation. In a précis you do not need to get at the causation, for the writer of a précis is responsible only for the sequence of events.

The differences between the two techniques may be best shown by a double-column comparison. On the left is a précis of the final section of Fitzgerald's story "Babylon Revisited." On the right is the final paragraph from the sample theme included at the end of this chapter.

Wales goes to the Ritz bar to find Lorraine and Duncan, who are not there. After talking with Paul, the bartender, Wales considers the mistakes of his past. He then calls Lincoln and learns that Marion is emotionally overwrought. Lincoln does not want to make her worse, and thus he cannot bring up the subject of returning Honoria again for six months. Returning to the bar, Wales refuses to get drunk and resolves to come back again for his child.

The third, final, part of the story (section V) opens and closes with the idea that Charles is strong and resolute despite this reversal. Talking with Paul, the head bartender at the Ritz, he recalls that his own life had crashed because of the giddiness and unreality of the old bull market days. In other words, the real crash came because of easy wealth, not financial ruin. Although Charles phones Lincoln and learns that he must wait six months before talking again to Marion about Honoria, he is not discouraged. Under other circumstances, when he might have dissolved his disappointment in liquor, he is firm and steady. The story concludes on this note of stability:

[quotation]

It should be clear that the summary theme is an interpretive piece of writing. This is not to minimize the précis, for a great deal is to be learned from writing one. The essential requirement of the précis is to put a story or argument into your own words—not an easy task—and the test of the précis is fidelity to the story. The essential requirement of the summary theme is to develop a central idea and to show how the events in the work fit the central idea. The single most common fault in writing about literature is that it so easily becomes précis writing. A précis is all right if that is what you are required to write, but it is wrong if anything else is assigned. If you can recognize the problem, however, and preserve the distinction, you should be able to plan and write a good summary theme.

Planning Your Theme

The first thing to do is to study your notes on the story or play or poem carefully. Observe whether the events you noted fit into any sort of pattern. What seem to be the main points of the story? How do these events fit the main points? In *Oedipus Rex,* for example, you might determine that the events occur as part of a plan to illustrate Oedipus's pride; that is, you might say that all the events in the play are either caused by his pride or cause him to realize that he is proud; his realization may be regarded as the climax of the play. The plot may then be stated as an attempt to show that excessive pride causes destruction.

You may observe that there is usually disagreement and discussion about plot; indeed, some of your classroom discussions have shown that different persons may make entirely different interpretations. Such diversity is no problem, for instead of being a cause of uncertainty, it is a means of enrichment. Use your study to draw your own conclusions; decide what the main points are and what events are important in making these points. Above all, remember that events in works of fiction do not simply happen; they are always included by the author as part of a plan or idea. *Discover that plan or idea.*

Once you have made your decision about the main idea of the work, you should write it down (e.g., "In this novel the main theme is the growth from childhood to adulthood," or "In this play the main character realizes the folly of trying to set himself above Fate," and so on). Without doubt it is difficult to make sure that your interpretation of the main point will coincide with that of your instructor, but remember that he will prefer any interpretation to none at all. You might realize that your interpretation is not necessarily the final and only answer to the question of plot. What you are trying to present here is an idea that will serve you as a basis for your *theme.* You should attempt an interpretation and use it as your central idea. Once you have done so, you are on the way to developing your critical powers in using your central idea throughout your theme, and your instructor will honor your interpretation. Where you can go wrong is not in your interpretation, but in failing to maintain that interpretation as a central idea everywhere in your theme; in that event, it is your theme, not your interpretation, that is bad.

You should state your central idea in a thesis sentence, which will (1) state the plan of the work, and also (2) organize your own theme and enable you to bring out your central idea. A thesis sentence might be, "This growth is described by Mark Twain in an extensive trip on a raft down the Mississippi River, during which numerous adventures cause the narrator, Huck, to grow to maturity despite the restrictive background from which he has come." Once you have decided on a central idea and thesis sentence, fill in the details of your theme and do the job of writing it.

How Much Detail to Include

In writing you need to follow through with your plan as outlined in your thesis sentence and to include enough detail to bring out your central idea. If you were summarizing *Huckleberry Finn,* for example, you would build on the thesis sentence by mentioning (1) the early events before the trip, and (2) the principal events on and off the river, in such a way that you would emphasize Huck's increasing maturity. Naturally you cannot summarize everything in the story; nor would everything be desirable, for your mythical reader could go to the novel itself if he wanted to know everything. Your use of topic sentences will help you here, for if you say that "The first part of the work describes the common sense of Huck when he is faced with Tom Sawyer's mental extravagances," you do not need to describe every detail but only the most significant ones. Similarly, after you have discussed the "first part," let us assume that there is a second, or third, or fourth part. Before you start summarizing each part, it is absolutely essential that you inform your reader of the new section. Then you need to include only as much detail as exemplifies your topic sentences. The object of your theme is to summarize, accurately, the work of literature assigned; the problem is to stay in control of the material, not merely to say "This happens" and "That happens," but instead to say "This happens as part of this pattern," and "That happens as part of that pattern." Control the material; do not let it control you.

How much detail should you include? You must give your reader as thorough but as brief a knowledge of the work as is possible within the limits of the assignment. If a man is murdered in your story, it is worth saying that "X shoots Y, who dies," or if a man steals a horse, it is interesting and perhaps important to say "Z steals Sheriff Q's horse." Unless details of this sort are essential, however, you should not lengthen your theme by including them. For example, in the ancient *Epic of Gilgamesh,* the hero Gilgamesh is reverent toward the gods and goddesses Anu, Shamash, Ishtar, and Ninsun, but in a summary theme there is no particular advantage in including these names; it is wise simply to say that the hero is pious or reverent. In this way the point is made without the inclusion of interesting but unnecessary details. The intelligence you show in selecting details—distinguishing the essential from the nonessential—will be extremely important in the quality of your finished summary theme.

Organizing Your Theme

Usually there will be two parts in a summary theme.

PART I: INTRODUCTION

The introduction identifies the work, the most significant character or characters, and the general situation; it is the place for your *central idea* and *thesis sentence*. In the introduction you should also describe the most noticeable physical characteristics of the work summarized—that it is a play, essay, or novel; that the work is mainly in dialogue, or narration; that the narration of events is accompanied by descriptions of the hero's thoughts; that the story is told by the hero himself; that the description of present events is augmented by reminiscences of past events; that the reader must infer the relationships among the characters; that much of the story is in dialect, and so on.

PART II: THE SUMMARY

The summary itself grows out of your thesis sentence. The development of your theme should follow the form of the work that you are summarizing. That is, you should present the main events as they occur in the story, even if much of the story is related by a flashback method; you should try to re-create the actual movement of the story itself. Remember, however, that what characterizes your theme *as a theme* is your central idea—your general interpretation of the work—and your guiding topic sentences that give unity to each of your paragraphs. Remind yourself constantly as you write that (1) you should closely follow the work you summarize, (2) you should write accurately, precisely, and vividly, and (3) you should use an occasional word, phrase, or passage from the work in order to give your reader a taste of the original.

SAMPLE THEME

The Story of F. Scott Fitzgerald's "Babylon Revisited" [2]

The short story "Babylon Revisited" is set in Paris shortly after the stock-market crash of 1929. The main character, Charles Wales (i.e., "wails") has experienced a crash too, a moral crash, and is attempting to reconstruct himself. In the indulgent days before the crash, he had become alcoholically negligent of his family. When he was in a sanitarium to be cured of his alcoholism, his wife died and he relinquished legal control over his daughter Honoria to his sister and brother-in-law (i.e., his dissipations made him forsake his

---

[2] In Maurice Baudin, Jr., ed., *Contemporary Short Stories, Volume II,* The American Heritage Series (Indianapolis and New York: Bobbs-Merrill Co., Inc., ca. 1954), pp. 117–40. Parenthetical page numbers refer to this edition.

honor). Now, able to provide a home for her, he has returned to persuade his in-laws to give Honoria back. *Fitzgerald's theme is that such reconstruction can be effected only with great difficulty; past irresponsibility constantly endangers and frustrates healthy aims in the responsible present.*   **CENTRAL IDEA**

In what here will be called the first section of the story, Fitzgerald concentrates on Charles's present moral worthiness; in the second he concentrates on the past and how it foils Charles's present plans for happiness; in the third Fitzgerald re-emphasizes Charles's strength of character and his anticipation of future triumph because of this strength.   **THESIS SENTENCE**

The first part of the story comprises Fitzgerald's sections I and II, in which he emphasizes that Charles has successfully overcome his past, as far as his own character is involved.   **TOPIC SENTENCE: FIRST PART OF THESIS SENTENCE**

Currently back on his feet and working prosperously in Prague, Charles returns to Paris to see his daughter, and his in-laws. He visits the Ritz, a bar that he had frequented in former days, and discovers that everything there is hollow and empty. His one joy is his visit with his daughter Honoria, but his past returns to haunt him when he converses with her legal guardians, Lincoln and Marion Peters. (Marion is a distrustful, vengeful, and nearly hysterical woman.) Their conversation brings out Marion's belief that Charles's drinking had been a major cause of the death of his wife, Helen. After Charles leaves, he wanders through the Parisian scenes of his former extravagances, pondering his loss. His present moral worthiness is made clear by his refusal to go with a prostitute to her room.

Fitzgerald's second section continues the theme of Charles's moral reform that had concluded the first section, and hence these two sections form a coherent whole.   **TOPIC SENTENCE**

Charles has lunch with his daughter, who declares her love for him and her dependence on him. In the café he is met by two former companions in dissipation, Duncan Schaeffer and Lorraine Quarrles, whose frivolousness makes a discord in his present, harmonious sobriety. He and Honoria flee the two, even though they meet later at a variety show. It is as though Fitzgerald is showing that the past still encumbers Charles, no matter how strongly he tries to escape it.

The story's second part, composed of Fitz-   **TOPIC SENTENCE:**
gerald's sections III and IV, demonstrates the   **SECOND PART OF**
harmful effects of the past on the present. In   **THESIS SENTENCE**
section III, the theme of Charles's determination to overcome the
past is pursued to a temporarily successful climax. His manner and
conversation convince Marion, the chief skeptic about his reforma-
tion, that he is now fit to care for Honoria, although Marion is not
enthusiastic. Before she consents to release Honoria, the conversation discloses more details about the past, which Charles has worked
so hard to conquer and which Marion so bitterly resents: Charles
had begun drinking after stock-market successes had made him rich
and idle. In a drunken rage one night, he had left Helen, gone
home, and locked the door. When Helen came home with no key,
and was unsuccessful in rousing Charles, she left and wandered hys-
terically in the snow for an hour before going to Marion's home.
Subsequently the marriage became more unstable, and Helen became ill. Before dying, she arranged for Honoria's going to Marion;
Charles consented because he was then in the sanitarium and did
not have the self-confidence to resist.

Just as the preceding section of the second   **TOPIC**
part shows Charles victorious over his past, the   **SENTENCE**
next (section IV) shows the past victorious over
him. When he is speaking with Marion and Lincoln about details of taking Honoria back, Duncan and Lorraine
burst in. They are drunk, and their behavior scandalizes Marion,
who out of loyalty to the dead Helen had always distrusted
Charles's attachment to Lorraine. It was with Lorraine, this section
shows, that Charles had indulged in impossibly frivolous and child-
ish pranks, though nothing more intimate is suggested. Charles
brusquely ushers the drunken pair out, but all talk of his taking
Honoria has now ended, and Marion is more adamant than ever
against his attempt to establish a new life with his daughter.

The third, final, part of the story (section   **TOPIC SENTENCE:**
V) opens and closes with the idea that Charles   **THIRD PART OF**
is strong and resolute despite this reversal. Talk-   **THESIS SENTENCE**
ing with Paul, the head bartender at the Ritz, he recalls that his
own life had crashed because of the giddiness and unreality of the
old bull market days. In other words, the real crash came because
of easy wealth, not because of financial ruin. Although Charles
sees Lincoln and learns that he must wait six months before talking
again to Marion about Honoria, he is not discouraged. Under

other circumstances, when he might have dissolved his disappointment in liquor, he is firm and steady: the story concludes on this
note of stability:

> He would come back some day; they couldn't make him pay for-
> ever. But he wanted his child, and nothing was much good now,
> beside that fact. He wasn't young anymore, with a lot of nice thoughts
> and dreams to have by himself. He was absolutely sure Helen
> wouldn't have wanted him to be so alone (p. 140).[3]

[3] Reprinted with the permission of Charles Scribner's Sons and The Bodley Head
Ltd. from "Babylon Revisited" (Copyright 1931 The Curtis Publishing Company; re-
newal copyright © 1959 Frances Scott Fitzgerald Lanahan) from *Taps at Reveille* by
F. Scott Fitzgerald.

THE REPORT

CHAPTER
2

This assignment will generally be simply to "Write a report or paper about such-and-such a story, novel, poem, or play," or "In this course you will be expected to submit X number of book reports." Assignments of this sort will be made not only in literature courses, but in many others. For such an assignment, you are generally on your own and, since what to say is entirely up to you, you may understandably feel ill at ease. "What does my instructor want?" "What should I say?" "How should I organize the material?" "Should I write a summary?" Reactions like these naturally arise if you have received no other directions.

As you begin to think and to write, you should consider the subject of your theme in the following light: though your instructor has made a general assignment, he probably wants to see evidence that (1) you have read and followed the work, (2) you have understood it and can say something intelligent about it, and (3) you have reacted to it in some way and have formed an opinion about it. Assuming that your report is well written and punctuated correctly, the quality of what you write will depend on the success with which you fulfill these three requirements.

Questions as a Means of Analysis

The report stands at a mid point between the summary theme on the one hand, and the various sorts of analysis, including evaluation and appreciation, on the other. That is, you will find here a need for the kind of summary that provides a reader with a quick, thumbnail sketch of a work with a minimum of delay. Also, you will deal in this theme with the principal objects of writing about literature; namely, analysis and evaluation.

For a report you should be concerned with literary analysis in a general sense only. You do not need to exhaust all the possibilities of a particular analytical approach. In fact, you may be able to make your analysis mainly by answering several major questions. Here are some of them. Do not feel limited by them, but go further and raise some of your own:

1. Did you notice if the author emphasized any particular ideas? To deal with such a question, you must (a) state the idea, (b) show its importance in the work as a whole, and describe its relationship to the layout or form of the work, and (c) evaluate the idea; that is, is the idea good, bad, helpful, dangerous, harmless, and so on?

2. Did you notice the form or organization of the work? Describe the various parts and their relationships. Try to explain what you think are the reasons for the relationships.

3. Did the work contain a great deal of dialogue, or narration? Was the dialogue well written? In what way? Was the narration such that it held your attention? How did it do so? Can you provide any information about particularly interesting passages and supply reasons for the interest?

4. Was the work written to satisfy any specific need or demand at the time it was first published? For example, Walt Whitman's poem "When Lilacs Last in the Dooryard Bloomed" was written in reaction to the assassination of President Lincoln. If you can point to an occasion or demand, try to state whether the writer dealt successfully with the issues he faced as a result of the occasion.

5. Can you engage in any other kinds of analysis that will show that you have made an effort to comprehend the work? For example, in poetry it is sometimes helpful to count stanzas, lines, and words, for by determining the positions of things you can also determine developments of ideas and relationships of one part to another. Analyzing or parsing sentences may also yield insights that you did not have when you first read through the work. Studying words to see whether they are vivid or non-descriptive, specific or general, may give you an insight into the author's style.

In your analysis you are free, of course, to try writing answers to all these questions, though if you provide full answers you may find your report becoming too long. Pick and choose. The experience of many students has shown that in a free choice, most students will discuss ideas or "meaning." Perhaps the ideas you choose to discuss may have social importance, or political or personal significance. Whatever the import, always try to focus your attention on the areas in which you feel the ideas have the greatest bearing.

Organizing Your Theme

You should include the following parts in your report:

INTRODUCTION

Here you should name the work, the author, and any relevant data about the writing and reception of the work. Be brief on biographical and background information, however, for these matters quickly can divert you from actually talking about the work itself. Begin describing the main characteristics of the work you are reporting on; i.e., is it a novel, an essay, a long poem? Is it written in narrative, dialogue, argument? Does it contain dialect, slang? Is there anything else a general reader should know about it? After dealing with questions like these, move to your central idea and thesis sentence.

A SHORT SUMMARY

The summary meets the requirement that you have read the entire work. Concentrate on a short, succinct summary, not to take up more than about one-fifth of your theme. (This proportion will be smaller in longer reports, in which most of your attention should be devoted to analysis.) Remember that an intelligent summary should be interpretive in a limited way; this one should almost exclusively summarize plot as distinguished from story. If the work you are reporting on is divided into parts, chapters, stanzas, or some other ascertainable divisions, your summary should take these matters into account. The summary should also rely on short quotations from the text in order to root itself as deeply as possible in the original work.

AN ANALYSIS

In this section you analyze the principal meanings and qualities of the work on which you are reporting. This section should occupy the largest part of your theme. Your instructor will likely place greatest weight on the skills you show in this section. You should therefore be at pains to demonstrate that you have examined the assigned text closely and that your understanding is beyond what is required simply for following the idea or story.

When you write, you might try to answer many questions like those listed above, or perhaps you might deal with only one, depending on the nature of the questions and your interest in them. If you deal with a question about ideas, for example, your analysis might very well be taken up entirely with that question. You may prefer to write on style, structure, and meaning separately. One thing to bear in mind is the general nature of the assignment: if you discuss a main idea, it is wise to show how that idea affects and is affected by the style and structure. You are concerned here with the general techniques of literary analysis. The more specific and detailed techniques will come later. Show that you are a good, alert reader and your book report will have achieved its aim.

You can make this section unnecessarily difficult if you allow yourself to wander. You must always remember that a theme, even a report, should have a *thematic development* (see the Introduction, pp. 4–10). Your analysis should therefore be tied to the summary, perhaps by an introductory remark like, "This work's outstanding quality, which my summary cannot show, is the uncanny way *Y* author's style creates powerful anxiety in the reader . . . ." (Then would follow an analysis of how that effect is created, together with other related matters.) Throughout this analytical section you should make sure always that your sentences are relevant to your central idea. All your insights, word counts, and general interpretations will lose effect if they do not cohere to a definite point. In short, your analysis should show continuity and development.

THE FINAL SECTION: YOUR ATTITUDES

Your theme should conclude with an explanation of your attitudes toward the work (about one-fourth to one-eighth of your theme). Although not the largest in terms of space, this section is nevertheless important. Your remarks here should take on greater weight because of your work on the analysis. It is usually gratifying to describe your own opinions if they are based on calm, rational thought, not prejudice. (Prejudice is usually the result of unconsidered emotion. It might lead to your rejecting a poem "because I don't like poetry." A considered opinion, on the other hand, is the result of thought; it might result in your criticism of a work because it does not succeed in doing what it tries to do, and so on.)

Your likes and dislikes have a definite place in this section, however, if you combine them with your judgment to answer questions that are really important. How did the literary work affect you? Did you feel satisfied, complete, happy, after reading it? Did you think that the work was good? Bad? Did you feel that the author should have done something more? This section is the place for your individual thoughts and reactions. Do not be afraid to speak your mind, but do not do so unless you have a sound basis in ideas from the text. Good literature is always interesting and moving, and it should be enjoyed by all. If the particular work did not affect you, therefore, it is your duty to say so, but try to assess the blame for failure properly: if you did not like the work, is the fault in you or in the work? In dealing with these questions, you will perhaps learn something about yourself, but you will also be dealing with questions of *evaluation* and *appreciation*. These words are fundamental to the study of literature. You will quickly see that this third section, instead of being the easiest, is the hardest of all, because evaluation and appreciation are not to be taken whimsically. When you write about literature more frequently, you will also notice that your evaluative powers will increase as you develop into a more disciplined reader.

Cautions

These, then, are parts of the book report. This type of theme is not vague, but extremely specific. What you say is up to you, as long as you say it about the work assigned, and as long as you remember that your instructor is interested in seeing (1) the evidence of your general analytical ability, and (2) the nature and degree of your individual reactions. Remember that good writing is always your aim. Make your theme coherent; be sure that your paragraphs start with transitional phrases. Your theme will have three parts, but do not make them seem like three lumps. Work out a good thesis sentence that will help your reader to understand the organization and plan of your paper, and write a brief but interesting introduction. In short, keep in control at all times.

Keep in mind that this suggested organization should be adapted to the specific directions of your instructor. If there are no other directions, the three parts of the general critique should give you an acceptable organization and should enable you to write a well-rounded theme.

The Report and the Review

If you are writing your report in a freshman or sophomore class, the form as described in this chapter should be sufficient for your purposes. For more advanced classes, however, you should consider writing a review rather than a report (see Chapter 17). The review is similar to the report because it, like the report, is a general piece of writing about literature. The review, however, assumes a greater skill and more experience in analyzing and discussing literature than are assumed for a report.

SAMPLE THEME

A Report on Ralph Ellison's Story "Flying Home" [1]

"Flying Home" was first published in 1944, during World War II. At that time, according to Ellison, Negroes were trained as pilots but were not actually sent into combat. This fact provides the cause of the frustration of the major figure in the story, a young black pilot named Todd. The story has about an equal amount of dialogue and narration, and is not marked by sections or divisions. *Ellison's principal idea in the story is that a black person's ambitions are strait-jacketed in a predominantly white society. This point is made clear in the principal action of the story and in the major characteristics, and it is made emphatic by the power of the story to evoke compelling and sympathetic emotions.*

CENTRAL IDEA

THESIS SENTENCE

The difficulty of being black in a white society is made clear in the principal action of the story. Todd is black, and on a training mission has crashed his plane in a white man's field in Alabama. Seriously injured, he is consoled by an aged black named Jefferson, whose young son Teddy goes to find help. Todd is fearful that he might be seen as a failure by white people for having crashed. When Jefferson diverts him from his pain by telling a story, the story is about the difficulty of the blacks. Specifically, Jefferson's tale is about how he was ordered out of heaven by a white St. Peter. Todd is racked with pain, and, prompted by pain and by Jefferson's narrative, he thinks about how, even from earliest youth, he had wanted to fly but had been told that such aspirations were inappropriate for a black. At this point the owner of the field, a white named Graves, appears with two attendants who put Todd in a straitjacket, because "you cain't let the nigguh git up that high without his going crazy" (p. 269). After enjoying his "joke," Graves orders Todd off his property, and the blacks, not the whites, carry him off. The action clearly shows both the hostility and indifference of whites to blacks.

TOPIC SENTENCE

[1] In James A. Emanuel and Theodore L. Gross, eds., *Dark Symphony: Negro Literature in America* (New York: The Free Press, 1968), pp. 254–270. Parenthetical page numbers refer to this edition.

In presenting the black characters, Ellison **TOPIC**
shows that they have been limited by the same **SENTENCE**
racial hostility and indifference. Todd is young
and determined and is trying to cope in the real world of the air
force. Jefferson is old and also determined, but his efforts to cope
have turned mainly to fantasy. Todd's crashing and Jefferson's being turned out of heaven for "speeding" suggest how normal aims
and aspirations, which may reach fruition for whites, always are
thrust against a barrier for blacks. Todd has been given a plane but
not allowed to fight during the war, while Jefferson, in his dream,
has been given wings but not allowed to fly. By this means Ellison
shows that both men have the ability to function well—just as by
implication all blacks, like all human beings, have this same ability
—but because they are black they will not be allowed to.

A similar parallel is drawn between Todd **TOPIC**
and Teddy, the young son of Jefferson. First, of **SENTENCE**
course, their names are similar. Second, even
though Teddy does not figure prominently in the story—during
most of it he has been away getting help for Todd—Ellison brings
out details about him that show his similarity to Todd. Teddy is
a competent boy, being entrusted to get help and to carry Todd on
the stretcher. In addition, he is humming at the end. Here is
strength of character, similar to the strength of Todd, whose childhood dreams of being a pilot are so important in the story. If the
parallel is followed, of course, much the same kind of frustration
that happened to Todd and Jefferson will be the lot of Teddy.

Because of these parallels, it seems to have **TOPIC**
been no accident that Ellison created the three **SENTENCE**
black persons as possessing youth, maturity, and
age. All have the same past, present, or future;
namely, being frustrated or truncated. The three whites in the
story, by contrast, are all in the full power of their maturity, which
is the apparent inheritance of the white race in the social structure
criticized by Ellison. Interestingly, too, the whites do not directly
assist Todd from the field. They provide the stretcher, but make
sure that Jefferson and Teddy do the actual carrying. If there is to
be any improvement for blacks, Ellison may be suggesting, it will
be brought about only by blacks of all ages pulling cooperatively
together.

Primarily because of such a clear, direct
view of the predicament of the black in the
society geared to whites, this story is compelling
but also disturbing. If a man is injured to the
extent of having a broken ankle, as Todd is, it should be a human
thing to help him. Yet Ellison shows that the attendants put a
straitjacket on him in an enactment of Graves's grim joke. This
incident is powerfully disturbing as a symbol: when a person falls
into quicksand he needs help, not a push. Yet the effect of the
symbol is that he gets the push. Because of the outrageousness of
this action, together with the aspirations so clearly portrayed by
Ellison, such as the letter of Todd's sweetheart and the story of
Todd's grasping at the empty sky for an airplane, "Flying Home"
creates a highly sympathetic response. Here is a story with a coherent,
richly symbolic texture. The study of almost any passage is illuminating and most rewarding.

The Theme of
CHARACTER ANALYSIS

CHAPTER
3

An extremely popular theme subject, particularly in courses in drama and novel, is the analysis of character. Writers in ancient times wrote character sketches and novel-like stories, and many medieval and Renaissance writers, like Chaucer, were adept at creating character, but real interest in particularized fictional characters did not develop until the seventeenth century. In the eighteenth century the novel emerged as an important literary form. With the advent of modern psychology, interest in patterns of human behavior has come of age. Of course drama, with its emphasis on a main character, has been popular since the time of the ancient Athenians. In our own times it is one of the more vital literary forms.

If you recollect some of the novels and dramas you have read or seen, you will realize that they are about characters, their reactions to an extended series of actions, and their attempts, both successful and unsuccessful, to shape those events. The novel and the drama are similar because they show the interactions of character and action in rather full detail. To these genres one might add epic and narrative poetry, which also center on character and action. Short stories and poems do not aim at the broadness and fullness of the larger forms but concentrate instead on the essential high points of human experience.

What Is Character?

Although sometimes we use the word *character* synonymously with "person," "human being," and "literary figure," more often we use it in reference to an individual's personal qualities and characteristics. Both senses should be retained (we can speak about the "character" of a character), but the second sense will be amplified here.

Other words used as either equivalents or modifications of character are *psyche, soul, ego, consciousness, moral fiber, being,* and many others. What all these terms probably mean, however, is the sum total of typical qualities and propensities in any given individual that are controlled by that individual's drives, aims, ideals, morals, and conscience. These qualities are manifested in his behavior under any set of circumstances, and we make observations about his character by drawing inferences from this behavior. Always, the character we are talking about is something that exists somewhere and somehow *within* that individual, or simultaneously *with* him. It is the uniqueness or typicality of that something that concerns us as we discuss the character of the individual. Most persons desire to get ahead in the world, but what makes our friends John and Tom unique is that John works ten hours a day to get ahead while Tom works five. In discussing John and Tom, we would point out this behavior (assuming that it results from choice) and attempt to make inferences about their characters from it and from other behavior.

It is by such an inferential process that we learn about our fellow human beings, and if our inferences lead us to admiration, this process (on both sides) leads us to form our friendships. We perceive the qualities of the person who is our friend by our contacts with him. We learn about his strengths and weaknesses by observing his speech and action and by listening to him as he communicates his thoughts and emotions to us. If we want to learn more about a particular quality, we ask him about it. With people who are not close to us, however, we are unable to acquire such information, and hence we have no very clear idea of their characters. This difficulty is even more pronounced when we, as voters, are asked to pass judgment on men who run for public office. These men therefore spend much time and energy, as do their campaign managers and aides, to project an "image" of themselves as men of fine, worthy character. The information we gain about them, however, must be supplemented with the comments of political analysts and opponents.

In studying character in literature, we approach a situation more like that of getting to know the public man than that of getting to know our friend. (Notice this difference: the author usually attempts to describe every facet of the character, good and bad, not just those traits that create a one-sided view.) We can understand the qualities of a literary character only by interpreting what the author has written about him. All the character's actions, plus what he says and what is said about him, provide us with the only material from which we can make inferences, and we can expect no more than what the author has chosen to disclose.

For this reason, we may define *character* in literature as the author's creation, through the medium of words, of a personality who takes on actions, thoughts, expressions, and attitudes unique and appropriate to that personality and consistent with it. Character might be thought of as a reasonable facsimile of a human being, with all the qualities and vagaries of a human being.

How Is Character Disclosed in Literature?

Before you prepare to write your theme, you should know the four ways in which a writer usually indicates character to you:

1. By what the person himself says (and thinks, from the author's third person omniscient point of view).
2. By what the character does.
3. By what other characters say about him.
4. By what the author says about him, speaking as either the storyteller or an observer of the action.

These four points require amplification.

1. What a particular character says about himself may frequently be accepted at face value as truth, but just as often it may be only a reflection of his intellectual and emotional state at a given moment. If a character in deep despair says that life is worthless, for example, you must balance that statement with what the same character says when he is happy. Then too, you must consider the situation in the literary work when a statement is made. If a character voices despair at the start, but is cheerful (or sad) at the end, there has been a development, or change, in that character's view of life. In *Crime and Punishment,* for example, Raskolnikov is convinced of his right to make judgments on the lives of other people, but at the end of the novel he doubts his right. A shift has occurred that any analysis of his qualities must consider. As you can see, you are free to interpret what a person says in the light of the context in which it appears.

Most of the above applies to what a person thinks as it is reported to us by the author acting as an omniscient narrator. If you detect differences between what the person thinks and what he says, you may be sure that the author is demonstrating some quality of character, either (a) favorable, if the discrepancy is part of a worthwhile strategy, or (b) unfavorable, if the discrepancy is part of a worthless or ignoble one.

2. You have heard that what you do speaks louder than what you say. The same is true in literature, and sometimes actions illustrate important character traits. An author may create a character who professes

honesty yet does dishonorable things. Uriah Heep in *David Copperfield* and Tartuffe in Molière's play *Le Tartuffe* have such characteristics. Iago in *Othello* is another case in point: he professes to be Othello's friend, but secretly behaves like a devil. In analyzing what characters do, you must ask whether the character's actions are consistent with his words. If not, why not? What does the author communicate by showing inconsistencies? In the three examples just cited, the authors succeed in showing the diabolical nature of hypocrisy.

Exposing hypocrisy, however, might not be the reason for showing gaps between statement and action. This technique may illustrate ideas like "Human beings have a great capacity for self-deception," or "Human beings are weak." An author may show characters behaving consistently with what they say as a mark of favor to these characters (or also as a mark of credit to a rogue who is honest with himself, like Peachum in John Gay's play *The Beggar's Opera*).

3. In literature, as in life, people are always talking about other people. What they say of course raises the problem of *point of view*, because the character and motivation of a person will condition whatever he says about someone else (see Chapter 4). You know, for example, that the word of a person's enemy is usually biased against that person. Therefore an author may frequently give you a favorable impression of a character by having a bad character say bad things about him. Similarly, the word of a close friend or political manager may be biased in favor of a particular character. In short, you must always consider the context and source of all dramatic remarks about a particular character. In Conrad's *Victory*, for example, an evil hotel manager named Schomberg always claims that the hero, Heyst, is a villain. The reader is to believe the opposite of what Schomberg says about Heyst, because Schomberg seems to be attributing his own evil motives to Heyst. By contrast, in *Macbeth*, when Macduff and Malcolm say that Macbeth and his rule in Scotland are bad, their statements should be accepted as truth because the two men are presented as honest, just, and good.

4. What the author says about a character is usually to be accepted as truth about that character. Naturally, the author must be accepted absolutely on matters of fact in the narrative or drama. But when in his own person he interprets the actions and characteristics of his characters, he himself assumes the role of critic, and his opinions are open to question. For this reason authors frequently avoid making overt interpretations, and devote their skill instead to arranging events in the drama or narrative so that their own conclusions are obvious to the reader. If the author chooses to present an analysis of character, however, he might resort to a person in the work who will then be bound by his own limitations as an observer. In this case, the dramatic commentator is like the characters discussed in paragraph 3.

Character, Reality, Probability, and Decorum

We are entitled to expect that the characters in a novel or play will be true to life. That is, the actions, statements, and thoughts of a particular person must all be what a human being is *likely* to do, say, and think under given circumstances. This is the standard of *probability*.

The phrases "true to life" and "given circumstances" need explanation, for they are vital to the concept of literary character as distinguished from real-life character. There are major differences between literature and life. First, literature presents a highly selective view of reality, even in the most "realistic" of works. That is, each action performed by a character within a work has organic significance; it may be interpreted either as a facet of character or sometimes as an example of an author's philosophy of life. Thus, those things in life that seem unpredictable, whimsical, and unaccountable are made to seem meaningful in literature. For example, the conversation of the soldiers on the watch at the opening of *Hamlet* is not there for just any reason at all, as it might be in real life when people sometimes simply "make conversation." Along with having a functional role in the exposition of the play, the talk shows the nervousness of the men, some of their characteristics, and their attitudes as midnight—the time the ghost walks—approaches. The speeches represent the way in which soldiers would likely talk under these circumstances; their speeches are not accidental, but are *probable* and relevant to the entire play.

In studying the characters in each work of literature, you may draw conclusions about the probability of the actions in this way. However, your judgment on this score requires a strong imaginative boost. You must not judge simply from your own point of view but must imagine what very different kinds of persons would do under exactly similar circumstances and with the same mental and philosophical outlooks. You must look carefully at the early parts of the work in order to see what tendencies the characters have exhibited. With these characteristics in mind, you must then ask yourself "Is the subsequent action a logical consequence of this man's qualities?" In the early scenes of *Macbeth,* for example, Shakespeare demonstrates that Macbeth is a loyal, strong, valiant, and almost foolhardy warrior; that he is ambitious; but that he is also kind and gentle. In view of Macbeth's later responsibility for a series of deaths and for a brutally oppressive regime as king, the question is how to square his characteristics with the subsequent action. If it is any consolation, keep in mind that you will probably not be able to please everyone by your answer to this question, or to most questions.

Ultimately, the best you can do is to make sure that your construction of the literary work is accurate and that your inferences are sound.

A second condition that you will meet in literature is that not all works are the same nor do they present probability or reality in the same way or in the same aspects. Fiction attempting to mirror life—the realistic or naturalistic or "slice-of-life" type of fiction—sets up conditions and raises expectations about the characters that fiction attempting to portray a romantic, fanciful world does not, and vice versa. A character might behave and speak "realistically" in the "realistic" setting, and these habits would be out of place in the romantic setting.

But the situation is more complex than this, for within the romantic setting, which is fanciful and dreamlike, a character might reasonably be *expected* to behave and speak in a fanciful, dreamlike way. Speech and action under both conditions are therefore *probable* as we understand the word, although different aspects of human character are presented in these two different types of works. In the Renaissance and eighteenth century, concern for adapting the notions of probability to fit the conditions of life as described in various types of works led literary critics to exalt the concept of *decorum,* or appropriateness. Authors of the period followed this principle in making their characters speak and act according to their class and circumstances and according to the type of literature in which they appeared. Thus, Shakespeare gave his noblemen elevated diction in poetic accents but gave his country bumpkins the slang of the Elizabethan streets.

Writers in the modern period have abandoned decorum as a practicing principle, but they still observe decorum to the extent that it coincides with common sense and also to the extent that their interest in various aspects of character leads naturally into certain types of literature. For example, modern psychology has had a far-reaching effect on this interest, and hence on the novel. Freud's metapsychology has led writers to explore means of delineating those aspects of character that in earlier fiction were not expressed except as they appeared in behavior. James Joyce's *A Portrait of the Artist as a Young Man* relies heavily on an "interior monologue" that takes place within the mind of the young Stephen Dedalus; much of the earlier part of the novel is written as the expression of Stephen's conscious observations and reflections as they cause new thoughts and associations to develop within his mind. This technique would not have developed had it not been for psychology. Similarly, the sections entitled "The Camera Eye" in *U.S.A.* by John Dos Passos are written as the conscious musings of an enlightened observer on the American social scene of the 1930's. Joyce pursued his explorations into the mind to such an extent that in *Finnegans Wake* he attempted to describe the mental activity—the "stream of consciousness"—of a sleeping man.

The drama has also been heavily influenced by the altered and modified ideas of reality provided by modern psychology. Eugene O'Neill's massive drama *A Long Day's Journey Into Night,* for example, is not realistic by the standards of our ordinary acquaintance with life, but is realistic nevertheless because the members of the troubled family represent enlargements of human character; through these characters the anguish and disappointments of life are focused. Recent dramatists like Samuel Becket and Harold Pinter do not aim at everyday realism; instead, they focus on the abstract parts or aspects of human character and personify these parts through their stage figures. The resulting characters are still realistic, but realistic in the way that a microscopic view of the skin of a frog is realistic, particularly if the rest of the frog is not seen. The same criterion is applicable to most works of literature in which the literary form limits full character development, such as detective fiction, science fiction, and romantic comedy. Edgar Allan Poe's detective C. Auguste Dupin, for example (in *Murders in the Rue Morgue* and other stories), is realistic in the sense that his character is concentrated on the reasoning and deductive human powers; many other aspects of character are neglected by Poe because they are irrelevant to the detective-story form.

Judging the Completeness of Character Development

With all these considerations in mind, you can see the usefulness of the idea that literary characters should be "true to life under given circumstances," and to this phrase should be added another one, "within certain literary specifications." The key to your study of character should always be to discover if the character—whether intended by the author to be a full, complete, round, lifelike person, a romantic hero, or an absurdist abstraction—is related to your concept of what human beings might reasonably be expected to do and say under the exact conditions presented by the author. Does the character ring true, or do the qualities of character presented in him ring true? In other words, does he come to life? Does he illustrate many qualities that add up to a really complete facsimile of a human being, or does he seem to be flat, one-sided, one-dimensional? Lola, a minor figure in Dreiser's *Sister Carrie,* is such a character; we see little in her beyond the fact that she is a worldly wise working girl in a chorus line. On the other hand, Stephen Dedalus in Joyce's *Portrait of the Artist* is totally realized, because his thoughts, words, responses, and actions are described fully from earliest consciousness to young adulthood. The degree to which an author can make a character come alive is a mark of his skill; if you think that your author is successful in this regard, you should say so in your theme.

Organizing Your Theme

INTRODUCTION

As always, your theme should have a clearly stated central idea that runs throughout your entire character analysis. Your central idea here will be whatever general statement you make to describe the character you analyze. Your thesis sentence must be a brief statement of the main sections of your theme.

BODY

Your organization is designed to illustrate and prove your central idea. You have much freedom in organizing your main points. Some possible methods are the following:

1. Organization around central characteristics, like "kindness, gentleness, generosity, firmness," or "resoluteness of will frustrated by inopportune moments for action, resulting in despondency, doubt, and melancholy." A body containing this sort of material would demonstrate how the literary work brings out each of these qualities.

2. Organization around central incidents that reveal primary characteristics (see, for example, the sample theme). Certain key incidents will stand out in a work, and you might create an effective body by using three or four of these as guides for your discussion, taking care to show in your topic sentences that your purpose in this arrangement is to illuminate the character you have selected, not the incidents. In other words, you would regard the incidents only as they bring out truths about character. In a discussion of the character of Stephen in *A Portrait of the Artist as a Young Man,* an effective arrangement might be to select the incidents of the pandybat, the prostitute, and the young girl standing in the water.

Naturally, with this arrangement, you would have to show how the incidents bring out the characteristics and also how they serve to explain other things the character might do.

3. Organization around various sections of the work. This arrangement is particularly effective if you are demonstrating that a character is undergoing changes and developments. In analyzing the character of Iago, for example, you might say that up to Act II, Scene iii of *Othello* he behaves in a reasonably motivated way, that from there to Act V he behaves like a devil, and that in Act V he becomes an enigma.

CONCLUSION

The conclusion should contain your statements about how the characteristics you have brought out are related to the work as a whole. If the person was good but came to a bad end, does this discrepancy elevate him to tragic stature? If he was a nobody and came to a bad end, does this fact cause you to draw any conclusion about the class or type of which he was a part? Or does it illustrate the author's view of human life? Or both? Do the characteristics explain why the person helps or hinders other characters in the literary work? Does your analysis help you to clear up any misunderstanding that your first reading of the work produced? Questions like these should be raised and answered in your conclusion.

A Warning about Diction

In view of the closeness between character analysis and psychology, you must realize that for a literary theme it is best to avoid technical terms from psychology. Even if you have acquired much skill in using these terms, your instructor will probably not receive them sympathetically if you substitute them for thoughtful analysis. Always explain yourself, and do not descend to jargon, as there is great danger of doing in this theme. Some words from psychology are admissible, however, without much amplification: words like *disturbed, frustrated, anxiety* are satisfactory because they are in common use, but if you start using words like *complex, neurosis,* and *psychosis,* you should explain the concepts, not just use the words. Be cautious, and use common sense. If you have any question about a word, ask your instructor.

SAMPLE THEME

**The Character of Jim
in Conrad's Lord Jim** [1]

Jim is difficult to understand. He is seen mainly through the eyes of Marlow, who imparts his own values to much of the story. He is also the subject of much interpretation by other informants in

[1] Joseph Conrad, *Lord Jim* (New York: The Modern Library, 1931). Parenthetical page numbers refer to this edition.

the story, so that we receive many views of him. In addition, Jim is the principal figure in a richly symbolic tapestry, so that much of what he does and says is relevant to most people at most times. In this respect his individuality is sacrificed to his existence as a symbol. Despite these difficulties, however, Jim emerges as a fully developed individual, even though we do not hear of every detail that might ever have concerned him. *The key to understanding Jim's character is that he is a man capable of imagining the best in himself and in men generally—a man whose action at any given moment is controlled by an idea of the best.** He is, in Stein's word, a "romantic," and I would add that he is an introspective dreamer. *His character is made clear by three incidents in the novel, all of which are connected with leaps, or jumps, that Jim either makes or does not make.* †

When Jim has his first opportunity to leap, he does not take it. This failure to jump is symbolic of Jim's preference for mental over physical heroism. It hurts his own high evaluation of himself. Imbued with the British ideals of manhood and adventure in the days of the naval empire, he has been dreaming of his own "devotion to duty" in a way "as unflinching as a hero in a book" (p. 6). But when the opportunity comes to join in a rescue operation, he misses the boat. He does not jump. From this point Jim becomes a drifter, for this failure has given him a hint of the basic indecision (*cowardice* would be too strong a word at this point) that is worrying the bubble of his own self-esteem. This one incident, in short, explains the moral laziness that finally causes him to ship aboard the *Patna.*

The bubble of Jim's esteem is totally destroyed by his second jump—from the *Patna* when it is listing heavily and supposedly near sinking. This jump is the major incident in the novel, since it brings out the depths of Jim's being, that inner panic that destroys all his conscious dreams by causing a single cowardly act despite his good intentions. This jump brings out Jim's sense of shame, which must be overwhelming, since it causes him to wander all over the Indian Ocean, fleeing whenever anybody mentions the *Patna* episode. With his depths thus exposed, I believe that Jim feels morally naked, without the privacy that most of us have, since we know, or hope, that the depths of our own souls may never emerge to haunt us. Jim's emerges, and he runs from it, as run he must.

But the *Patna* jump also emphasizes Jim's good qualities. He has a high sense of justice, and before he runs he therefore faces

* Central idea.
† Thesis sentence.

trial, which can end in nothing but his dishonor and disgrace. His conscious dream of what is right has enabled him to face the consequences of his real guilt. Perhaps this facing of the trial when all the other deserters flee is the start of Jim's awareness, acted upon but never clearly stated by him, that life constantly demands expiation for guilt that is caused not entirely by our own choice.

Jim's final leap results from his own choice, however, and as such it enables him finally to live out his dream. It is a kind of triumph. Leaping over the fence enclosing Rajah Allang's courtyard, he allies himself with Doramin, and proceeds quickly to justify the title *Lord Jim* by acting wisely, in concert with Doramin, in governing the forlorn outpost of Patusan. He is convinced of the value of his dream, and always behaves with justice, honor, and firmness, yet always with forgiveness. These are the conscious virtues, to which Jim adheres closely, since they are the embodiment of his character as a dreamer.

This adherence explains why he accepts the final responsibility for the death of Dain Waris. Beyond question, his third leap has enabled him to dedicate himself to the good life in Patusan as expiation for his guilt in the *Patna* episode. The personal quality of this dedication should be stressed, however, and contrasted with the quality of Jim's feelings after Gentleman Brown commits his treacherous act. In this affair Jim is responsible only for not having destroyed the Gentleman *before* the murder is committed. Yet, in Gentleman Brown, Jim apparently sees that the cowardly depths are common to all mankind, not just to himself. So Jim faces Doramin in expiation, just as he had earlier braved the court and the subsequent disgrace. But as Jim sacrifices himself, the best in him, his capacity to dream, triumphs over whatever it was that made him leap from the *Patna*. He is genuinely great at that moment of sacrifice, when he expiates for us all.

Admittedly, Jim is a puzzling character, since his characteristics show that human life is a mystery and since we never really get inside him. But Conrad uses him to demonstrate that, if life has its depths, it also has its high points. At the highest point, a human being willing to live out his dream, if this dream has value and ennobles mankind, can justify the claim that life is elevated and great. Jim, with all his frailty, is a truly great representation of a human being, since he has met and conquered life's greatest obstacle—the deflation of one's own high self-esteem.

The Theme About
POINT OF VIEW

4
Point of view refers to the position from which details in a literary work are perceived, considered, and described. Alternative terms are *viewpoint, central mind, unifying voice, persona, center of attention, focus,* and the like. Point of view deals with the credibility and probability of the writer's voice as he presents his narration or argument, and also with the interrelationships of this voice and the materials of the work.

The Author's Voice, or Persona

Most writers select a voice representing a phase of personality that is appropriate to the type of situation being presented. This voice, or persona, may be that of the author himself, as nearly as that identity may be determined with all the variant and complex shades of human personality; or the voice may be a separate and totally independent character that the author creates for the occasion. If the personality is taken as totally separate from the author, you may wish to call the voice the *speaker,* or the *persona,* or the author's *mask,* because you refer to an entity that is as much a part of the author's creation as the story itself.

Concern about speakers and masks is derived from the notion that literature is an imitation of life. The concern was not originated by literary critics, but by writers themselves. They conceived of literature as being bound by the same rules of truth and evidence that are operative in law courts and in the writing of history. If literature was to be like life, then it had to be told by a speaker who was similar to an authentic, believable human being. In narrative literature, the speaker had to tell the story as though he was a first-hand witness. If he was on the spot of an action, he may have acquired his knowledge because he was a participant; or he could have been in a building and looked out just as the action began developing; or he might have been in a room looking through a keyhole to see action in another room. If he was not on the spot, he had to acquire the information in some other believable way: he could hear it from someone who was there; or he could receive an informative letter; or he could overhear a conversation between first-hand witnesses. In lyric or discursive poetry, the speaker had to be shown as a person who was directly involved in the emotions or thoughts brought out in the poem. Perhaps he was a happy lover, or an unhappy lover; or perhaps he was a sophisticated human being concerned with philosophical problems. In a word, no matter what kind of literature was being written, the creation of an authentic, centralizing, unifying voice was of paramount concern as a *sine qua non* of a believable, lifelike work.

When modern fiction had its beginnings early in the eighteenth century, the writers were always responsive to problems of point of view. Some writers created a single voice to narrate an entire sequence of events as an account of personal experience. Other writers wove their works out of a collection of letters, thereby allowing a number of voices to describe and interpret events. Later writers, like James, Conrad, Fitzgerald, and Salinger, have paid similar attention to voices and narrators and to the means by which detail is authenticated.

Kinds of Points of View

When you read a work, you may easily detect the point of view by determining the way in which the action is narrated.

FIRST PERSON

If the story is told by an "I," the author is using the *first person* point of view, usually a fictional narrator and not the author himself. The first person speaker can report everything he sees, hears, and thinks, and as he does so he conveys not only the action of the work, but also some of his own particular background, mental characteristics, attitudes, and even prejudices. The speaker's particular type of speech will have a great effect on the language of the work itself. A sailor will use many nautical terms, just as a sixteen-year-old boy may use much slang. For these reasons, the first person speaker is often as much a subject of interest as the details he describes. Nick Carraway in F. Scott Fitzgerald's *The Great Gatsby* is such a speaker. Nick is ostensibly a minor character in the action who tells all about what is happening in the lives of Gatsby and the Buchanans. Sometimes the "I" narrator is the major character in the book, like Mark Twain's Huckleberry Finn or Swift's Gulliver. Often a seemingly minor character who happens to be the narrator may be seen as a major character because of his interest and involvement in the action, like Joseph Conrad's Marlow, the narrator of "Youth," *Heart of Darkness,* and *Lord Jim.*

THIRD PERSON

If the narrator is not introduced as a character, and if everything in the work is described in the third person (i.e., *he, she, it, they*), the author is using the *third person* point of view. There are variants here.

The third person point of view is called *omniscient* when the speaker describes not only the action and dialogue of the work, but also seems to know and report everything that goes on in the minds of his characters. In the third person omniscient point of view, the author takes great responsibility: by delving into the minds of his characters he assumes a stance that exceeds our ordinary experience with other persons. The reason for the term *omniscient* is therefore plain. Like God, the writer attempts to show the inner workings of a character's mind, workings that may be obscure even to that character himself. If you encounter the omniscient point of view, you may be sure that the writer is displaying great concern with psychological patterns and motivations. Writers like George Eliot, Dostoëvsky, Dickens, and Dreiser employed the omniscient point of view often. You may detect it whenever you see phrases like "He thought. . . ." or "As she approached the scene, she considered that. . . ." and so on.

If an author uses the third person, but confines the narration mainly to what one single character does, says, and sometimes thinks, then you have the third person *limited* point of view. While the omniscient point of view gathers in the thoughts of most of the characters, the limited focuses on only one. The limited viewpoint is thus midway between the first and the third person points of view. In Hemingway's story "Big Two-Hearted River," Nick Adams is the entire focus of the action. Hemingway confines his descriptions to what Nick sees and does, only occasionally referring to what he feels. Similarly, Joyce in *Dubliners* includes a number of stories (e.g., "A Little Cloud," "Counterparts," "The Dead") that are focused on the actions and thoughts of a major figure, while the reports on the other figures are confined to actions and statements.

DRAMATIC

A writer using the *dramatic* point of view confines his work mainly to quotations and descriptions of actions. He avoids telling you that certain characters thought this or felt that, but instead allows the characters themselves to voice their thoughts and feelings. Often, too, an author using the dramatic point of view will allow certain characters to interpret the thoughts and feelings of other characters, but then attitudes and possible prejudices of these speakers enter into your evaluation of their interpretations. The key to the dramatic point of view is that the writer presents the reader with action and speech, but does not overtly guide the reader toward any conclusions. Naturally, however, the conclusions may be readily drawn from the details presented. Guy de Maupassant is famous for creating stories rendered in the dramatic point of view, as are Hemingway and Sherwood Anderson.

It goes virtually without saying that many novels, being long works, often have an intermingling of viewpoints. In a largely omniscient narrative, the writer may present a chapter consisting only of action and dialogue—the dramatic point of view—and another chapter that focuses entirely on one person—the limited. Writers of short stories, on the other hand, usually maintain a consistency and uniformity of point of view.

Point of View and Opinions

Point of view should be carefully distinguished from opinions or beliefs, although in popular usage point of view and opinions are frequently confused. Point of view refers to the position from which things are seen; in its broad sense, *position* comprises everything that affects the speaker as an observer, including opinions. Point of view conditions opinions. Suppose that a speaker is blind, or deaf; suppose that he is a child, or an old man; suppose that he has just been married, or that he has been disappointed in love. The opinions of these speakers about a painting, a piece of music, or love, would be necessarily limited by their conditions as observers of these matters. Remember, therefore, that opinions are only a function of point of view. You might say that studying opinions is to study *effects*, while studying point of view is to study *causes*.

Point of View, Character Analysis, and Tone

There are places at which point of view overlaps with *character analysis* (see Chapter 3) and *tone* (see Chapter 12). Thus any consideration of point of view must necessarily treat those character traits of the speaker that influence what he says. Similarly, point of view has the same relation to tone that it has to opinions: tone reveals the attitudes of the speaker toward his material and toward his audience, and these attitudes must inevitably be a product of the speaker's point of view. When you consider these similarities, however, you should realize that there are differences in emphasis: character study emphasizes everything connected with character; tone emphasizes the way language and structure are manipulated to convey attitudes; point of view emphasizes the total vantage point from which things are perceived.

The Purpose of a Theme about Point of View

The purpose of this theme is to cause you to study the complex relationship between the author and the material he is presenting. You should try to identify the author's voice, to determine by inference the qualities and characteristics of the speaker behind the voice, and to determine the relationship between the speaker and the narrative or argument. Find out how the speaker's attitude, knowledge, and limitations have contributed to forming the literary work as it actually is. Also, judge whether the point of view has succeeded in making the work seem true, or authentic, or probable. To make such a judgment you will need to develop your skills in sifting evidence. This is not to say that you should begin by doubting everything that you read, but rather that you should become adept at capturing the qualities and nuances of the writer's art. Selecting a point of view is one of the first steps in the creative-writing process; studying point of view should thus help you to understand and appreciate the artistic mind.

Organizing Your Theme

The object of your theme is to analyze the relationship of the particular point of view to the work. Areas of concern are language, selection of detail, characterization, interpretive commentaries, and narrative development. Your theme might be organized to include analysis of one, a few, or all of these elements. Generally you should determine how the point of view has contributed toward making the story uniquely as it is, and also toward your interpretation of the story. In what way has it entered into your response to the story? Are there any special qualities in the work that could not have been achieved if the author had used another point of view?

INTRODUCTION

In your introduction you should get at the matters and problems that you plan to develop. Of the kinds of points of view, which one is used in the work? What is the major influence of this point of view on the work (e.g., "The omniscient point of view causes full, leisurely insights into many nuances of character," or "The first person point of view enables the work to resemble an exposé of back-room political deals.")? To what extent does the selection of point of view make the work particularly interesting and effective, or uninteresting and ineffective? What particular aspects of the work (action, dialogue, characters, description, narration, analysis) do you wish to analyze in support of your central idea?

BODY

The questions you raise and answer here will of course depend on the work you have studied. It would be impossible to answer all of the following questions in your analysis, but going through them should make you aware of the sorts of things you can include in the body of your theme.

If you have read a work with the first person point of view, your analysis will necessarily involve the speaker. Who is he? Is he a major or a minor character? What is his background? What is his relationship to the person listening to him (if there is a listener)? Does he speak directly to you, the reader, in such a way that you are a listener or an eavesdropper? How does the speaker describe the various situations? Is his method uniquely a function of his character? How reliable is he as an observer? How did he acquire the information he is presenting? How much does he disclose? How much does he hide? Does he ever rely on the information of others for his material? How reliable are these other witnesses? Does the speaker undergo any changes in the course of the work that have any bearing on the ways he presents the material? Does he notice one kind of thing (e.g., discussion) but miss others (e.g., natural scenery)? What might have escaped him, if anything? Does the author put the speaker into situations that he can describe but not understand? Why? Is the speaker ever confused? Is he close to the action, or distant from it? Does he show emotional involvement in any situations? Are you as a reader sympathetic to his concerns or are you put off by them? If the speaker makes any commentary, are his thoughts accurate or valid? To what extent, if any, is the speaker of as much interest as the material he presents?

If you encounter any of the third person points of view you should try to determine the characteristics of the voice employed by the author. Does it seem that the author is speaking in his own voice, or that he has created a special voice for the narrator? You can approach this problem by answering many of the questions that are relevant to the first person point of view. You should also try to determine the closeness or distance of the narrator to the action. How is the action described? How is the dialogue recorded? Is there any background information given? Do the descriptions reveal any bias toward any of the characters? Are the descriptions full or bare? Does the author include descriptions or analyses of a character's thoughts? What are these like? Do you see evidence of the author's own philosophy? Does the word choice direct you toward any particular interpretations? What limitations or freedoms devolve upon the story as a result of the point of view?

CONCLUSION

In your conclusion you should evaluate the success of the author's point of view: Was it consistent, effective, truthful? What did the writer gain (if anything) by his selection of point of view? What did he lose (if anything)? How might a less skillful writer have handled similar material? After answering questions like these, you may end your theme.

Problems in Writing Your Theme

1. In considering point of view, you will encounter the problem of whether to discuss the author or his voice, speaker, mask, or persona as the originator of attitudes and ideas. If the author is employing the first person point of view, there is no problem. Use the speaker's name, if he is given one (e.g., Nick Carraway, Huck Finn, Holden Caulfield), or else talk about the "speaker" or "persona" if he is not named. You face a greater problem with the third person points of view, but even here it is

safe for you to discuss the "speaker" rather than the "author," remembering always that the author is manipulating his narrative voice. Sometimes the voice will be the author's, but sometimes the author will write as though he is emphasizing a certain phase of his own personality through his speaker. There will naturally be many ideas common to both the author and his speaker, but your statements about these must be inferential, not absolute.

2. You may have a tendency to wander away from point of view into a synopsis or a discussion of ideas. Emphasize the presentation of the events and ideas and the causes for this presentation. Do not emphasize the subject material itself, but use it only as it bears on your consideration of point of view. Your object is not just to interpret the work, but also to show how the point of view enables you to interpret the work.

Obviously you must talk about the material in the work, but use it only to illustrate your assertions about point of view. You should avoid the following pattern of statement, which will always lead you astray: "The speaker says this, which means this." You must instead adhere to this pattern, which will keep your emphasis always on your central idea: "The speaker says this, which shows this about him and his attitudes." If a particular idea is difficult, you might need to explain it, but do not do so unless it illustrates your central idea.

3. Remember that you are dealing with point of view in the *entire* work, and not simply in single narrations and conversations. For example, an individual character has his own point of view when he states something, but in relation to the entire work his speech is a function of the dramatic point of view. Thus, you should not talk about Character *A*'s point of view, and Character *B*'s, but instead should state that "Using the dramatic point of view, Author *Z* allows the various characters to argue their cases, in their own words and with their own limitations. . . ." and so on.

SAMPLE THEME

Shirley Jackson's Dramatic Point of View in "The Lottery" [1]

The dramatic point of view in Shirley Jackson's story "The Lottery" is essential to the success with which the author is able to render horror in the midst of the ordinary. * The story is not just a horror story; it could also be called a surprise story, an allegory,

---

[1] Shirley Jackson, "The Lottery," in *The Lottery* (New York: Avon Books, 1969). Parenthetical page numbers refer to this edition.

* Central idea.

and a portrayal of human obtuseness, passivity, and cruelty. But the validity of all other claims for "The Lottery" hinge on the author's establishing the horror as stemming from a seemingly everyday, matter-of-fact situation—a situation that could not easily be maintained if another point of view were used. *The success of Shirley Jackson's rendering of horror is achieved through her rudimentary but expert characterization, her almost clinically detached selection of details, and her deceivingly simple diction.* †

The villagers are depicted as ordinary folks attending a normal, festive event—in contrast to the real horror of their ultimate activity. Because of the dramatic point of view within the context of a brief narrative, Miss Jackson prevents all but the most essential aspects of character from emerging. She chooses to see things from the outside, almost as though she is adopting the pose of a villager who is detached and emotionally uninvolved with the events that are unfolding. Her speaker thus records details about the villagers and reveals a certain knowledge of local gossip. The speaker presents enough background information about Mr. Summers, for example, to permit the conclusion that he is a middle-aged, pillar-of-society type who is the usual community leader. Tessie Hutchinson is the principal character in the story, but we learn little more about her than that she is chatty, illiterate, and relatively inarticulate—all facts that are essential to her behavior at the end of the story when she objects not to the lottery itself but to the "unfairness" of the drawing. So it is also with the other characters—and there are surprisingly quite a few—who appear in the story. Their brief conversations are recorded but no more. We see them from a distance, as we would likely see any representative group of human beings in a gathering that is too formal to permit intimacy. This distant, reportorial method of illustrating character is fundamental to the dramatic point of view, and the twist of cruelty at the end depends on the method.

While the dramatic point of view could theoretically permit the introduction of many details, Miss Jackson's method in "The Lottery" is to concentrate almost clinically on only those details that bring out the horror. Because her speaker is removed from the immediate emotions of the scene, we learn just enough detail, but no more. At the beginning of the story there must be at least some information about the background of the lottery so that the reader can make some sense out of it, but there should be absolutely no disclosure about the consequences of drawing the black spot. Thus, the speaker establishes that the villagers are gathering rocks, but

† Thesis sentence.

includes no mention of why. The short saying "Lottery in June, corn be heavy soon" is mentioned as a remnant of a more ritualistic kind of scapegoatism, but the speaker does not go into any sort of explanation (p. 215). All such references are at first presented innocently, and it is only after reading the ending that a reader can feel their sinister qualities.

Without exaggeration, if there had been more detail in the story, contrast could not have been brought out so well. The selection of some other point of view would inevitably have required more detail. A first person speaker, for example, could not have been credible if he had not explained the situation in advance, or at least if he had not described some attitude that would have anticipated the conclusion. An omniscient narrator would necessarily have expressed some commentary on the reactions of the townsfolk. But the dramatic point of view permits just enough detail to inform the reader, but not so much as to spoil the surprise conclusion.

Appropriate to the conclusion, and to the graceless, simple, unquestioning, overly conservative nature of the villagers, is the diction. The language is uncolored and unemotional, sufficiently descriptive but not elaborate. When Tessie Hutchinson appears, she dries "her hands on her apron" (p. 213)—a description that is functional and no more. Much of this sort of diction may be seen as a means by which Miss Jackson uses point of view to hide details from the reader. The piles of stones, for example, are to be used in the ritual stoning of Tessie Hutchinson, yet one could never draw this conclusion when they are first described:

> Bobby Martin had already stuffed his pockets full of stones, and the other boys soon followed his example, selecting the smoothest and roundest stones; Bobby and Harry Jones and Dickie Delacroix—the villagers pronounced this name "Dellacroy"—eventually made a great pile of stones in one corner of the square and guarded it against the raids of the other boys (p. 211).

The speaker's references to the nicknames, and to the association of the stones with apparently normal boyhood games, both divert the reader's attention and obscure the real horror of the fact that within two hours the stones will be used to kill someone. Even at the end, Tessie Hutchinson's son Davy is given a few "pebbles"; the implication of this word is that the boy is going to a game!

Because of such masterly control over point of view, it is obvious that Miss Jackson has created a supremely successful story. Her whole objective is to establish a superficial appearance of reality, which she maintains up to the last few paragraphs. Indeed, she is so successful that a possible response to the conclusion is that "such a killing could not take place among such common, earthy folks as the story presents." Yet it is because of the authenticity of the story that a reader sees the validity of Miss Jackson's vision. Horror is not to be found on moors and in haunted castles, but among the people we see everyday, like the villagers in Tessie Hutchinson's hometown. The story thus expands, and supports many applications to human life in general. Without Miss Jackson's skill in controlling point of view, there could be little of this power of suggestion, and it would not be possible to claim such success for the story.

The Theme About
SETTING

Setting refers to the natural and artificial scenery or environment in which characters in literature live, move, and have their being. Setting also includes what in the theater would be called props or properties—the implements and manufactured goods employed by the characters in various activities. Such things as the time of day and the consequent amount of light at which an event occurs, the flora and fauna, the sounds described, the smells, and the weather are all part of the setting. Paint brushes, apples, pitchforks, rafts, six-shooters, watches, automobiles, horses and buggies, and innumerable other items belong to the setting. References to clothing, descriptions of physical appearance, and spatial relationships among the characters are also part of setting. In short, the setting of a work is the sum total of references to physical and temporal objects and artifacts.

The setting of a story or novel is much like the sets and properties of the stage, and like the location for a motion picture. The dramatist writing for the stage, however, is physically limited by what can be built by carpenters and stagehands, and by what can be positioned and carried. A typical play today is often set in a single area, with differences in time of day or season suggested by lighting, costuming, and movable properties. In Shakespeare's day the stage was a bare platform with almost no movable scenery, and scenes were necessarily independent of place. The dramatist thus was compelled to focus his skill on language and action. Except for the use of various appurtenances of the stage, the effects of setting on Shakespeare's characterizations are negligible. In contrast to the dramatist, the writer of nondramatic works is limited only by his imagination. It is possible for him to include details of many places without the slightest external restraint. Therefore, for purposes of the present theme, the references to setting will be to stories, novels, and those poems that establish a setting either in nature or in man-made things.

It goes virtually without saying that the action of a story may occur in more than one place. In a novel, the locale may shift constantly. Although there may be several settings in a work, the term *setting* refers generally to all the places mentioned. If a story is short, all the scenes may be in one city or countryside, so that a theme about setting could include a discussion of all the locations within the story. If your assignment is on a novel, your discussion could best be devoted to the setting of only one major scene; otherwise you would necessarily be forced beyond the limits of a single theme.

Types of Settings

NATURAL SETTINGS

The setting for a great deal of literature is the out-of-doors, and, naturally enough, Nature herself is seen as a force that shapes character and action. It is true that the progress of civilization has been largely a process of overcoming and taming natural forces. It is also true that Nature has not been, and is not now, completely understood. As a result, writers have often seen the land, the wind, and the sea as forces that are wild, destructive, indifferent, unpredictable, and mysterious. Literature stemming from superstitious times emphasized the fabulous, the remote, the supernatural; hence the labyrinth of ancient myth, and places such as Scylla and Charybdis, Olympus, Valhalla, the Halls of Heorot, and the sea-washed coast of Cornwall. Medieval writers described fairy worlds, which included dark, brooding forests and fire-breathing dragons. Even in more recent times Nature has been perceived as still a hostile force. Destructive storms, blistering sun, drought, numbing cold, enveloping snow; high mountains, precipitous cliffs, burning deserts, quicksand; wolves, tigers, snakes, alligators, vultures—all these in the setting of a work are often presented as manifestations of Nature's hostility to human beings.

This is not to say that no writers show Nature as a benign, friendly force—a force to be enjoyed, loved, and protected. Nature may inspire joy by providing flowers, warm sunshine, balmy winds, groves of trees, refreshing lakes, butterflies, singing birds, and ripening crops. Even the wild and dangerous places of the earth may become the setting of quests for identity, and for comparisons between the vastness of God and the smallness of man. If Nature is seen as a positive benefit, she is also seen as something to be protected. Coleridge's Ancient Mariner violated Nature by shooting an albatross, and as a result he was destined to an eternity of expiation. James Fenimore Cooper described the wholesale slaughter of passenger pigeons and was affronted and depressed by such a wanton destruction of Nature. Today, when people have littered the land with trash and contaminated the air and water with pollution, many writers have perceived that Nature as we know her is threatened, as is man with her. We may expect future literature in which many aspects of natural setting will emphasize the precarious state of the natural world and the need for protecting it.

MAN-MADE SETTINGS

Artificial scenery always refers to the societies that created it. Hence a building, or a room, bespeaks the character of those who build and inhabit it, and ultimately it reveals the social and political orders that maintain the condition. A sumptuous artificial setting emphasizes the sumptuous and refined taste of the characters living in it, and also their financial and political resources. With a few cracks in the plaster and some chips in the paint or wallpaper, the same setting may well reflect persons of the same taste undergoing a decline in fortune and power. More recently the development of the idea that environment has a vital influence on human character has produced a number of stories that emphasize the deleterious effect of dirty, cold, ill-lit cities and drab rooms. D. H. Lawrence, who wrote many works in which environment is shown to have a shaping influence on character, wrote vehemently that ugliness hurts human beings—an idea that underlies much *realistic,* or *naturalistic,* fiction:

> Now though perhaps nobody knew it, it was ugliness which really betrayed the spirit of man, in the nineteenth century. The great crime which the moneyed classes and promoters of industry committed in the palmy Victorian days was the condemning of the workers to ugliness, ugliness, ugliness: meanness and formless and ugly surroundings, ugly ideals, ugly religion, ugly hope, ugly love, ugly clothes, ugly furniture, ugly houses, ugly relationship between workers and employers.[1]

This is not to say that an author cannot describe slovenly conditions to show that his characters are also slovenly, but it is to say that he may often include such descriptions to show that an ugly environment has contributed to the weariness, insensitivity, negligence, or even hostility in his characters.

Setting refers not only to place but also to time and everything that time implies. Morning, for example, is a time of beginning, and perhaps

[1] *The Portable D. H. Lawrence,* Diana Trilling, ed. (New York: The Viking Press, 1947, reprinted 1950), p. 620.

of optimism, whereas twilight is close to evening and hence a less optimistic time. The spirits of the hero Werther in Goethe's novel *The Sorrows of Young Werther* are directly related to spring, summer, autumn, and winter; as the seasons change Werther becomes more depressed until the winter of his soul overwhelms him. A happier mood is established by Wordsworth in "Lines Written in Early Spring," in which the title and the first two lines lead into a meditation on the discrepancy between the joyful season and the mismanagement of human beings by one another.

Studying the Uses of Setting

On the very primary level setting has served as a means of creating a semblance of realism in literature. Realism of course depends on the beholder, but men will always assent to the description of observable phenomena. Realism in a broad sense may be extended to include what is described from philosophical or religious points of view; psychological and political viewpoints will also color what is seen and described yet still determine what is called "realistic."

As a writer wishes to stress character, plot, or action, he may emphasize or minimize setting. At times a setting will serve as a mere location for events, as in Henry James's short story "The Tree of Knowledge." In this story the setting is minimal, and all the emphasis is on conversation and analysis of character. In other stories, however, the setting may become so significant that it virtually becomes an active participant in the action. A good example is the setting of Thomas Hardy's novel *The Return of the Native.* The desolate area known as Egdon Heath directly influences the characters who live there; it governs their lives and most of their activities. Although the Heath occasionally serves to bring characters together, more often it acts as a barrier, and it is even the active cause of the death of Mrs. Yeobright and Eustacia Vie.

In studying the setting of any particular work, your first concern should be to discover all details that conceivably form a part of setting and then to determine how the author has used these details. This concern is artistic. You might observe, for example, that the manipulation of setting may be a kind of direct language, a means by which the author makes statements that he may or may not interpret. In the concluding scene of E. M. Forster's *A Passage to India,* a large rock divides the path along which the two major characters are riding. This rock is a direct barrier between them, and Forster is at pains to point out this fact.

Another way to use setting as a kind of statement is to describe a setting in lieu of describing events, in this sense placing the setting on the level of metaphor (this technique has become common in motion pictures). The language used by the author to describe the setting is an important clue for you to follow in interpreting his story. Allan Seager's "This Town and Salamanca" provides such an example: the narrator describes the adventures of a childhood friend who spent his early manhood as a world traveler. The narrator dwells longingly and lovingly on the places visited by the friend, using language that gives them a romantic, heroic glow. At the same time, he describes his home town in matter-of-fact, flat language. As a result of this technique, Seager makes the assumptions and ideals of his narrator clear.

An author might also manipulate setting as a means of organizing his story structurally. It is often comic, for example, to move a character from one environment to another (provided that no harm is done in the process). Thus, Stephen Crane provokes smiles, if not laughter, in the first part of "The Bride Comes to Yellow Sky" by shifting a provincial town marshal into the plush setting of a Pullman car. Crane's description of the awkwardness of the marshal and the patronizing airs of the other characters, who are accustomed to the setting, is humorous. The same shifting of environment causes a bitterly comic and finally tragic effect in Aldous Huxley's *Brave New World,* in which the main character, John, leaves a primitive world for a hyper-modern, super-urbanized one.

Another structural manipulation of setting is the "framing" method: an author "frames" his story by opening with a description of the setting and then returns to the description at the end. Like a picture frame, the setting constantly influences the story. An outstanding example of the framing method is found in Hemingway's story "In Another Country," which is set in Milan in World War I. The opening picture is one of windy, autumnal chill, with dusky light illuminating dead poultry and dead animals hanging in a butcher's shop; the twilight casts a pall over a hospital courtyard, from which many funeral processions begin. At the story's end, one of the principal characters, a major, receives news that his wife has died of pneumonia (caught, presumably, because of the chill). He has been wounded in action and is at the hospital undergoing physical therapy by machine, and the news of his wife's death leaves him despondently looking out the windows. What he sees is obviously the same gloomy scene described at the opening of the story. By concluding in this way, Hemingway has framed the events in a setting of dusk, depression, and death.

A more full use of setting is the "enclosing" setting—a setting that serves as the place of the entire action and that is constant and prominent throughout the story. A notable example is the Usher mansion in Poe's "The Fall of the House of Usher." The house is approached, entered, and left by the narrator after a short lapse of time, which comprises the entire action; all attention in the story is focused on the house and its owners, Roderick Usher and his sister. Details of the house itself are vital to the action, and the condition of the house is symbolic of the condition of its occupants. Few stories have had setting, character, action, and mood so skillfully integrated as this one.

To the degree that a setting can add metaphoric energy to its purely mechanical functions, the discussion of setting fuses with that of *imagery* (see Chapter 11). Setting is often a form of imagery, for the qualities of a setting, like anything else, can be abstracted; if these qualities are generally true, then the setting is metaphorical and may become symbolic. The ease with which the language itself becomes metaphoric assists this process. Thus, when Poe writes that the stones of the Usher mansion possess a "still perfect adaptation of parts and the crumbling condition of the individual stones," it is obvious that he speaks not only of the house but also of the deteriorating psyche of Roderick Usher. Robert Frost's poem "Mending Wall" describes the scene of two men mending a stone wall in the springtime. Frost makes it clear that the wall refers metaphorically to those barriers that prevent close relationships between human beings, those protections of silence and indifference that allow a person to refuse understanding and compassion to others. Once this metaphorical significance is established, it is possible to carry the meaning of the wall still further; it can refer to political or social boundaries or more generally to any barrier between individuals or groups. Another wall that is symbolic is the one in Jean Paul Sartre's story "The Wall," in this case a wall against which prisoners are lined up and shot. The wall serves as a symbol of Sartre's idea that the terminataion of life is arbitrary and ridiculous and that the activities of life itself are similarly arbitrary and ridiculous. So well known is this use of setting that Sartre's wall has been claimed as a symbol of modern Existentialist philosophy, of which Sartre is a leading advocate.

The fact that setting merges into metaphor and symbol should make you constantly on the alert to determine when the two become one. You might note that the description of an action requires only a functional description of setting. An action set in a forest needs no more description than that the forest is there. But if a writer describes the trees, the colors, the shapes, the light, the animal inhabitants, or the topography, you should try to determine his purpose. That is, descriptions of setting may vary from the purely functional and appropriate to the evocative and to the outrightly symbolic; but they are almost never purely accidental or gratuitous. A full, colorful description may be designed as an appropriate setting for a happy action; but it might just as easily be interpreted as an ironic backdrop for an unhappy one. You can make your determinations as you read the story carefully, and you can see when the setting becomes evocative and symbolic. In Dickens's *Bleak House*, for example, Dickens describes a district called "Tom All Alone's" as a shadowy, dark, unhealthy, hopeless place. The district is symbolic of the bleak fate of all those human creatures doomed to live there. By contrast, Dickens creates a cheerful symbol in his constant references to the bubbling fountain toward the end of *David Copperfield*. The fountain suggests the upsurging fortunes of David and his growing love for Agnes.

Just as setting performs a vital functional role and also contributes to overall meaning because of metaphoric significance, it also affects the *atmosphere* or *mood* of stories and poems. The styles and shapes of things described, their colors, the language used to describe them—all have their own connotative life that an author may utilize to fulfill his aims. A description of happy colors (like reds, oranges, yellows, and greens) may contribute to a mood of gaiety, whereas one of somber colors (like blacks and greys) may suggest sobriety or gloom. References to smells and sounds bring the setting even more to life by asking more responses from the reader than those merely to sight. The setting of a story on a farm, or in a suburban split-level home, or in a large apartment, may evoke a response to these habitats that may contribute to a story's atmosphere.

The style with which things are described may have an effect on atmosphere, for a writer may make his scene static or still with many linking and passive words for one mood, but evoke another mood in a lively scene through the use of active verbs. Sometimes a setting may speak for itself, without authorial comment, but often the author will introduce comments designed to connect the setting with the characters or else to suggest the proper response to the reader. Here is a fragment from a lengthy description of a setting in Sir Walter Scott's *Kenilworth*. This description performs both functions, skillfully linking description to reader and character:

> . . . Formal walks and avenues, which, at different points, crossed this principal approach, were, in like manner, choked up and interrupted by piles of brushwood and billets, and in other places by underwood and brambles. Besides the general effect of desolation which is so strongly impressed, whenever we behold the contrivances of man wasted and obliterated by neglect, and witness the marks of social life effaced gradually by the influence of vegetation, the size of the trees, and the outspreading extent of their boughs, diffused a gloom over the scene, even when the sun was at the highest, and made a proportional impression on the mind of those who visited it. This was felt even by Michael Lambourne, however alien his habits were to receiving any impressions, excepting from things which addressed themselves immediately to his passions.[2]

Although the description of a setting may thus contribute to atmosphere in a number of ways, it is important to remember that atmosphere is a broad concept and is affected by everything in the story, not just the setting. Action, character, dialogue, idea, allusion, and style are all elements that contribute to atmosphere.

[2] *Kenilworth* (London: Everyman's Library, 1906), p. 25

Organizing Your Theme

The object of this theme should be to relate the setting to some aspect of the work being studied. You should not simply describe the setting and be satisfied. You should make your description a part of a point such as "The author's description of setting reveals an eye for detail, spatial relationships, and color," and so on. Then, your discussion would take the shape required by your central idea; your own detail would be functional. Your theme should move from a discussion of setting toward a discussion of its effects.

INTRODUCTION

Here you should limit that aspect of the setting you wish to discuss and relate it to your central idea and thesis sentence. Any special problems and qualifications should be mentioned here.

BODY

Here are some ideas about what to include in the body of your theme. You may concentrate on one of these, or two or three, depending on the story or poem that you are analyzing. Your principal aim should be to say as much as possible about the setting within the assigned length.

1. The relationship of physical characteristics of the setting to some general observation about these characteristics. If the author has been particularly careful to mention many details of the setting, you could fruitfully discuss these details in an attempt to re-create what you think the author envisaged and to make observations about the qualities of the setting. The settings of Shirley Jackson's "The Lottery" or Franz Kafka's "In the Penal Colony" could be treated in this way. Among the questions you might attempt to answer are these: Can the setting be re-created and imagined by the reader? Are the details about the setting specific, or are they vague? How great a bearing do the details have on the action of the story? Are they constantly used, or are they put aside once the action has begun? What details are neglected that the author might possibly have mentioned? On the basis of your study, what conclusions can you draw about the author's ability to paint a verbal picture (does the author describe shapes and distances better than colors, or vice versa)? Is he perceptive to smells and sounds? Does he introduce new details as the need seems to arise, or does he rely on his first descriptions?

2. The relationship of the setting to character. In many instances the author emphasizes the effect of environment on character, as in O. E. Rölvaag's novel *Giants in the Earth*, Melville's story "Bartleby the Scrivener," or Theodore Roethke's poem "Dolor." Your aim in a theme on this subject is not, as in the first type, to describe the details of setting, but to select those details that have the most bearing on character and to speak about their effects. Questions that would lead you into the topic might be the following: What tasks do the characters perform that involve them in the setting? What particular physical and moral strengths do these tasks require? What weaknesses do they bring out? What traits enable a person to adjust to these conditions and to prevail against them? What outlooks toward God, life, and Nature do the characters have that may be traced specifically to their environment? That is, does the world seem difficult, easy? Does God seem benevolent, all-powerful, harsh, or nonexistent? Does Nature seem to be an enemy or a friend? Are the views justified in terms of the life envisaged in the story, or do some characters receive false impressions? Do they ignore aspects of their environment? What other character traits may be traced to the way of life on the soil or before the mast or within the sweatshop or behind the desk? Emphasize constantly the interaction of setting and character.

3. The relationship of setting and (a) atmosphere (b) structure and action and (c) ideas. This theme attempts to deal with artistic relationships and effects. A theme on atmosphere and setting should establish the prevailing atmosphere or mood of the work and then attempt to fit the setting into this whole. Colors, shapes, time of year (or day), and the effects that these things generally produce are relevant here. If the atmosphere of the setting is at variance with the general effect of the story, you should emphasize this variance and attempt to determine why it exists.

A theme about the relation of setting to structure and action should attempt to show how significant the setting is in the form and principal actions of the story. Is the setting a frame, an enclosure? Is it mentioned at various divisions or shifts in the action? Is it brought in as a natural place for the characters, or does it become significant accidentally? That is, does a character move naturally from, say, a park to a pastry shop to home, or does he move from the park and then accidentally walk down a street he never walks down, where the main action takes place? How important a role does the setting play in the action? Do the characteristics of a room seem appropriate for a private conversation, for private grief, or for personal isolation? Do the characteristics of a natural scene enter directly into the action as land that is to be plowed, trees to be cleared, or great nautical distances to be traversed? Does the setting afford any natural pleasures of which the characters take advantage? Does it afford natural dangers that the characters either avoid or to which they fall prey?

A theme about setting and ideas should emphasize the setting as statement and metaphor. A writer, for example, may establish that a ship, where the action occurs, is similar to the world at large and, therefore, that his ideas about life aboard ship are also true of life in general. A natural setting that is crisp, clear, and bright, with precisely defined relationships, might be created by an author as a way of saying that truth in the universe can be readily grasped; yet a setting that emphasizes haziness, difficulty of determining things at a distance, or vastness might be construed to mean that truth is not easily found and that much of life is mysterious. Similarly, the conditions of buildings, rooms, and tools might be interpreted as statements about the conditions of life generally. When settings become symbolic, as discussed earlier in this chapter, then the value of the symbols should be described. In this theme you should stress not only the ideas represented by the setting but also the means by which the setting lends itself to statement. Before attempting a theme about setting and symbol, you would do well to read the chapter on imagery (Chapter 11).

SAMPLE THEME

The Setting of Conrad's Story
"The Secret Sharer" [1]

If the setting of Conrad's "The Secret Sharer" were not as descriptive and detailed as it is, the story would not be effective. The setting aboard ship in the Gulf of Siam, described in the Captain's words, leads to the relevant action in the first part of the story; namely, the Captain's decision to conceal Leggatt both from his own crew and from the Captain and crew of the *Sephora*, the ship aboard which Leggatt "committed" his crime. By law, the Captain does wrong in aiding and abetting Leggatt, and a great deal of explaining and describing on Conrad's part is necessary to justify this baffling of courtroom justice. The concealment itself, to be plausible, requires detailed description of the Captain's cabin and the adjacent parts of the ship. Conrad's picturesque and detailed description of the setting therefore serves first to persuade the reader to see things as the Captain sees them—to focus attention on his human, personal considerations—and second to act as a passive agent in the sometimes melodramatic action of the story.

Although the only essential actions in the first quarter of the story are the Captain's conversations with Leggatt and the decision

1 Morton Dauwen Zabel, ed., *The Portable Conrad* (New York: The Viking Press, 1950). Parenthetical page numbers refer to this edition.

to shelter him, the section contains much description both of the seascape and of the ship. Because the Captain is the observer and narrator, the setting reveals his broad, full perspective. He is an inquisitive, understanding man who sees and notices much. His perceptions take in shapes, distances, and colors:

> . . . when I turned my head to take a parting glance at the tug which had just left us anchored outside the bar, I saw the straight line of the flat shore joined to the stable sea, edge to edge, with a perfect and unmarked closeness, in one leveled floor half brown, half blue under the enormous dome of the sky (p. 648).

Because of this eye for detail, the reader is inclined to accept the Captain's generalization, which concludes the opening descriptions:

> In this breathless pause at the threshold of a long passage we seemed to be measuring our fitness for a long and arduous enterprise, the appointed task of both our existences [i.e., the ship's and the captain's] to be carried out, far from all human eyes, with only sky and sea for spectators and for judges (p. 649).

Indeed, Conrad's main reason for the opening detail is to establish confidence in the Captain. If the reader can accept the Captain's sensitivity toward the natural world, it will be possible then to accept his judgment and protection of Leggatt, for Leggatt is portrayed with characteristics so similar to those of the Captain that he is constantly referred to as the Captain's "double." The two characters have much in common; the sea links them in the brotherhood of naval life, and the sea itself is the means by which they meet. It is also the Captain's observations of the effects of the sea on Leggatt's appearance that emphasize their kinship. Leggatt comes to the ship at night through the dark water, cast in a "ghastly, silvery, fishlike" and "greenish cadaverous glow" (pp. 655, 654). The setting itself underscores the Captain's unspoken but clearly felt awareness, personified in Leggatt, that within each human being is the potentiality for trouble and that this danger stems from our very origins, symbolized by the darkness (of the soul) and the water (from which life comes). Some are lucky enough to avoid trouble, but when it emerges, we must protect ourselves from it. Something like this reasoning makes understandable the Captain's decision to protect Leggatt, whose claims of innocence are not necessary to the Captain's feeling of kinship with him. By using the setting to show the Captain's sensitivity, Conrad makes his actions acceptable.

To make the events acceptable to the reader is also the purpose of Conrad's attention to detail throughout the story, particularly to those details of the ship and the coast of Cambodia that permit the successful concealment of Leggatt. It is vital to the story's credibility that the details of the Captain's cabin be presented. The L shape of the cabin is mentioned as providing a number of hiding places—the hanging coats, the bathroom, the curtained bunk. The tension resulting from the near-discoveries by the steward all depend on details about the cabin being known. Similarly, touring the ship itself becomes a means by which the Captain preserves his composure when the *Sephora*'s captain comes aboard searching for Leggatt. The noise made by sailors walking on the deck above the Captain's cabin permits the Captain and Leggatt to speak together without fear of being overheard. The sail locker is the place of concealment for Leggatt as he prepares to leave the ship.

Many details of this sort could be mentioned, for it would be difficult to refer to any action in "The Secret Sharer" that is not closely related to the setting of the ship. The section of the story in which details about the setting become most important, however, is the conclusion, when the ship itself is in danger of foundering on the Cambodian shore. With the "black mass of Koh-ring" hovering over the ship, the Captain steers dangerously close to land, in an action symbolic of the decision he has made to save Leggatt. The closeness of Koh-ring to the ship and the consequent danger to the Captain's future suggest the difficulty and danger men generally must face if they are to carry on in life. Symbolically, even though the tugboat at the story's beginning leaves the Captain's ship and thus emphasizes man's independence of action, Koh-ring emphasizes the threat hanging over man as he exercises this independence.

The setting of the story thus verges between the real on the one hand and the symbolic on the other. Without the realistic details about the ship and navigational methods, the story would not be as believable or as exciting as it is. The setting permits the reader to accept the story on the easiest level, that of the action, without becoming involved in the aura of symbolism that surrounds the action.

If one chooses to savor the incidents, however, the details support conclusion after conclusion. The setting of the tale within the tale—Leggatt's narration of how he strangled the sailor—might be construed to mean that men are sometimes faced with circumstances in which by doing right (putting up a sail to rescue a ship in a severe storm) they also inadvertently do wrong. Judgment in such cases, if possible in view of the facts, must be tempered with understanding. The Captain shows such understanding, for clearly he can see himself behaving the same way under the same conditions. Such possible interpretations enable one to conclude that Conrad's use of setting provides a dynamic image of the world that men must face. This world is vast and mysterious, and the consequences of action in it are not predictable. If a good action produces a bad effect, this action should be judged fully, in view of the resultant good and character of the actor, and should never be considered apart from all its effects.

The Theme Discussing
IDEAS

CHAPTER 6 The word *idea* is closely related to the actions of seeing and knowing. At one time it was defined as a mental image, picture, or perception; an idea was an image of something you could bring to mind when that thing was no longer present before you. That meaning has been largely replaced. An idea to most people today is a concept, thought, opinion, or belief. When you discuss ideas, then, you are concentrating on thoughts and concepts. If you start talking broadly about *meaning* you are discussing ideas. When you consider questions like "What was on the author's mind?" or "What is the implication of this or that work?" you are in fact considering ideas. As you respond to the question "What is this work about?" you will be dealing with ideas.

You have spent much of your reading time in discovering and profiting from ideas, just as much classroom time on literature is devoted to the discussion of ideas. But bear in mind that although ideas are important, they are not all. Try to find a "message" in Keats's "To Autumn," and you will realize that looking for ideas and *only* for ideas has limitations (e.g., searching only for ideas might make a reader oblivious to literary pleasures derivable from things such as the artist's diction, manipulation of sound, comic techniques, and control over structure). Within these limitations, however, the study of ideas is valuable. If you have been asked to write about ideas, your purpose should be to analyze the literary work in order to name, discuss, and evaluate the ideas contained within it. Ususally it is best for you to concentrate on one major idea rather than several.

The Place of Ideas

In expository literature there are few special obstacles to understanding the principal idea or ideas, because a major purpose of exposition is to present ideas. Except for the special kind of exposition known as dialogue, exposition offers only the ordinary difficulty of understanding the ideas as they are presented—a difficulty that every college student encounters when he listens to a lecture or reads a textbook.

In imaginative literature, however, which tells stories, dramatizes human conflicts, idealizes or attacks various attitudes, and deliberates generally on the human condition, perceiving ideas is more difficult. Ideas in imaginative literature are usually presented indirectly, and often they are couched in metaphorical language. They are therefore subject to interpretation. In most stories, poems, and dramas, ideas are subordinate to the situations and actions. Although such works are usually enjoyed without reference to ideas, it is true that ideas are important reasons for which the author originally took pen in hand. An author is above all a person with something to say. Sometimes an idea will have caused him to shape his story in a certain way, or to create characters with certain distinguishing traits. Suppose a writer has an idea that a particular custom or institution of society is wrong, or suppose that he has an idea that human beings should be free. He may then write a story or novel to make these ideas apparent. Suppose he believes that human beings in the twentieth century have lost their intolerance of cruelty; might such an idea have prompted W. B. Yeats to write these lines that conclude his poem "The Second Coming":

> And what rough beast, its hour come round at last,
> Slouches towards Bethlehem to be born?

Lines such as these should make you realize that in much literature the original meaning of *idea* as an image or figure is still operating. Yeats embodied many ideas about political and military conditions in the twentieth century within the image of the "rough beast." How many ideas about war, genocide, and displacement of peoples could you suggest from this image?

Many works similarly exemplify or dramatize political, psychological, or social ideas. Sometimes a writer may introduce the same idea into different works, perhaps to test the idea by varying it and seeing how far it can be pursued. Ideas, in short, are vital in the content and form of literature, and an analysis of ideas necessarily implies a consideration of their artistic effect.

How to Find Ideas

You should therefore know the ways, direct and indirect, by which authors express ideas. The following descriptions are for convenient analysis only, because in a literary work the methods described may all occur simultaneously.

DIRECT STATEMENTS BY THE AUTHOR.   Often an author makes direct statements of ideas in order to guide or deepen your understanding of his story. George Eliot, for example, is noted for the many discussions about human character and motivation interspersed throughout her novels. Also, an author manipulates literary devices such as metaphors, similes, settings, and physical descriptions in such a way that these may be interpreted as statements of his own ideas. In the stories of J. D. Salinger the introduction of a bright, intuitive child has the importance of a symbol, for the child always suggests Salinger's idea that the insights of children, who are close to God in time, serve as evidence of God's being and for this reason are spiritual and emotional stimuli to jaded adults.

When an author states ideas in his own person or through literary devices, you should consider these at face value. It is reasonable, when you discuss these ideas, to attribute them to the author. Remember, however, that your attribution should not have the weight of absolute biographical fact. You are reading an author's work, not his mind, and an author may well exercise his right to express ideas of the moment or ideas with which he does not agree. When in writing a theme you say "George Eliot believes . . . ." or "It is Faulkner's idea that . . . ." you must always realize the limitations of your statements: you are really not talking absolutely about the *authors* but instead are talking about their *works*. With this reservation your remarks about an author's ideas should usually be acceptable.

DIRECT STATEMENTS BY THE AUTHOR'S PERSONA.   Frequently, instead of narrating in their own persons, authors will write from the point of view of a character in the work (for example, Frederick Henry in *A Farewell to Arms* and Gulliver in *Gulliver's Travels*). Such a character is called a *persona,* with life and independence of his own and with the freedom to state ideas peculiar to himself. Whereas the author unquestionably might agree with the ideas of his *persona,* you can never know exactly when this agreement takes place. Although the statements of a *persona* may be direct, you must use your ingenuity and intuition in deciding how closely the *persona's* ideas correspond with the author's.

DRAMATIC STATEMENTS MADE BY THE CHARACTERS IN THE WORK. In any dramatic work, and in most novels, stories, and poems, the characters will state ideas. What the characters say will often be in conflict, for an author may sometimes present thirteen ways of looking at a blackbird and leave the choice up to you. He may provide you with guides for your choice, however. For instance, he may create an admirable character whose ideas presumably coincide with his own. The reverse would be true for a bad character, and so forth.

CHARACTERS WHO STAND FOR IDEAS. The characters themselves often represent ideas. In this case, interactions of the characters may represent the interweaving of ideas, and the conflicts between characters may represent conflicts between ideas. For example, in allegories like *The Faerie Queene* and *Pilgrim's Progress,* the characters stand for ideas in conflict. Aldous Huxley, in his novels, evolved a form called *the novel of ideas,* in which the various characters in the story are made to represent ideas that in Huxley's opinion gave his novels intellectual life.

THE WORK ITSELF AS IT IMPLIES IDEAS. Perhaps the most important method by which authors embody ideas in a literary work is to manage carefully the total impression of the work. All the events and characters may add up to an idea that is made particularly powerful by the emotional impact of the story itself. Thus, although an idea may never be stated in the work, it will be apparent after you have finished reading it. In the novel *A Passage to India,* E. M. Forster shows that political institutions and racial and national barriers prevent men from realizing that they are brothers. He does not use these words, but this idea is clearly embodied in the novel: the separation of the Indian and Anglo-Indian communities even after the charges against Dr. Aziz are dropped and the differences in customs between the English and the Indians, and even between the Hindus and the Moslems among the Indians themselves, all point toward this idea. Your reading would be incomplete if you did not see this implication. Similarly, Shakespeare's *Hamlet* might be interpreted as an illustration of the idea that evil breeds evil upon evil, sweeping both the innocent and guilty before it. You will recognize that this act of interpreting the basic idea in a work of fiction is the same that you have been performing whenever you form a central idea for any theme you write.

It should be apparent that your easiest task in determining ideas will occur when the author speaks directly. In all the other cases you must interpret indirect and dramatic statements and be alert to the implications of each work that you read. You must be certain that there is adequate justification *in the literary work* for the points that you are making about it.

Two Critical Problems

Two critical problems are raised by the analysis of literature for ideas. The first is whether or not literature should be purely "instructive" or purely "pleasing" or both. The classical or "Horatian" view is that it should be both. Some writers have denied one or the other of these two aims (e.g., Poe, who said that the writer should aim only at giving pleasure, and Shaw, who said that the only justification for writing was to instruct). The issue is not only how pleasing ideas themselves are but also how relevant they are to literature. You are free to decide this issue for yourself, but you should realize that the Horatian view has been the most influential, historically, and that therefore many writers have written with both an instructive and a pleasure-giving intention.

The word *intention* brings up the second problem, for it is often difficult and sometimes almost impossible to claim that an author *intended* that you derive a certain idea from his work. For example, there has been a long controversy over Shakespeare's idea about Shylock in *The Merchant of Venice:* did Shakespeare present Shylock as a farcical outsider in a Christian society or as a sympathetic outcast and a victim of religious prejudice? Similarly, in reference to Shakespeare's *Henry V,* many critics have thought that Henry is engaged in a righteous war that brings out the valor and strength of the English people and that he is one of England's great kings. But other critics have thought that Henry cynically embarks on a war of aggression and is responsible for many needless deaths. These differences of interpretation bring up the question of whether the writer's intention is even relevant, because the author seldom states his intention explicitly.[1] Many critics have asserted that great works have new meanings for each succeeding generation, in spite of the writer's intention. There is some validity to this claim, and one must assent to it to the degree that the ideas in every work are to be regarded as having value for the present, unless their irrelevance can be proved. Still other critics, as a result of research into the intellectual milieus of the various literary periods, have claimed that an author's probable intentions can be discovered and that his work is an important piece of evidence in determining his intentions. This kind of research is essential in the historical study of literature. As with the first problem, of course, you are free to weigh the relative merits of these views and to decide what your position will be.

---

[1] See W. K. Wimsatt, Jr., "The Intentional Fallacy," *The Verbal Icon* (New York: The Noonday Press, 1960), pp. 3–18.

Choosing and Limiting
Your Central Idea

There are two major steps in analyzing imaginative literature for ideas. The first is to recognize that to talk about an idea is not the same as to re-tell the story or simply to define the literary type to which it belongs. To talk about ideas you must discuss meaning in your own expository prose. The phrasing of your central idea is crucial in this process, for if you go wrong here you might go wrong in the rest of your theme. For example, Jane Austen's novel *Northanger Abbey* (completed in 1803) is commonly recognized as a satire on the supernatural, Gothic novels popular at the end of the eighteenth century. If you were writing a theme about a major idea in this novel, however, you would go wrong if you framed central ideas like *"Northanger Abbey* is a story about a girl who learns to recognize truth" or *"Northanger Abbey* is a satire on Gothic novels." Instead, you should take some aspect of the story or of its satiric thrust that can be analyzed and discussed *as an idea.* Possibly your central idea might become, "Jane Austen's idea is that human nature and human drama are best seen in incidents of everyday life, not in imaginative fantasies." Another idea for a theme might be, "Jane Austen's idea is that the true qualities of heroism are stability and common sense." Both these ideas can be derived from the satire of *Northanger Abbey* and could be treated readily within theme limits. But if you tried to explain the satire of the work you would probably wind up explaining how certain events and attitudes in the novel parallel similar events and attitudes that are characteristic of Gothic novels. With this type of treatment, your discussion of ideas would become secondary, and you would no longer be writing a theme about ideas. Remember that an author's decision to employ a literary mode like satire stems from an idea like the two that we used as possible central ideas. Try to get through the story and the mode into the idea or ideas that are expressed or implied in the work.

The second major step in writing on ideas is to select and phrase one idea from among the many and to determine the form of your own theme by pursuing this idea and its ramifications within the work being studied. Your theme is to be about a major idea, not a helter-skelter of many ideas. The idea you select usually does not require many words to express (e.g., "Fitzgerald's main idea in the novel *Tender is the Night* is that human energies are depleted and destroyed by wealth."); but in order to write a good theme about it you must, in addition to naming and describing it, show how and where it is exemplified; you must demonstrate its importance in the work as a whole. A theme on the second idea about *Northanger Abbey,* for example, might demonstrate that the development of the heroine's character takes the pattern of increasing awareness of the truth that heroism is stability and common sense. Everything that happens to her in the novel may be seen as demonstrating this truth.

In forming your own theme, you might help yourself by answering questions like the following about the idea you are discussing: What is the best statement of the idea that you can make? What has the author done with the idea? How can the actions of the major character or characters be related to the idea? Can the organization of the story be seen as a function of the idea? Does the setting have any relationship to the idea? Is there imagery or symbolism that develops or illustrates the idea? Does this imagery or symbolism recur? Are there any characters, or actions, who may be measured according to how they fail to live up to the idea? In short, develop your theme by interpreting the work in light of the major idea you have chosen for discussion.

You can easily see that your discussion will lead you into statements with which someone else might take issue. Remember, however, that your interpretation will usually be respected as long as you base your statements accurately on the story itself. If for some reason you happen to make errors, either because of faulty understanding or because of your own prejudgments, you will of course be subject to correction. Be sure that your reading is accurate and that your interpretation can be defended at each point by material within the work.

Organizing Your Theme

In your themes your instructor will look for the intelligence, skill, and accuracy with which you make use of the literary materials as a base for your discussion of ideas. The general form of your theme will probably be (1) statement of the idea, and (2) discussion of the relevance and place of the idea in the work.

INTRODUCTION

In the introduction naming the idea will in fact be the central idea of your theme. You should state that the idea has interest and importance in order to arouse your reader's curiosity about your paper. You might also show how you arrived at your decision to write about that particular idea. Conclude your introduction with a thesis sentence.

BODY

The body of your paper should show the ways in which the writer has brought out the idea in his work. You might wish to explore the importance of the idea in the organization of the work (e.g., "The writer's idea that no human being can hold himself above respect for life causes him, first, to have the main figure commit a horrible crime, and second, to show this figure enduring a long and painful expiation for the crime."). It might be that you would study the importance of the idea in certain characters (e.g., "Eliot's Prufrock is an embodiment of the idea that man in the twentieth century has been deprived of his identity and importance."), or in certain actions (e.g., "Wordsworth's having crossed the Alps is an action showing the idea that high moments of achievement are possible in human life."). Though you might wish to bring all these aspects into your theme, it would be difficult to discuss everything fully. Therefore you must, as always, be selective in what you choose to discuss. Use only those details that are essential and clearly relevant.

It is easy, when you illustrate your point, to let the detail become an end in itself rather than a means toward asserting the truth of your central idea. Once you start describing the story and move away from your point, you actually have started to summarize. Remember, *your central idea must always be foremost in your reader's mind.* The unifying element in your theme is this idea, and you must keep mentioning it. As you are writing, stop at various times and ask yourself: "Is this material relevant to my point so that my reader could immediately see its relevance, or is it just synopsis?" It is advisable to keep restating the original idea, in order to remind your reader of your purpose in writing. Everything you say should be relevant, and you must remember that your reader is not likely to be as aware of your point as you are. How can he know unless you tell him? Don't force him to do too much guessing, or he may stop reading your paper.

CONCLUSION

In your conclusion you ought to evaluate the idea and its function in the text. The evaluation of the idea is sometimes external to the text, because it may include individual attitudes (e.g., a student considering Bunyan's idea of Christian salvation in *Pilgrim's Progress* would probably discuss his own ideas too). However, the consideration of the idea's function is artistic. How forcefully is the idea presented? How convincing is it in the story? With answers to these questions you may conclude.

The Idea in D. H. Lawrence's
"The Horse Dealer's Daughter"
that Man's Destiny Is to Love [1]

Lawrence demonstrates so many ideas about the love between man and woman in this story that I cannot possibly discuss them all here. A few separate ideas are: that love is a part of the uncontrollable side of man's life—the emotions; that love starts with the body, and that no satisfactory relationship between man and woman can be achieved without this basis; that love transforms life into something new; that love gives security since it fills an otherwise unfillable void in one's life; that only love gives meaning to life; that love is not only something to live for but something to be feared. Perhaps the one idea that takes in all these is that loving is an essential part of man's nature—that it is man's destiny to love. Lawrence's story seems to be one grand embodiment of this basic idea. It controls the form of his story, and all characters seem to be judged on the basis of how successfully they live up to this idea. I will therefore discuss the idea as it appears in what I consider to be the two main divisions of the story.

In the first part Lawrence shows us characters who are without love and whose lives are therefore incomplete. Thereby he illustrates the idea that men who are not living according to their destiny will be frustrated, cantankerous, and sullen, and that they will try to find fulfillment in some other way (which will not, however, make them happy). Their lives are virtually like those of the great draft horses, which Lawrence describes as moving with "a massive, slumbrous strength, and a stupidity which held them in subjection" (p. 115). Time, Lawrence implies, is running out on people in this condition, and unless they do something they are doomed to misery. But, according to the main idea, an evasion of the destiny to love will not avert this doom. Joe, the oldest of the Pervin brothers, has arranged for an apparently loveless marriage to achieve economic security. With deliberate finality, Lawrence disposes of Joe, who thereby becomes an example of the main idea: "He would marry and go into harness. His life was over, he would be a subject animal" (p. 115).

---

[1] "The Horse Dealer's Daughter," in Cleanth Brooks, John T. Purser, and Robert Penn Warren, eds., *An Approach to Literature,* Alternate 4th ed. (New York: Appleton-Century-Crofts, 1967). Parenthetical page numbers refer to this edition.

This idea that life virtually ends without love is finally brought to bear on Mabel, the lone girl in the Pervin family, and the figure for whom the story is named. Just as the death of her father has precipitated the breakup of the family (who melt away at this point), the breakup is precipitating some drastic action on her part. Here the operation of Lawrence's idea is brought out clearly: since it is man's destiny to love and since life without love is a kind of death and since Mabel has no love on earth to anticipate but only the love for her dead father to remember, she stolidly and deliberately chooses real death with dead love, which she prefers to a life on earth without any love at all. The first section of the story closes as Mabel attempts to drown herself. She walks "toward the centre of the pond, very slowly, gradually moving deeper into the motionless water, and still moving forward as the water got up to her breast" (p. 119).

But this pond—symbolic of death as Mabel walks into it—is also a symbol of life and regeneration (for example, infant baptism employs water, and the major symbol for life in Freudian psychology is water). This generative symbolic value is dominant in the second part of Lawrence's story and also puts into operation the second part of his idea (which has frequently been described by the old saying "Love finds a way"). Rescuing Mabel from the death to which she has consigned herself is Dr. Fergusson, who has previously been introduced as a person leading a life of quiet desperation, even though he also has derived a power from his closeness to the lives of his patients. (Is he living a vicarious life, or is he simply sublimating his desires?) Perhaps the good doctor's common cold, mentioned when we first meet him, is to be interpreted as a symbol of the sickness of the soul without love, and therefore the need to be well would become a strong support for Lawrence's basic idea. Whether this interpretation is right or not, however, it is important to note that Dr. Fergusson's rescue of Mabel is therapeutic not only for Mabel, but also for himself.

For the rescue follows the pattern of Lawrence's idea and is actually a symbol of the attainment of this idea: that love rescues the life without love. But love is complex, suggests Lawrence (and in this case, it is mildly comic), and it creates new problems once it has been realized. Therefore, Lawrence builds the idea that love is something to be desired but also something to be feared. It brings out emotions that are new and strange; it violates man's naturally conservative nature; it upsets previously established equilibrium; it changes life so fundamentally that no life will ever be the same after having been touched by love. Is it any wonder that Lawrence concludes his story in the following words:

"No, I want you, I want you," was all he answered, blindly, with that terrible intonation which frightened her almost more than the horror lest he should *not* want her (p. 123).

This complexity of emotions raises Lawrence's treatment of his idea above the level of the popular, romantic, "Hollywooden" conception of love, and answers all potential objections that love between Mabel and the doctor happens too rapidly. (Incidentally, Lawrence carefully demonstrates that there were emotional contacts between the two lovers before the outpouring of their love in the deserted room of the Pervin house.) Lawrence's idea is mature and profound. Clearly, he suggests, love itself creates problems as great as those it solves, but it also builds a solid platform of emotional strength from which these new problems can be attacked and solved. The idea is that this strength can be achieved only when a man and woman know love, because only then are they living life as it was designed. The problems facing them then, Lawrence suggests, are the real problems that man and woman should face, since the problems are a natural result of their destiny. By contrast, the men and women without love, like those at the beginning of the story, have never reached fulfillment and consequently they face problems that, though certainly severe and immediate, are really peripheral to life as it should be lived. The entire story of Mabel and Jack is an extensive example of Lawrence's dominating idea that it is the destiny of man and woman to love.

The Theme on
A CLOSE READING

One of your main tasks as a reader is to understand and appreciate the page before you. Beyond the words, phrases, clauses, and sentences are implications, shades of meaning, and beauty. For a full understanding and appreciation you should, theoretically, spend as much time reading a work as the author spent writing it; that is, you should spend this much time, using all your alertness and skill, if you really want to grasp everything. Unfortunately, time is prohibitive, and therefore you must settle for something less. With good reading skills, however, you can perceive and appreciate a great deal of the expressed and implied meaning.

To assist you in developing good reading techniques, your instructor will probably spend much classroom time in explaining and discussing with you various poems, novels, plays, and stories. As you experience this classroom guidance, you should develop the ability to read well without guidance. The theme asking you to perform a close reading of a passage is an important means by which your instructor can verify your progress as a reader.

The close-reading theme can be either very general or very technical, depending on the skills you have acquired when you undertake to write it. Mainly, however, the aim of the assignment is to give you a chance to exercise your general perceptions and knowledge as a reader. The theme can take the form of your abilities and interests. You may, for example, be concerned with the character of the principal male in Willa Cather's novel *The Lost Lady,* for most of the story's action is presented more or less as he sees it. You might therefore wish to concentrate on what a particular paragraph reveals about him. Or you may have acquired some interest and knowledge of political science and may wish to concentrate on the political implications of a passage in Shakespeare's *Richard II,* and so on. In short, the close-reading assignment can change as you change. It might be interesting to write such a theme early in your college days and then to write another one later, perhaps even about the same passage, after you have acquired more experience as a reader.

The assumptions behind the close-reading theme are these: if you can read a page, you can read the entire book of which the page is a part; if you can read a speech, you can read the entire play; if you can read one poem by a poet, you can read other poems by the same poet. Underlying these assumptions are others: in a good literary work, each part is absolutely essential; nothing could be eliminated without damage to the work. In the same way, all the writings of each author form a homogeneous unit, with each work contributing something to that unity. A close reading of an individual passage, therefore, or of an entire work, should indicate essential truths about the work or about the author being studied. Your reading of a passage or of a poem should indicate your ability to handle entire works. This is not to say that the writing of an analytical-reading theme automatically qualifies you to read every work by the same author. Few people would maintain that the reading of passages from Joyce's *Dubliners* makes it possible to read passages from *Finnegans Wake* immediately. What you are showing instead is a skill, an ability to bring your knowledge and understanding to bear on a specific passage and to develop a thematically conceived response and interpretation.

A close reading of a passage requires a certain awareness of *style* and *prosody* (see Chapters 13 and 14), but your focus in this theme will only touch on these elements indirectly. Instead, you are to focus attention on everything in the passage or work assigned. If the work is particularly rich in meaning, you will need to select from the superabundance; if the work seems thin, you can cover everything. Works by good writers, however, generally offer God's plenty for your study.

Various Assignments

A close-reading theme will frequently be assigned in courses in drama or the interpretation of poetry, although it can be assigned in any course, including courses in novels and short stories. Your instructor might give you the assignment as "Write a paper on this passage" or "Write an analysis of this poem." When you have received this assignment, you have the job of writing a theme based on close reading.

Although you are concerned here with writing a theme, you might be given the assignment as part of a classroom impromptu or examination (see Appendix A, on tests). Either you might be required to analyze a poem or passage, or you might be given a number of passages as identification-and-comment questions. If you have a passage to identify, concentrate on its subject matter and position in the work and in the philosophy of the writer.

Preparing to Write

Your first job is to read the entire work in order to make sure that you understand the relation of the passage to the whole. If you do not read the entire work first, you are likely to make inexcusable blunders in your reading of the specific passage. Read carefully. Then study the passage you are to write about. First, be sure to use the dictionary for all words that are even slightly obscure. Sometimes you may not be getting the sense of a passage at first or even second reading. Remember that even the simplest looking words may offer difficulties. Therefore, you must look up *all* the words in the passage that is giving you trouble, and frequently you will discover that your trouble resulted from attaching the incorrect meaning to a word. Use the dictionary whenever you have the slightest question. In Shakespeare's Sonnet No. 73, for example, this famous line appears:

> Bare ruined choirs, where late the sweet birds sang.

If you regard *choirs* as an organized groups of singers (as you are likely to do at first), you simply will not understand the line. The dictionary will tell you that *choirs* may be an architectural term referring to the part of a church in which the singers usually are placed. Let us take another line, this time from John Donne's first Holy Sonnet:

> And thou like Adamant draw mine iron heart.

Unless you look up *Adamant* and realize that Donne uses it to mean a magnet, you are likely not to know the sense of *draw,* and you will thus miss the meaning of the entire line.

You also ought to use your imagination to find whether the words in the poem or passage convey any consistent patterns, as a pattern of references to flowers, to water, to high finance, or to political life. In your preparation for writing, do not hesitate to pick out such references in each line. Try to classify them into categories, for you can frequently achieve an extremely good reading by making drawings and schemes.

Once you have understood the words, pay some attention to the sentence structures, particularly in poetry. If you read the line "Thy merit hath my duty strongly knit," be sure that you figure out the proper subject and object of the verb ("Thy merit hath strongly knit my duty"). Or, look at these lines:

> Let such teach others who themselves excell,
> And censure freely who have written well.

> —Pope, *Essay on Criticism,* lines 15-16

On first reading, these lines are difficult. A person might even conclude that Pope is asking the critic to censure (for an assignment, look up *censure* in the O.E.D.) those writers who have written well, until the lines are unraveled thus:

> Let such who themselves excell teach others,
> And [let such] who have written well censure freely.

There is quite a difference here between the correct reading and the mis-reading. What you must keep in mind is that your failure to understand a sentence structure that no longer exists in everyday English can prevent your full understanding of a passage. Therefore you must be absolutely sure, in your preparation, that you have untied all the syntactic knots.

With this preparation done, you may go on to plan and write your theme.

Organizing Your Theme

INTRODUCTION

Your introduction should describe the particular circumstances of the passage or work. Who is talking? To whom is he talking? Under what circumstances is he talking? Why? What is the general subject matter of the passage or work? These questions are relevant to whole poems as well as to fragments from a drama or story.

When you have answered these questions, you should make plain your central idea. Never begin to write until you have developed a general reaction to the passage or work assigned; your description of this reaction, or consideration, will be your central idea. The sample theme argues that in the passage analyzed Hamlet is speaking about himself—giving a self-revelation, as it were. The remainder of the theme develops this idea. In a theme involving a close reading it is sometimes difficult to arrive at a central idea, but if your theme is to be good, you must produce some guiding point that makes sense out of your reading.

BODY

Your plan in the body of the theme is to combine the results of your close reading with the central idea you have asserted. You might be guided by the following:

SPECIAL CIRCUMSTANCES. Observe the special circumstances of the passage or work to see how they influence the language, and therefore how they illustrate your point (e.g., suppose that the speaker is in a plane crashing to the ground or suppose that he is on his way to meet his sweetheart; either of these circumstances must be mentioned and kept in mind throughout your discussion). The sample theme analyzes Hamlet's disturbed state of mind when he is addressing the ghost, who has just left the stage. The presence of the ghost is a special circumstance that accounts for Hamlet's shock and confusion.

DICTION. Discuss the meaning of the words as related to the speaker's background and state of mind. In Browning's "Soliloquy of the Spanish Cloister," for example, the speaker is a jealous, worldly monk. His language is the kind a monk might use, but his interjections and schemes all show that he is a spiteful, petty person, certainly not a saintly, holy one. The language in Keats's "Ode to a Nightingale" indicates that the speaker is despairing, disappointed, and uncertain, but it also shows his joy in life's fullness and in the beauty provided by the imagination. The sample theme demonstrates that Hamlet's diction is that of a student; therefore it is natural for him to use the references to *tables* in the academic sense.

When you discuss diction it is also proper to make observations on both the direct statements in the work and the implications and suggestions. Also, if there are any special problems with words, describe these problems and show how their solution (by aid of the dictionary) has assisted you in your reading.

OTHER ELEMENTS. Discuss all other things that are relevant to your point. Here you might include either or both of the following:

1. Any noteworthy ideas. Your emphasis, however, should not be on the ideas *as ideas,* but on the way they are related to the central idea of your theme. For example, the sample theme briefly discusses the Renaissance theory of faculty psychology but is less concerned with explaining this theory than with relating it to the central idea of Hamlet's self-revelation.

2. The sentence patterns and rhythms of your passage. Because this analysis is fairly technical, it anticipates the prosodic analysis of poetry and the stylistic analysis of prose. In the present theme, however, you need to show only those qualities of style and versification that are relevant to your point. The sample theme demonstrates that at the end of the passage there are falling, trochaic rhythms that are sympathetic to the spirit and mood of Hamlet's speech. By emphasizing relationships of this sort, you can make your discussion of technique contribute to the thematic unity of your paper.

CONCLUSION

If the passage you have analyzed is a paragraph in a story or a portion of a play, as in the sample theme, you should conclude by making statements about the relationship of the fragment to the rest of the work. You are in effect pointing out the organic nature of the entire work, because you are emphasizing that your passage is essential to the whole (for more detail on this topic see Chapter 10, on *Structure*). The sample theme asserts that the passage being analyzed is the climax of the first act of *Hamlet* and that it anticipates much of what Hamlet does later.

It is also possible that the passage you have analyzed has meaning that is worthy of discussion independent of its context. You might then conclude by discussing the implications of this meaning. If you have been analyzing an entire poem, you might then conclude by discussing the relationship of the poem to other works by the same poet, or by other poets, on the same theme. Such a conclusion might involve you briefly in *comparison and contrast* (see Chapter 9). Whatever you write about in your conclusion, be sure that you touch once more on your central idea before you end your paper.

A Note on Mechanics

For quick, easy reference, you should include a copy of the passage you are analyzing. If the passage is not numbered, number it, by lines or sentences, beginning with *1*. If you are quoting a passage that is already numbered, you should use these numbers in your duplication. (The following fragment from *Hamlet,* for example, is numbered according to the Neilson and Hill edition of Shakespeare.) Whenever you quote from your passage, indicate in parentheses the line number or numbers of your quotation, for example: (21), (26–28), (24, 43, 38), and so on.

Hamlet's Self-Revelation:
A Reading of Hamlet, I. v, 95–109 [1]

Remember thee!	95
Ay, thou poor ghost, while memory holds a seat	96
In this distracted globe. Remember thee!	97
Yea, from the table of my memory	98
I'll wipe away all trivial fond records,	99
All saws of books, all forms, all pressures past,	100
That youth and observation copied there,	101
And thy commandment all alone shall live	102
Within the book and volume of my brain,	103
Unmix'd with baser matters. Yes, yes, by heaven!	104
O most pernicious woman!	105
O villain, villain, smiling, damned villain!	106
My tables, my tables—Meet it is I set it down	107
That one may smile, and smile, and be a villain!	108
At least I'm sure it may be so in Denmark.	109

In this passage from Act I of *Hamlet,* Hamlet is alone on stage immediately after the ghost has left, and so the character addressed is the ghost, at least at first. Actually, the speech is a soliloquy, because Hamlet almost immediately seems to be talking to himself or to the open air. Although Hamlet speaks about the ghost, his mother ("O most pernicious woman"), and his uncle (the "villain"), the real subject of the speech is himself. His words describe his state of mind; his selection of words indicates his background as a student, his awareness of what is happening to him, and his own highly agitated mental condition at the moment.

For Hamlet has clearly been disturbed by the ghost's message that Claudius is a murderer. Whereas previously the young prince has been melancholy and ill at ease, feeling the need to do something but without any reason for action, he has now realized that definite action will be necessary in the future. His desire for revenge here reaches the fury that he will later feel in the "rogue and peasant slave" soliloquy. His passionate dedication to vengeance is sworn "by heaven!" His disturbance, which he himself recognizes in line

[1] *The Complete Plays and Poems of William Shakespeare,* William Allan Neilson and Charles Jarvis Hill, eds. (Cambridge, Mass.: Houghton Mifflin Company, 1942). Line numbers refer to this edition.

97, is demonstrated first by his decision to wipe away "all trivial fond records" from the "table" of his memory (99, 98), and then by his writing down (or so we presume) in his "tables" (i.e., his commonplace book, his notebook) that "one may smile, and smile, and be a villain" (108). Can this distinction between his declaration and his action do anything but indicate his mental confusion?

Regardless of this confusion, Hamlet's selection of words related to *tables* indicates that his existence as a character has been completely visualized and perfected by the dramatist, Shakespeare, who has created a diction that is in perfect accord with Hamlet's background as a student. Hamlet's speech is therefore the most telling indication that his subject is really himself. *Table, records, saws of books, copied, book and volume of my brain, baser matter, tables, set it down*—all these smack of the classroom, where Hamlet has so recently been occupied. And in lines 96 through 104 there is a complicated but brief description of Renaissance psychology, a subject that Hamlet has just been learning, presumably, at Wittenberg. Briefly, he states that his mind, or his memory, is like a writing tablet, from which he can erase previous experience and literature (the "pressures past" of line 100), and which he can then fill with the message that the ghost of his father has just transmitted to him. In short, his mind will never be quite the same, since the new message will occupy it entirely.

Once Hamlet has decided to erase all previous impressions, it is as though he has killed his past, and once he has made his resolution, his future project will be to murder Claudius. It seems deliberate, then, that the last lines of this passage are characterized by many trochaic rhythms, which would have been described in Shakespeare's day as having a *dying fall*. There are falling rhythms on *yés, bý héaven,* and *Ò villain, villain, smiling, damned villain!*

The last two lines end with trochees (*villain, Denmark*). This rhythm is unlike most of what went before, but will be like most of what follows, particularly the interjections in the "To be or not to be" soliloquy and the conclusions in that soliloquy (on the word *action*).

Since this passage reveals Hamlet's character so clearly, it is startlingly relevant to the rest of the play. From this point onward Hamlet will constantly be spurred by this promise to the ghost, that the ghost's "commandment all alone shall live / Within the book and volume of . . . [his] brain" (102, 103) and Hamlet will feel guilty and will be overwhelmed with self-doubt and the urge for self-destruction because he does not act on this promise. His attitude toward Claudius, which previously was scornful, will now be vengeful. His budding love for Ophelia will be blighted by his obsession with vengeance, and as a result Ophelia, a tender plant, will die. Truly, this passage can be regarded as the climax of the first act, and the prediction of the remainder of the play.

The Theme on
A SPECIFIC PROBLEM

CHAPTER

8

The theme on a specific problem is frequently assigned in literature courses, just as the solution of problems is required in every course you will ever take. The question-and-answer discussion method, with which you have become familiar in your classes, is perhaps the best previous experience you have had with the general method of writing a specific-problem theme. In answering a question like "In *Heart of Darkness* why does Conrad state that Kurtz has made a lengthy study aimed at improving the lot of the natives?" you have been putting facts and conclusions together in the way you will follow in writing a theme on a specific problem. Only rarely can you answer such questions merely by summarizing subject matter or identifying characters in the work.

The idea behind the specific-problem theme is this: too frequently a person takes for granted everything that he reads, only to discover when challenged that he has not really understood or thought about the material. Therefore, if the material he reads can be seen as a problem, or as containing immediately unanswerable questions, he will search the material more deeply and develop more command over it. As he does so, he is also developing those skills and habits that characterize the educated person. Few people would dispute the assertion that education can aim at little better than putting students into the frame of mind of asking questions and seeing problems.

The active reader, which you are trying to become, is always inquisitive. He constantly asks questions such as "What would this work be like without that?" and "What would this character do in other circumstances?" As he raises these questions, he learns about art and broadens his general ability to read and think. In attempting to find answers he must try out a number of provisional solutions; he must organize and structure his material convincingly and originally. He can solve some problems by simple exposition, whereas he can solve others only by presenting an argument or by making a certain major assertion seem valid or invalid.

How Assigned

The problems you deal with in this type of assignment may be assigned by your instructor (for both papers and tests), or they may arise in classroom discussion. Suppose that a particular question puzzles the members of your class. You might well find yourself with that problem as the subject of your next theme.

You might also be asked to make up your own problem for a theme assignment. In this event you must conceive of a problem and formulate it. Write down all questions that occur to you as you read. You might easily make one of these the problem you deal with in your theme. Here also you can use your classroom experience, which will help you eventually to develop feelings for the relevant sorts of questions that you should raise. Now, suppose that in class you have discussed a work in which the principal character is under a sentence of death. What questions arose? How were these questions answered? By contrast, suppose that the work which you have been assigned concerns people with an undetermined future (e.g., "they lived happily ever after"). Can you raise problems about this work similar to those that were raised in class? Or, suppose that in class you have discussed a comic work, and have answered questions about what makes it comic. If your assigned work is comic, you might bring some of the classroom discussion to bear on a problem of your own about the causes of laughter.

Your Problem in Writing This Theme

Your main job in this theme is to provide a convincing solution to the specific problem with which you are faced. You must perceive the most significant implications of the problem and decide on a suitable order in which to deal with them. Then you must judge the relevance of materials from your text. Choose only those that have an immediate bearing on the problem. Of course, both your sharpness as a reader and your close study of the text will bear fruit here, because much material seemingly irrelevant to a careless reader can be interpreted as vital by a keen, knowledgeable reader. As in all your assignments, your first objective is therefore to think carefully.

The Nature of Literary Problems

Problems may be of any kind, and in this respect all writing about literature may be fitted into the *problem* category. For convenience, the problems may be classified as *artistic* (concerning style, arrangement, and general content), *conceptual* (concerning ideas), and *historical* (concerning influences, background, and genre).

You should realize that a problem will often cause a fusion of these three classifications, because they are all interlocked in the literary work itself, and because the problem may certainly be relevant to any and all classifications. You should also realize that your method of handling the theme will depend on the way in which the problem is put. For example, the question "What is the influence of the pastoral machinery on Milton's 'Lycidas'?" would require an expository treatment of how the pastoral elements figure in the poem. The aim of a theme on this problem would be mainly expository. But a related problem might be "Does the pastoral convention spoil 'Lycidas' by making it seem too artificial?" You can see that writing a theme on this second topic would require argument rather than simple exposition. Naturally a certain amount of exposition would be necessary in the treatment of this problem, but the exposition would be used only as it related to the argument.

ARTISTIC PROBLEMS

Almost anything in a literary work can be dealt with in artistic terms, but you are here concerned with problems as they relate to matters of style, structure, and—by extension—motivation and character. Suppose, for example, you were asked the question. "What meaning does the name 'Joe Christmas' have in the novel *Light in August* (by William Faulkner)?" This question is directed toward the novel, and implies that you would answer it as it relates to the artistry of the novel, even though in doing this job you would need to answer the question of Faulkner's idea in the novel. If you interpret Christmas as a "reverse image of Jesus Christ" (as some critics have done), then it is necessary for him to be killed at the end, if your parallel is to be exact. Your consideration would therefore involve you in a discussion of *structure*.

As another case, suppose you ask why Browning, in "The Pied Piper of Hamelin," created "such a rhythmic verse and such happily jingling rhymes." To solve this problem, you would need to decide how true the assumption about the verse is, and then relate the quality of the verse to Browning's subject and intended audience (the subtitle "A Child's Story" suggests that the poet had a certain audience in mind). Your method, as you see, would not be simply to analyze and scan the verse, but to bring to bear the results of your analysis and scansion on your conclusion.

Similarly, suppose you ask why the Polyphemus episode appears where it does in Odysseus's narrative in *The Odyssey*. Solving this problem really involves a discussion of *structure* in relation to your interpretation of the epic. Your solution might be something like this: "Since Polyphemus's curse is the cause of Odysseus's ten-year journey, it must come at the beginning of his wanderings, after his leaving Troy. Also, if *The Odyssey* is to some degree a story showing how Odysseus's ideas of personal responsibility grow, Odysseus must have time to recognize his guilt where Polyphemus is concerned and must also reconcile himself to what is essentially a tragic view of life."

You can see that dealing with a problem like this also involves a consideration of motivation and, necessarily, of character. If your problem, for example, is to answer the question of "How does Hurstwood change in Dreiser's *Sister Carrie?*" or "Why do the Schlegel sisters feel obligated to befriend Leonard Bast in E. M. Forster's *Howards End?*" and so on, you are dealing with causes, effects, and relationships among characters. All these problems are artistic.

CONCEPTUAL PROBLEMS

Problems of this sort are about ideas. Your intention in dealing with a problem about ideas, however, is not expository, but argumentative. For example, after reading Aldous Huxley's novel *Point Counter Point,* you might ask how valid his ideas are about the role of politics in modern life. This problem requires not only that you describe Huxley's ideas on the subject (perhaps as expressed through the character Mark Rampion), but also that you criticize these ideas, showing their validity and perhaps stating the degree of their applicability to modern society. And, if you conclude that they are not applicable, what other answers might be more applicable? You can see that solving a problem about ideas sometimes requires subjective responses; on many occasions you might dispute with your author, at other times you might agree with him. How, for example, would you solve the problems implied in "Wordsworth's ideas on 'The Old Cumberland Beggar' and modern welfare"? Or try "Did the ideas of Dos Passos on politics really change from *U.S.A.* to *Mid-Century?*"

HISTORICAL PROBLEMS

Most problems of this sort require a certain amount of research. Suppose that you are dealing with a problem of influences (you should know that many instructors object strongly to the assumptions underlying the word *influence,* and would probably not give you such an assignment). You are given the problem of Virgil's influence on Chaucer. You probably could not solve this problem yourself and so would have to consult a secondary source or sources in your library. If this problem were put in a different way, however—let us say "The similarity of ideas in certain works by Virgil and certain works by Chaucer"—you could probably solve the problem yourself by recourse to a comparison-contrast method, though you would certainly not claim that one poet influenced the other. Even in this inquiry, however, you would probably help yourself by using a secondary source. (A *secondary source* is a book *about* the works or authors you are reading; a *primary source* is usually the work itself.)

Problems of *background* and *milieu* also require varying degrees of research. Background information about the position of the Jewish people in medieval history would assist you in solving a problem like "How did Chaucer's audience interpret *The Prioress's Tale?*" *Milieu* refers to the intellectual and artistic currents prevailing at the time of a particular writer. If you were asked to solve the problem: "What was the milieu of Shaw's *Mrs. Warren's Profession?*" you would need research in secondary sources to help you with your answer.

A similar need to do research would occur in problems of *genre* or *type.* As with *influences,* the study of genre has fallen into some critical disrepute. But if you determine the genre of a work, you will know what to expect from it and can thereby make a reasoned evaluation. It would be folly for you to read a Greek tragedy and compare it unfavorably with *Hamlet* because "*Hamlet* has more action than the Greek tragedy, and besides, the Greek choruses are dull." You must understand that the conventions of Greek tragedies were different from those in Shakespeare's plays. A consideration of genre would permit you to understand the differences and lead to a better appreciation of both kinds of plays. As another example, you may fail to appreciate certain works of poets who wrote during the neoclassic period of English literary history. A realization that these writers wrote according to rules of genre would make you able to recognize the requirements that they set for themselves (i.e., epic satire, Horatian satire, mock-epic satire, pastoral poetry, discursive poetry, heroic drama). Once you recognized the limits of their achievements, you would be better able to recognize their merits. In this way, the study of genre brings a wider range of appreciation than you could gain without

it. Remember one thing, however: when genre leads to unwarranted conclusions (for example, pleading that because Housman was a great poet
within the limits he set for himself he is to be regarded as Milton's equal),
it has defeated its own purpose—reasonable appreciation.

In dealing with a problem of genre, then, you will need to learn the
special conditions under which the work was composed and the type that
the work was supposed to be. Some problems of genre would be: "*Hamlet*
as a revenge play," "*Gulliver's Travels* as a travel book," "Dryden's *Annus
Mirabilis* as a 'historical' poem," "*An American Tragedy* as a realistic
novel," "*The Nun's Priest's Tale* as a beast epic," "*The Rape of the Lock*
as a mock-heroic poem," and "Virginia Woolf's *Mrs. Dalloway* as a stream-
of-consciousness novel." Your problem would be to set up an idea of what
to expect from the work that you have considered and then to show how
it successfully lived up to these expectations.

Problems of genre can also require a treatment employing argument.
For instance, "To what extent is *Gulliver's Travels* more than just a
parody of contemporary travel books?" or "Did the revenge motif in
Hamlet limit Shakespeare in treating Hamlet's responses to Claudius?"
Questions like these can be multiplied indefinitely. In dealing with one
of them you would (1) examine the truth of the assumption about genre,
and (2) deal with the relation of the genre to the problem at hand.

Your Approach in Writing

As you may conclude from the types of problems discussed, it is impossible to predict all the various problems that will occur not only in your
classes but also in your mind as you read literature. For your theme,
however, remember the following: Your job is to convince your reader
that your solution to the problem is valid. Your theme will therefore
most often require an argument designed to support your central idea
(which is in fact a short statement of your solution to the problem).
The various parts of your theme will be subpoints supported by evidence.

As you read your literary work, take notes on relevant details. Study
your notes carefully after you have finished reading. From your notes you
should arrive at a major conclusion, which you will make the central
idea of your theme. The material in your notes may then be arranged in
an order suitable to the logical steps of your argument. When you begin
to write, you may suddenly realize the importance of other material that
you did not include in your original notes. Work in this new material,
but take care to illustrate its relevance to your central idea.

Depending on the degree of argument required by your topic, you
will find a need to examine closely the key words in the statement of your

problem. It is always wise to study these words carefully. If your instructor has phrased the problem for you, his phrase may contain words having implications with which you do not agree. That is, some of his words may "beg the question." You will also find it necessary to determine the limits within which you wish a certain word to operate. Or, if you object to the way a problem is phrased, you may wish to rephrase it. What would you do, for example, with problems phrased like these: "How much misanthropy does Swift show in *Gulliver's Travels?*" or "Show why Faulkner is the great American novelist." You can quickly see that these are "loaded" questions. To answer the first you would need to determine the meaning of *misanthropy* and if you admitted the word at all, you would need to limit its use to Swift's meaning. For the second question you would need to spend time on the meaning and admissibility of the phrase *is the great* before you could write a good theme. The sample theme considers the meaning of the term *successful* when applied to Robert Frost's poem "Desert Places." This theme sets up reasonable conditions for determining whether or not the poem is successful and proceeds to argue and demonstrate that the conditions are met. It thereby develops from the discussion of one of the major terms presented in the original statement of the problem. You might profit from employing a similar method whenever you are confronted with a similar literary problem.

As with all themes except the summary, you may assume that your reader is familiar with the literary work you have read. Your job is to arrange your materials convincingly around your main point. You should not use anything from the work that is not relevant to your central idea. You do not need to discuss things in their order of appearance in the work. You are in control and must make your decisions about order so that your solution to the problem may be brought out most effectively.

Organizing Your Theme

INTRODUCTION

If your problem requires an examination of any of its key words, the introduction is the proper place for this examination. Once that is done, your introduction should describe the problem in terms of either its importance in the work you have read or its general importance in life and literature. Thus, say you have the problem: "Is Moll Flander's bad life justified by her economic circumstances?" You might wish to look first at the phrase "bad life" and may conclude that it is properly descriptive. Then you might wish to deal with the issue of justification in either or both of two ways: (1) whether, and to what degree, the immediate circumstances justify the sins of which Moll is guilty; (2) whether environment is generally a justification for human conduct. Ultimately, you might find yourself raising other perplexing moral and artistic questions that develop from these; for once you have raised the original problem, more problems usually follow, and they should be used to strengthen your argument. Although the original problem is particular, it raises general implications that should also be dealt with if a solution is really to be found.

Your introduction should also describe your solution to the problem in a brief statement, which will be your central idea. Your thesis sentence should include the introduction.

BODY

The body should contain the main points of your argument. Another way to look at the body is to think of it as stating the main reasons for which you have arrived at your solution. Generally, you will state a point (topic sentence) and then show how a certain amount of representative material from the work supports that point, and so on throughout the body. Always keep emphasizing how the material supports your point. Just to present the material is to write a synopsis, and this theme is not to be a synopsis.

CONCLUSION

Your conclusion should affirm your belief in the validity of your solution in view of the supporting evidence. You must recognize that in nonscientific subjects like literature there are rarely absolute proofs, so that your conclusions will not actually be proved. But your conclusions, along with the evidence, should be *convincing,* and you should always give the impression that you have not been grinding an axe. The conclusion of your theme should therefore build conviction in your reader. If you think your reader may have doubts, you should satisfy these doubts in your conclusion. It is a good rhetorical method to answer any objections or contrary claims that might be raised against your solution. Whether you state the objections fully or only make them implicit, you ought to answer them. In this way you convince your reader that your solution has been reasoned wisely and that you have omitted nothing in seeking out evidence and in thinking of solutions.

In the Poem "Desert Places" (1936),
Is Frost Successful in Shifting the
Meaning of the Term "Desert Places"?

This question is another way of asking whether the poem itself is successful, for Frost's shift of meaning is both the emotional climax and the physical end of the poem. If the shift does not work, the poem does not present its major point successfully. Frost first uses the term in his title to refer to "places that are deserted." In the first lines of the poem he applies this meaning specifically to the field on which snow is falling, and in lines 13 and 14 he applies it to interstellar spaces. In the last line of the poem he uses the term both metaphorically and pejoratively to suggest that the speaker's soul is a desert place. Presumably, the shift from a natural to a human application would not be successful if it were totally unrelated to everything before it, but it would be successful if the contrary were true. One might also claim failure if the term did not acquire the clarity necessary for full effectiveness, since nothing at all comes after it as explanation and development. It seems clear, however, that Frost's shifting of the meaning is accomplished successfully and hence that the poem itself is successful. Both the general metaphor of the poem and Frost's reliance on a well-acknowledged tradition of the humbling of the self answer any objections that might be made to his semantic shift.

The primary cause of Frost's success is the general metaphoric quality of the first three stanzas. To the reader who is accustomed to finding more than one level of meaning in a natural description, the introduction of the field suggests a comparison with the human soul: the field is a broad expanse enclosed by a woods; weeds and grain or hay both grow there; sometimes the summer sun shines on the field and at other times the night of winter reigns. Now, only weeds and stubble show through the accumulating snow, which covers the hibernating animals. All these details suggest a state in which life is being overgrown, cut off, buried, and enveloped in darkness.

When Frost connects this "lonely" scene with the "absent-spirited" speaker, the invitation to read the details metaphorically has been made clearly. The darkness, the surrounding woods, the weeds, the stubble, the smothered animals, the cold, the loneliness—all these metaphorically suggest that not only snow, but men themselves, are benighted. Along this avenue of suggestion, one might take the date of the poem, 1936, to make a reading of lines 9 and 10: the prediction in these lines of a dark future suggests the despairing state of mind of a sensitive person during those ominous years preceding World War II—certainly an episode that sprang from the uncultivated wilderness of the human soul. In other words, even before the final lines, the reader has been readied for the suddenness of Frost's metaphoric shift of meaning—a climax that may thus be seen as integral to the poem.

All the above details are pulled together and focused by the shift of meaning at the end. The final words crystallize the poem, providing the reader with a second view of it and putting everything into a meaningful pattern. Although nothing follows, the placement of the words makes it seem as though something indeed has followed. The term "desert places" thus achieves clarity. It can be construed as a reference to something like spiritual isolation, human indifference, lack of human warmth, or what is sometimes called the "emptiness" of human existence. The meaning is not exact, but it is sufficiently clear in view of human experience; and the condition referred to is real enough to "scare" the speaker (line 16). Frost thus emphasizes the speaker's self-realization as much as the meaning of the metaphor.

By this means Frost limits the metaphor and in effect answers the potential charge that he is generalizing. Specifically, if some mythical reader were to object by saying that not everyone possesses "desert places" (an unlikely claim), the phrase "my own" in line 16 has confined the desert places only to the speaker, and to the speaker's self-awareness. The meaning is thereby limited and for this reason is not an issue for dispute. Because of the metaphor, however, it can reach a wide application, for there are many readers willing to assent to it.

Frost is actually relying on such assent, for the poem is in a long tradition of self-analysis and self-abasement. The proper Christian attitude of the prayerful person is to declare his unworthiness before God and to state his fears of being alone without God's kindness and protection. Although the speaker does not mention God, Frost is touching this habit of self-study and criticism. Uriah Heep to the contrary, we tend to trust someone who expresses fear at his own limitations and shortcomings. Such is the building block of human progress; all of Frost's poem fashions this block, which is given final shape in the concluding metaphor. Prompted by the discoveries of the galaxies and intergalactic distances in the 1920's and 1930's, the poem is seen as an expression of the human idea that men should solve human problems before they ponder outer space (or enter it). Therefore, nothing about the final metaphoric shift is unusual; the meaning is both a logical turn within the poem and a natural turn of mind in our own culture.

Despite these arguments, the shift of meaning may still be open to the charge that Frost has been too brief in his development of the idea; he simply states it and leaves it. Of course, a long psychological study about all the worst aspects of human personality would tell more than Frost does. His aim, however, is to employ his material briefly in order to produce the reader's assent in a flash of insight. A poetic wholeness is Frost's goal here; his wish is to use the idea in a poetic structure, not to explain it. A better charge might be in fact that the final meaning of "desert places" is trite and therefore that the poem is unsuccessful. If one were to lift the term out of its context, this charge might be maintained. But the phrase must be kept in context, and there it offers freshness and surprise. Frost has used it to connote the cold, the distant, the blank, the emotionless aspects of human beings—the ice of human neglect, not the fire of human passion. This connotation of the term is particularly meaningful as world population increases and as men develop callousness toward the plight of others. Frost's term is carefully wrought and skillfully presented, an element of success in a successful poem.

The Theme of
COMPARISON-CONTRAST

A popular theme subject is the comparison of different authors, of two or more works by the same author, of different drafts of the same work, or of different characters, incidents, and ideas within the same work or in different works. Your instructor may assign this theme in many ways, such as "Compare *X* and *Y*" or "Discuss the idea of *Z* in such-and-such works." No matter how the assignment is made, your job is to write a comparison-contrast theme. This assignment requires a detailed study and a thorough consideration of a much wider range of material than is needed to write a theme about a single work, idea, character, or author.

Comparison-Contrast as a Way to Knowledge

Comparison and contrast are important means to gaining understanding. For example, suppose that you are having trouble understanding separately the poems "War is Kind" by Stephen Crane and "The Fury of Aerial Bombardment" by Richard Eberhart. When you start comparing the two poems, however, you will immediately notice things that you may not have noticed at first. Both of course treat the horrors of war, but they do so differently. Crane is ironic, while Eberhart, by contrast, is quietly bitter. Though Eberhart's topic is the "fury" of bombardment, he does not describe explosions and anguished death, but rather draws attention to mankind's collective stupidity and to the regrettable deaths of men with great potential. Crane, on the other hand, achieves his ironic effect by speaking of "slaughter" and "corpses" at the same time he also speaks of war's being "kind." Both poems ultimately agree on the irrationality of war. Making a comparison and contrast in this way enables you to see each poem in perspective, more clearly than you might have done if you had continued to study the poems separately. The comparison-contrast method is similarly rewarding whenever you apply it, for perhaps the quickest way to get at the essence of an artistic work is to compare it with another work. Similarities are brought out by comparison, and differences are shown by contrast.

You will quickly perceive that the comparison-contrast method is closely related to the study of *definition,* because definition aims at the description of a particular thing by identifying its properties while also isolating it from everything else. Comparison-contrast is also closely allied with Plato's idea that we learn a thing best by reference to its opposite; that is, one way of finding out what a thing *is* is to find out what it is *not.*

As you study literature, your use of comparison-contrast will enable you to define and describe the particular characteristics of a particular writer or work by showing the general category to which your subject belongs and also by differentiating it from all other members of the category. To a great degree, the method of comparison-contrast can be used to set off a great literary work by comparison with inferior works. In these senses, this type of theme is an integral part of literary classification, literary history (because it takes time differences into account), and literary evaluation (it implies that along with separation goes the cause for separation, including the rating of works and authors into orders of superiority and inferiority). When your instructor asks you to "Compare Pope and Tennyson" or to "Compare and contrast Chaucer with Edgar Guest," you should realize that he is asking you to bring out some of the important points that make the study of literature a true discipline.

Clarify Your Intention

Do not begin to write this, or any theme, without a plan or intention. Your first problem is to decide your objective. You ought to relate the material of the assignment to the purposes of the course, for the comparison-contrast method can be focused on a number of points. One focal point may simply be the equal and mutual illumination of both (or more) subjects of comparison; thus, in a survey course, where your purpose is to gain a general understanding of all the writers in the course, a theme about Milton and Pope would serve to describe the methods of both poets without throwing primary attention on either. But suppose you are taking a course in Milton—then your comparison-contrast theme could use Pope's methods as a means of highlighting Milton's; your theme would finally be about Milton, and your discussion of Pope would be relevant only as it related to this purpose. Conversely, if you were taking a course in eighteenth-century literature, you might use a discussion of Milton only as it illuminated Pope, and your theme would ultimately be about Pope. Your first task is therefore to decide where to place your emphasis. The sample theme illustrates the first type, namely the illumination of both works being considered. Unless you want to claim superiority for one particular work, you will find this type suitable for most comparisons.

Find Common Grounds for Comparison

Your second problem is to select the proper material—the grounds of your discussion. It is useless to compare essentially dissimilar things, for then your basic conclusions will be of limited value. Therefore your task is to put the works or writers you are comparing onto common ground. Compare like with like; that is, style with style, subject with subject, idea with idea, structure with structure, characterization with characterization, prosody with prosody, milieu with milieu, evaluation with evaluation, and so on. Putting your subjects on common ground makes you arrive at a reasonable basis of comparison and therefore a legitimate occasion for contrast. Nothing can be learned, for example, from a comparison of "Pope's style and Milton's philosophy." But much can be learned from a comparison of "the influence of philosophy on style in Milton and Pope." The first promises little, whereas the second suggests common ground, with points of both comparison and divergence and with further implications about the ages in which the two poets lived.

In attempting to find common ground, seek possible similarities as you prepare yourself by reading and taking notes for the assignment. Here your generalizing powers will assist you, for apparently dissimilar materials may meet—if you are able to perceive the meeting place. Thus a comparison of *The House of Mirth* by Edith Wharton and *The Catcher in the Rye* by J. D. Salinger might put the works on the common ground of "The Treatment of the 'Outsider' " or "Corrosive Influences of an Affluent Society on the Individual" or "The Basis of Social Criticism," even though the works are about different characters living in different ages. As you can see, what appears at first dissimilar can often be put into a frame of reference that permits analytical comparison and contrast. Much of your success in writing will depend on your ingenuity in finding a suitable basis for comparison.

Methods of Comparison

Let us assume that you have decided on your rhetorical purpose and on the basis or bases of your comparison: you have done your reading, taken your notes, and know what you want to say. The remaining problem is the treatment of your material. Here are two acceptable ways.

A common, but inferior, way is to make your points first about one work and then to do the same for the other. This method makes your paper seem like two big lumps, and it also involves much repetition because you must repeat the same points as you treat your second subject. This first method, in other words, is only satisfactory—it is no better than a *C* method.

The superior method is to treat your main idea in its major aspects and to make references to the two (or more) writers as the reference illustrates and illuminates your main idea. Thus you would be constantly referring to both writers, sometimes within the same sentence, and would be reminding your reader of the point of your discussion. There are reasons for the superiority of the second method: (1) you do not need to repeat your points unnecessarily, for you can document them as you raise them; (2) by referring to the two writers in relatively close juxtaposition in relation to a clearly stated basis of comparison, you can avoid making a reader with a poor memory re-read previous sections. Frequently such readers do not bother to re-read, and as a result they are never really clear about what you have said. As a good example, however, here is a paragraph from a student theme on "Nature as a basis of comparison in William Wordsworth's 'The World Is Too Much with Us' and Gerard Manley Hopkins's 'God's Grandeur.' " The virtue of the paragraph is that it uses material from both poets as a means of development; the material is synthesized by the student (sentence numbers in brackets) as follows:

[1] Hopkins's ideas are Christian, though not genuinely other-worldly. [2] God is a God of the world for Hopkins, and "broods with warm breast and with ah! bright wings" (line 14); Hopkins is convinced that God is here and everywhere, for his first line triumphantly proclaims this. [3] Wordsworth, by contrast, is able to perceive the beauty of Nature, but feels that God in the Christian sense has deserted him. [4] Wordsworth is to be defended here, though, because his wish to see Proteus or to hear Triton is not pagan. [5] He wants, instead, to have faith, to have the conviction that Hopkins so confidently claims. [6] Even if the faith is pagan, Wordsworth would like it just so he could have firm, unshakable faith. [7] As a matter of fact, however, Wordsworth's perception of Nature gives the contradiction to the lack of faith he claims. [8] His God is really Nature itself. [9] Hopkins's more abstract views of Nature make me feel that the Catholic believes that Nature is only a means to the worship of God. [10] For Hopkins, God is supreme; for Wordsworth, Nature is.

If H and W are allowed to stand for ideas about Hopkins and Words-worth, the paragraph may be schematized as follows (numbers refer to sentences):

$$1 = H. \quad 2 = H. \quad 3 = W. \quad 4 = W. \quad 5 = W, H. \quad 6 = W.$$
$$7 = W. \quad 8 = W. \quad 9 = H. \quad 10 = H, W.$$

This interweaving of subject material (two of the sentences contain references to both poets) gives the impression that the student has learned both poems so well that he is able to think of them together. Mental "digestion" has taken place. When the student discusses Hopkins's idea of Nature, he is able to think of it immediately in relation to Wordsworth's, and brings out references to both poets as he writes. You can profit from his example. If you can develop your comparison-contrast theme in this interlocking way, you will write it more economically and clearly than you would by the first method (this statement is true of tests as well as themes). Beyond that, if you have actually digested the material as successfully as the interlocking method shows, you will be demonstrating that you have fulfilled one of the primary goals of education—the assimilation and *use* of material.

Avoid the "Tennis-Ball" Method

As you make your comparison, do not confuse an interlocking method with a "tennis-ball" method, in which you bounce your subject back and forth constantly and repetitively. The tennis-ball method is shown in the following example from a comparison of A. E. Housman's "On Wenlock Edge" and Theodore Roethke's "Dolor":

> Housman talks about the eternal nature of men's troubles whereas Roethke talks about the "dolor" of modern business life. Housman uses details of woods, gales, snow, leaves, and hills, whereas Roethke selects details of pencils, boxes, paper-weights, mucilage, and lavatories. Housman's focus is therefore on the torments of man close to Nature; Roethke's on civilized, ordered, duplicated, grey-flanneled man. Housman states that the significance of human problems fades in the perspective of eternity; Roethke does not mention eternity but makes men's problems seem even smaller by showing that business life has virtually erased human emotion.

Imagine the effect of reading an entire theme presented in this fashion. Aside from its power to bore, the tennis-ball method is bad because it does not give you the chance to develop your points. You should not feel so cramped that you cannot take several sentences to develop a point about one writer or subject before you bring in comparison with another. If you remember to interlock the two points of comparison, however, as in the example comparing Hopkins and Wordsworth, your method will be satisfactory.

Organizing Your Theme

First you must narrow your subject into a topic you can handle conveniently within the limits of the assignment. For example, if you have been assigned a comparison of Tennyson and Pope, pick out one or two poems of each poet and write your theme about them. You must be wary, however, of the limitations of this selection: generalizations made from one or two works may not apply to the broad subject originally proposed. If you state this qualification somewhere in your theme, your comparison will have much value, and your instructor will probably be pleased with the wisdom of your selection.

INTRODUCTION

State what works, authors, characters, and ideas are under consideration, then show how you have narrowed the basis of your comparison. Your central idea will be a brief statement of what can be learned from your paper: the general similarities and differences that you have observed from your comparison and/or the superiority of one work or author over another. Your thesis sentence should anticipate the body of your theme.

BODY

The body of your theme depends on the points you have chosen for comparison. You might be comparing two works on the basis of *structure, tone, style,* two authors on *ideas,* or two characters on *character traits.* In your discussion you would necessarily use the same methods that you would use in writing a theme about these terms in a single work, except that here (1) you are exemplifying your points by reference to more subjects than one, and (2) your ultimate rhetorical purpose is to illuminate the subjects on which your comparison is based. In this sense, the methods you use in talking about *structure* or *style* are not "pure" but are instead subordinate to your aims of comparison-contrast. Let us say that you are comparing the ideas in two different works. The first part of your theme might be devoted to analyzing and describing the similarities and dissimilarities of the ideas *as* ideas. Your interest here is not so much to explain the ideas of either work separately as to explain the ideas of both works in order to show points of agreement and disagreement. A second part might be given over to the influences of the ideas on the *structure* and *style* of the particular works; that is, how the ideas help make the works similar or dissimilar. Or, let us say that your subjects of comparison are two or more characters. Your points might be to show similarities and dissimilarities of mental and spiritual qualities and of activities in which the characters engage.

CONCLUSION

In this section you should bring out the conclusions that have emerged from your study. If your writers were part of a "school" or "period," you might show how your findings relate to these larger movements. You also should illustrate the limitations and implications of your treatment; you might show that more could be done along the same lines, and what might be the effects of pursuing the method further.

SAMPLE THEME

Alienation and Triumph: A Comparison of
Down These Mean Streets *by Piri Thomas and*
A Portrait of the Artist as a Young Man *by James Joyce* [1]

Down These Mean Streets by Piri Thomas and *A Portrait of the Artist as a Young Man* by James Joyce are similar in many ways. Both books are autobiographical. Joyce gains a degree of fictionalized distance from the autobiography by changing his hero's name and presenting the story in the third person limited point of view. Thomas is more directly involved; he keeps his own name and uses the first person point of view. Thomas's work is thus more clearly recognized as autobiography than Joyce's, which is usually seen as a novel. Though the substance of *Down These Mean Streets* is admittedly autobiographical, however, the work is organized and developed as though it is a novel. *A Portrait of the Artist as a Young Man* may be called an autobiographical novel, while *Down These Mean Streets* could be termed a novelistic autobiography.

There are many other parallels between the two works, but

[1] Quotations and parenthetical page numbers refer to Piri Thomas, *Down These Mean Streets* (New York: New American Library, 1967), and James Joyce, *A Portrait of the Artist as a Young Man: Text, Criticism, and Notes,* Chester G. Anderson, ed. (New York: The Viking Press, 1968).

the most important similarity is that they are both about alienation and triumph—alienation from forces that are shown as stultifying or destructive, and eventual triumph over them. Triumph is achieved by both protagonists, negatively, through both formal and informal education, and, positively, through the conscious choice of a new and different way of life.

Formal education is as different as it can be for the middle-class Stephen and the lower-class Piri, but in both works it is shown as a process accompanied by unnecessary suppression. For Stephen, education at Clongowes and Belvedere is highly formalized; many of the impressions and recollections of early childhood included in the first chapter are concerned with school and with religious training. By contrast, very little is mentioned in *Down These Mean Streets* about Piri's early school experiences. The book is unlike *A Portrait,* in fact, because it begins when Piri is about thirteen, while *A Portrait* opens with Stephen's earliest experience at about three. But if the schools attended by both boys are compared, they are both shown as negative and suppressive forces that certainly influence if they do not cause later alienation. While Stephen endures the pandybat and successfully gains a superb education, however, Piri escapes from school almost daily, runs away from a pursuing principal, and absorbs little if any formal instruction. His trouble understanding words like *psychology* and *introspectively* (p. 284) when he finally starts to develop his intellect in prison at the age of about 25 is in stark and sad contrast with Stephen's learned discourses on art at the age of 20 in the final chapter of *A Portrait.* Thus, for Stephen, the negative aspects of school do not interfere with intellectual growth; in fact, school is actually a liberating as well as a restricting force. For Piri, school is almost entirely negative, a force imposed by the white establishment to keep Blacks and Puerto Ricans in line. When Piri develops an increasing consciousness of his identity with Blacks, therefore, he rejects school and everything it represents.

In both works, the business of living and interacting with others—informal education—is seen as a more influential and thus a more destructive force than formal education. Virtually everything that Piri knows about life is gained on the streets, and it is the code he learns there that leads him to commit acts of violence. Stephen's experiences with home, friends, and acquaintances are all dominant in the way of life he finally rejects. Life for him, of course, is incomparably more peaceful than life for Piri, but Stephen too suffers from unnecessary violence on the streets. Heron, Nash, and Boland beat him because he has indicated a liking for the poetry of Byron and also has shown independence of mind with regard to church doctrine (p. 82). Stephen never adopts the ways of violence, seeing them as potential means by which he would be assimilated into the mediocrity around him:

> This spirit of quarrelsome comradeship which he had observed lately in his rival [Vincent Heron] had not seduced Stephen from his habits of quiet obedience. He mistrusted the turbulence and doubted the sincerity of such comradeship which seemed to him a sorry anticipation of manhood. The question of honour here raised was, like all such questions, trivial to him. . . . (p. 83).

By contrast, violence for Piri is a normal condition of existence. Without a willingness to fight and even to kill if necessary, Piri would lose his reputation for bravery, his *corazón*. It is not until he has followed his code into prison and is almost on the verge of joining a prison riot in order not to "punk out" on his fellow prisoners that he finally decides to reject violence, and even then he allows the decision to be made for him:

> "Hold it," a hack [prison guard] said. They were now all over the place [the prison yard]. I looked at them, the guys looked at them, we looked at each other. Our decision was being made for us, and we could save face. I let myself be molded into a line, my eyes and heart at the west wall but my mind out in the wild, wide street (pp. 269 f.).

As this decision shows, a final authority in all human relations is a system of law and morality, a system that allows freedom of rebellion up to a certain point but descends on an individual once he has gone too far. Because Piri does not decide to abandon violence until late, much of his story is about his own anger and rage and the consequences of many criminal acts. While he becomes a rebel against American legal structures, Stephen strains against the tight moral and religious structures of late nineteenth-century Ireland. Stephen's indulgence in illicit sex is purely lustful and normally rebellious, uncomplicated by anything like Piri's racial awareness and hostility, but it is followed by a long, drawn-out sermon threatening his soul with ageless torment in hell. Stephen's visual encounter with the girl standing in the middle of a stream results in "an outburst of profane joy" (p. 171), which leads him to conclude that life should be led as freely as possible. How different this experience is from Piri's encounter with the white girl on the subway between 42nd Street and 14th Street (pp. 136–138)! In all of Piri's acts, whether his experience with the white prostitute in Texas, his robberies, his beating the car dealer, or his shooting the man during the nightclub robbery, his anger and his hatred of "Paddies" (whites) are foremost, and it is this rage that he has acquired on the mean streets. For both Stephen and Piri, the result of encountering a suppressive, distasteful moral code is alienation. Stephen's alienation is manifested in his decision to leave home, fatherland, and church (p. 247), and Piri's is demonstrated in his being forced to serve six years of a possible fifteen-year prison term at Comstock.

If nothing but alienation were common to both protagonists, then frustration and not affirmation would be the keys to the works. But there is something affirmative and triumphant. Stephen's growth away from home and country and church is balanced by his growth toward what he thinks is the higher value of life as an artist. While a new life is not so clearly established for Piri, it is clear that in his rejection of violence and many other elements of his past he will find a new life. Like Stephen, Piri realizes his own personal value, and the value of his identity as a Puerto-Rican American. He has learned that "Free Side is the Best Side" (Chapter 33), even if pursuing freedom means compromise with anger and his "rep." Symbolically, Piri's final act is to walk away from Carlito the junkie. This is a triumph, for he presumably walks into a new life, still on the mean streets that he loves, but free of the destructive influences on the streets. For both Piri and Stephen, then, the past is truly prologue for a different and better life to come.

In addition to the theme of alienation and triumph, there are many other points of comparison between the two works. The fathers, for example, exert strong negative influences on the two protagonists, while the mothers are gentler and more moderating. Both Piri and Stephen have love involvements: Thomas develops the Trina relationship at some length, but Joyce leaves the E.C. relationship vague. There are parallel interactions in both works between the protagonists and their male peers, most of these relationships being negative in one way or the other. The list of other similarities could be extended, but there are major points of contrast. As a genre, *A Portrait of the Artist as a Young Man* is a pioneering book, and *Down These Mean Streets* is a kind of personal testimonial following in its wake. Then, too, Joyce's book is more general in import than Thomas's. Though Joyce's locale is Ireland at the end of the nineteenth century, the problems faced by Stephen are like those faced by any young person attempting to establish an independent, adult identity. *Down These Mean Streets* is much more about a specific social condition in America—the problems of growing up as a member of a suppressed minority. But if this topicality is for the moment laid aside, Thomas is as successful in his way as Joyce in probing the feeling and fears of the young who criticize and revolt against their environment and aspire to improve their lives. Both *A Portrait of the Artist as a Young Man* and *Down These Mean Streets* are books of great impact.

The Theme Analyzing
STRUCTURE

CHAPTER
10

Structure in literary study may be defined as the organization of a literary work as influenced by its plot (in fictional works) or main idea (in expository works). The work is also sometimes defined as the pattern of emotions in the literary work. Although these two definitions are distinct, they are closely connected and under most circumstances are virtually inseparable. The word *structure* is in fact a metaphor implying that a work of literature, both topically and emotionally, is as connected and unified as a building —a structure.

In imaginative works, structure refers to the chronological position of parts, scenes, episodes, chapters, and acts; it also refers to the logical or associational relationships among stanzas, ideas, images, or other divisions. In expository works, the word necessarily refers to the arrangement and development of ideas. Structure is a matter of the relationships among parts that are usually described in terms of cause and effect, position in time, association, symmetry, and balance and proportion (the last two are usually concerned with evaluation, whereas the first three are more closely involved with description).

Literary artists universally aim at a unified impression in their works, and because literature is a time art (it cannot be comprehended as a whole in one moment, as can a painting or a work of sculpture), the study of structure attempts to demonstrate that the idea and the resulting arrangement of parts produces a total impression. You can see, therefore, that a study of structure is one avenue to the evaluation of literature, because such a study would bring out any lack of unity in a work and make that work subject to adverse criticism.

The Importance of Structure

In a very real sense, all studies of literature are either directly or indirectly concerned with structure. If you talk about the happy or unhappy ending of a short story, for example, you in fact consider the conclusion in relation to what went before it; inevitably you mention whether the earlier parts of the story demonstrated that the characers earned or deserved what happened to them. This consideration must touch on the logic of the story's action, and hence it is a subject of structure. Similarly, in considering Shakespeare's Sonnet No. 73 (quoted below, pp. 122–23), you may observe that the first quatrain compares the speaker to dead trees, the second to twilight, and the third to a dying and self-extinguishing fire. Whether or not you determine that there is a logical or topical relationship among these quatrains, you are discussing structure.

Since structure is so closely tied to all phases of literary study, you might ask in what way structure is unique. How, for example, does a theme about ideas, or a summary theme, differ from a theme about structure? The difference is one of emphasis: in studying structure you emphasize the logic, or the causes, underlying the major divisions in the work being analyzed; in a summary theme you emphasize the events or ideas that you have cast in a reasonable plan of organization; in a theme about ideas you emphasize the ideas and their importance as they are made apparent in the work. In fact, no matter what topic you are writing about, your finished theme is usually related to the structure of the work; for the major parts of your theme can be conveniently dictated by the organization of that work. Always, however, in studying structure, the organization of the work and the causes for it are your primary concern. Ideas, events, and other things such as tone, point of view, and imagery are relevant only as substance for your discussion of structure.

In a good work of literature, the parts are not introduced accidentally. One part demands another, sometimes by logical requirement. Elder Olsen's study of Pope's poem *Epistle to Dr. Arbuthnot*,[1] shows that in the first sixty-eight lines Pope illustrates a comic idea that constitutes a minor logical premise; namely, that a number of bad poets and other people have been waving ass's ears in his face. Then in the next ten lines Pope illustrates a major premise, namely that when people have ass's ears, you have to tell them about it. Finally, in four following lines, Pope draws a logical conclusion (which is also a defense of himself as a satirist); namely, that he had written a lengthy poem, *The Dunciad*, to tell the world that the people mentioned in the first sixty-eight lines had ass's ears. In short, the first eighty-two lines of the poem form a syllogism,

---

[1] "Rhetoric and the Appreciation of Pope," *Modern Philology* XXXVII (1939), 13–55.

not necessarily valid logically, but certainly valid comically and rhetorically.

Some works may have similar logical coherence, and in others the guiding plan may be chronology. It is never enough simply to assert that events happen in time; time is important only as it permits human reactions to occur, and hence chronology in literature is primarily a convenient classification for the logic of human motivation. For example, in Frost's poem "The Road Not Taken," the first three stanzas describe the speaker's taking one road at a fork in the road he was already traveling. As the stanzas progress it becomes clear that the road taken was actually the way of life chosen by the speaker. In the final, fourth stanza, the speaker observes that his choice was a major landmark in his life, affecting his present and future and making him different from what he would have been had he taken the road not taken. The structure of the poem is such that the stanzas move naturally from a brief account of events to their human effects and implications. The last stanza stems inevitably and necessarily from the first three; it could not be transposed and still make the same sense.

Aids in Studying Structure

In studying structure, be sure to take whatever assistance the author has given you. Has he made divisions in the work, such as stanzas, parts, chapters, cantos, or spaces between groups of paragraphs? Try to relate the subjects of these various divisions, and develop a rationale for the divisions. Is there a geographical location (or several locations) that lends its own mood and color to the various parts of the story? How can these be related to the events? Does the time of the day—or time of year—shift as the work progresses? Can the events be shown to have a relationship to these various times? Does one event grow inevitably out of another; that is, do the events have logical as well as chronological causation? Is a new topic introduced because it is similar to another topic (see, for example, Joyce's *A Portrait of the Artist as a Young Man*)? All these and like questions should assist you in your study.

You might also help yourself by following a suggestion made by Aristotle in his *Poetics*:

> . . . the plot [of any work], being an imitation of an action, must imitate one action and that a whole, the structural union of the parts being such that, if any one of them is displaced or removed, the whole will be disjointed and disturbed. For a thing whose presence or absence make no visible difference, is not an organic part of the whole.[2]

[2] Ch. VIII. 4, in S. H. Butcher, *Aristotle's Theory of Poetry and Fine Art*, 4th ed. (New York: Dover Publications, Inc., 1951), p. 35.

As an exercise, you might imagine that a certain part of the work you are studying has been taken away. You might then ask what is wrong with the work remaining. Does it make sense? Does it seem truncated? Why should the missing part be returned? As you answer these questions, you are really dealing with the logical necessity of structural wholeness. For example, let us suppose that the second stanza of Frost's "The Road Not Taken" is missing. The poem immediately becomes illogical because it omits the chronological event leading to the conclusion, and it also omits the logic of the speaker's choice of the road he selected. If you attempt similar imaginative exercises with other works, you can help yourself in determining whether these works are organic wholes.

You might also aid yourself by drawing a scheme or plan to explain, graphically, the structure of the work you are analyzing. Not everyone can benefit from drawings, and some people might even be offended by them as an aid in literary study. But if you have the kind of visually oriented mind that can be helped by a drawing or sketch, then making a drawing might help you to organize your thoughts and to improve your final theme. The story "Miss Brill," by Katherine Mansfield, for example, may be conveniently compared with a person running happily along a narrow path deep within a dark forest and making a turn only to plunge suddenly and unexpectedly off a steep cliff. You might graph this comparison like this:

In writing a theme about the story, you could employ this scheme as a guide for your discussion. This is not to say that the structure of the story could not be profitably analyzed in another way but that the scheme would help to give your own study penetration, meaning, and form.

Sometimes the use of an illustration can create an insight or series of insights that might at first not have been clear to you. For example, Shakespeare's Sonnet No. 73, already mentioned, has three quatrains and a concluding rhymed couplet:

Stanza I   That time of year thou mayst in me behold,
                When yellow leaves, or none, or few do hang

Upon those boughs which shake against the cold,
Bare ruined choirs, where late the sweet birds sang.

Stanza II

In me thou seest the twilight of such day,
As after sunset fadeth in the West,
Which by and by black night doth take away,
Death's second self that seals up all in rest.

Stanza III

In me thou seest the glowing of such fire,
That on the ashes of his youth doth lie,
As the death bed, whereon it must expire,
Consumed with that which it was nourished by.

This thou perceiv'st, which makes thy love more strong.
To love that well, which thou must leave ere long.

Let us assume, without proof, that the poem is an organic whole. (This is an assumption that you should make at first about every work you read, and you should maintain it until or unless your experience disproves it.) The quatrains, then, are connected in some way, and the couplet is similarly connected with everything going on before it. Allowing for the fact that each part must be unique as well as connected, an ideal plan of this distinctness and connection might be graphed with the use of four overlapping triangles, with the areas of overlap representing the subject matter common to the three quatrains and also to the concluding couplet:

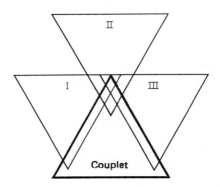

As yet, no connection has been demonstrated, but in attempting to justify the drawing, you will discover many connecting elements. In each quatrain the phrase "in me" appears with the phrases "thou mayest behold," "thou seest," and "thou seest" again. In the couplet the phrase "thou perceiv'st" and the word "that" as a pronoun referring to the speaker appear, so that each major unit contains references to the speaker and his listener. In addition, a common subject of the three quatrains might be various stages of light or conditions affecting light; in quatrain one, referring to late autumn, the sun would be low in the sky, just as in quatrain two the sun has set, and in the third the coals retain only a dull glow. Similarly, in quatrains two and three, death is mentioned specifically, and quatrain one refers to barren branches from which dead leaves have fallen. All three quatrains either imply or refer to something that has passed; namely, summer (I), daylight (II), and a bright fire (III), and all these are analogous to the speaker, so that the statement "To love that well, which thou must leave ere long" in the concluding couplet is a fitting résumé of the poem. With all these connecting links supplied, the drawing may be filled in, with the list of common elements placed next to it as a "key":

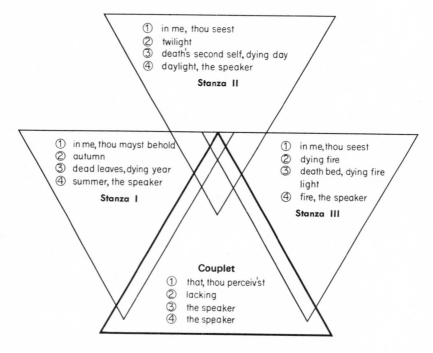

Stanza II
① in me, thou seest
② twilight
③ death's second self, dying day
④ daylight, the speaker

Stanza I
① in me, thou mayst behold
② autumn
③ dead leaves, dying year
④ summer, the speaker

Stanza III
① in me, thou seest
② dying fire
③ death bed, dying fire light
④ fire, the speaker

Couplet
① that, thou perceiv'st
② lacking
③ the speaker
④ the speaker

CONNECTING LINKS

1. (a)*"in me"* (b)*"thou . . .st"*
2. Time of low or absent light.
3. Death or something dead.
4. Things that have passed or will pass.

In the above sketch, triangles work successfully to show the structure and the connecting links, but in analyzing a work you might try circles, lines, planes, or other geometric figures. If you wish, you might make a list, or you might do nothing more than study and take notes carefully. What is important is that you attempt to look at the work you are studying as a *structure* of some sort and that you write a theme about this structure. Making a drawing or a graph has the virtue of giving you a visual grasp of the fact that the parts of a unified work are distinct and connected—important discoveries both for your understanding of the work and your writing a theme.

The Structure of Emotions

In keeping with the second definition of structure, it is important to realize that planning and organizing a literary work has little meaning if it is not designed to create some emotional impact on the reader. Accordingly, you should try to consider the relationship of the physical and logical structure to the emotional effectiveness of the work. This element is so important that it is included as a part of the first sample theme and is the entire subject of the second. One should never forget that authors arrange their material in order to build interest and emotional involvement, and that very few people would do much reading if they did not feel a sense of involvement in what they read.

Each work of literature may justly be regarded as a pattern capable of producing a complex set of emotions in a reader. The emotions that you feel while reading are the result of an interaction of involvement, time, and the structure of the work. To see that each of these elements is essential, let us regard an experience common to many readers. Often a reader irritated by remaining in suspense may read the conclusion of a story or novel before beginning to read seriously at the start. If you have ever "peeked" in this way you may recall that you knew the facts of the ending, but had little if any feelings about them. When you read that same conclusion after reading the work in proper sequence from beginning to end, however, you probably had an emotional response to it, even though you knew the facts in advance. The difference in the two readings was that the entire structure of the work itself had no influence on your response the first time, but strongly influenced you the second time. Involvement, time, structure—all these make up the basis of emotional response.

For this reason, even when you focus attention on a particular emotion that you felt at a particular moment in response to a work, you must necessarily relate this emotion to the sense of involvement, expectation, and apprehension that were more or less ongoing emotions as you approached the particular moment of emotion. In a word, discussing one emotion entails the discussion of the ways in which a literary work organizes and brings out related emotions. For example, Shakespeare's Sonnet No. 73 builds feelings of regret, sadness, and resignation, but concludes on a note of affirmation (although in a minor key). Any account of an emotional response to the conclusion of this poem must also attempt to deal with the fact that the impact of the last lines depends on the effect of the three preceding quatrains.

Each work of literature may thus be seen as a complex emotional structure. Emotional responses to even a relatively simple literary form like detective fiction, for example, are complex. Such fiction creates suspense by introducing inquisitiveness, doubt, and anxiety, with related emotions of various shades of horror, fear, and sympathy. Detective stories also create both properly and improperly directed hostility (at the true criminal and at the "red herring"), and finally produce satisfaction when the solution of the mystery ends all doubt and anxiety. It is not at all uncommon for such stories to end according to the age-old advice of the theater to "leave them laughing." A joke or a comic description thus may produce a smile that ensures the final defeat of anxiety—at least as far as that story was concerned.

The creation of a certain degree of anxiety is perhaps the principal means by which authors maintain interest. The author of a story about a pioneering trip across the American plains, for example, creates anxiety about whether the forces of Nature will permit the journey to be concluded successfully. If human agents such as outlaws are introduced as antagonists, then this anxiety can be related to hostility and fear, and if the principal characters are virtuous, they usually become objects of admiration. Many western stories and detective stories build strongly on the indignation that is usually aroused by an outlaw committing some outrageous crime or taking advantage of the momentarily helpless hero. The hero's eventual triumph over the outlaw is therefore made much more satisfying.

Such emotions are also coextensive with the structure of drama. Each play develops a major *conflict,* which is structured in such a way that maximum tension is produced. In the nineteenth century, a German novelist and critic, Gustav Freytag, suggested that the rising and falling actions and tensions in the typical five-act drama resemble a pyramid: emotions are incited with the exposition of the drama and are heightened as the plot complications develop until a climax is reached in the third act; after this point, the falling action begins until the final catastrophe, or denouement, is reached. The emotions preceding the climax are those that spring from uncertainty; those afterward spring from inevitability. One major idea in the Aristotelian idea of tragedy is that tragedy aims at the purgation—catharsis—of pity and fear. In the Freytag pyramid, you might observe that fear is touched most heavily before the climax, whereas pity becomes predominant after it, although the two are intermingled throughout a tragedy. The point here is that Aristotle's description of the aims of tragedy presupposed a proper arrangement of incidents and that this concern, like his other commentaries on plot in *The Poetics* (VI–XIV), was mainly structural.

If a literary work is an emotional structure, it should reach a satisfactory emotional conclusion—a relaxation of tension. In Greek tragedy, the concluding action, the *exodos,* consists of choral speeches that ponder the meaning of the action. This relatively intellectual section provides the opportunity to relax after the emotional peak of the play. In Milton's "Lycidas," although anger and indignation are strongly brought out in Milton's famous "digressions" (which are integral in the poem), the conclusion permits relaxation and satisfaction. Indeed, one major distinction between art and propaganda is that propaganda is deliberately designed to create dissatisfaction. Art is complete emotionally, whereas a political speech is as emotionally unfinished as the political work remaining to be done. This is not to say that art cannot be propagandistic nor propaganda artistic but that this distinction can help you to analyze and judge works of literature.

Examples could be multiplied. The important point, however, is that the study of structure is not confined exclusively to the physical placement of scenes, acts, episodes, and so on, in the work under consideration. Structure is equally concerned with the logic and unity of a work, and the patterning of emotions is a significant element in literary logic and unity.

It is most important that in discussing the structure of a work with emphasis on emotions, you should focus your efforts on the work itself, on the way in which the physical, lexical structure is also an emotional structure. Many persons respond individually and often unpredictably to what they read. But if you emphasize your observations about the work, you can rule out this possible avenue into complete subjectivity (another name for complete subjectivity is the "affective fallacy").[3] In writing on such a topic, concentrate on the author's skill in creating suspense, interest, resignation, happiness, sympathy, pity, satisfaction, and whatever other emotional states are brought out in the work.

Problems

You will of course encounter problems in your theme about structure. You must interpret the idea of the work properly, and you must also arrive at a sound conclusion about the work's effect. This problem is extremely subjective, but your interpretation will always be respected as long as it is reasonable.

[3] See W. K. Wimsatt, Jr., *The Verbal Icon,* 2nd ed. (New York: Noonday Press, 1960), pp. 21–39.

Even more difficulty will be encountered when you attempt to relate your analysis and description of the parts in the work to your interpretation of the work's idea and effect. It is here that you must be especially careful. If your first judgment is that one part is not relevant, be sure that you have not missed some essential idea that would make it revelant. Make sure that your central idea is accurately comprehensive. One well-known writer, for example, stated that the last section of *Huckleberry Finn* is "just cheating." It seems apparent that his judgment resulted from an inadequate idea about the meaning of the novel. If he had considered that the novel contrasts common sense (Huck's idea of freeing Jim) with quixotism or faulty judgment (Tom's idea of freeing Jim with "style"), he would have modified his statement in keeping with this consideration.

You also have the usual problem of selectivity. What you choose to discuss will be made on the basis of your initial analysis of the idea and the effect of the work you analyze. A mere description of what happens in the work and where it happens is nothing more than a synopsis. Your instructor is of course interested in your ability to describe the organization of the work, but he is much more interested in what you *make* out of your description. Do not employ summary in your theme, but refer to events as they are relevant to the point you are making about idea and effect. As always, your point is of primary importance and should be kept foremost.

Organizing Your Theme

INTRODUCTION

You should consider what you think is the most important idea in the work that you have analyzed, and you should also consider the principal emotional pattern in the work; make an attempt to relate these two. The problem here is finding the lowest common denominator that will take in all the principal events or statements in the work; you must make a general statement that is true for the work and that therefore makes purposeful all the events or statements in the work. Thus, a principal idea governing Milton's "Lycidas" is that life and effort have a final purpose (that life has meaning); a discussion of this idea would take into account the structure of the poem. Similarly, the main idea in Hemingway's *A Farewell to Arms* is that happiness is not to be found on earth. Once you have arrived at an idea in this way, you should make it the central idea of your theme. Conclude your introduction with a thesis sentence.

BODY

Work from your introduction into a discussion of the way in which the idea influences the form of the work. If the work is arranged according to stanzas, cantos, books, scenes, acts, chapters, or sections, try to determine the logic of this arrangement. Your emphasis should be on the way in which each of the parts bears on the idea or statement you have accepted as the governing idea or plan of the work, and upon the relationship of part to part. You might talk about *movement* from one part to the next. Does one part end on a note of expectation? Does the next part present material that satisfies that expectation? Does the logic of one part require that other events follow? Does the author provide these events, or does he exceed the ordinary requirements of logic? Does the movement of the work depend on the mental functioning and consequent action of a certain character? Does the author demonstrate that such functioning and actions are truly a part of this character? If you have made any graph or drawing that helps to explain the structure, you could use that as an aid in discussing the relationship of part to part.

If you are concentrating on emotions and structure, you might wish to discuss the pattern or progression of emotions in the work. What relationship does one emotion have to emotions felt earlier or later? Do the emotions occur as you might, on reflection, expect them to occur? What complications develop in the emotions (e.g., Is sorrow tempered by satisfaction at seeing justice done? Is happiness complicated by the insult or injury of one or more of the characters?)? Or you might wish to concentrate on a dominant emotion such as anxiety or empathy. What techniques, what control over materials, does the author employ throughout the work in order to maintain this emotion? Does he disclose everything at once, or does he hold things back? Does he create a mystery? Does he provoke tension by illustrating the depths of a character's dilemma?

CONCLUSION

You should conclude your theme with an evaluation of the authors' success as far as structure is concerned. Are all the parts of the work equally necessary? Do they occur in the best order? Would the work be damaged if any parts were left out, or if any parts were transposed? Are the parts successful in creating a total impression? If your answer to any of these questions is no, you have grounds for saying that the structure of the work is faulty. If your answer is always yes, you should probably conclude your theme with praise for the author, for you have been analyzing a perfectly unified work.

An Analysis of the Structure
of "The Three Strangers"
by Thomas Hardy [4]

Hardy's principal aim in "The Three Strangers" is to show the warm, kind, human qualities of the Wessex natives who are so prominent in the story. To bring out this human kindness, Hardy demonstrates the reactions of the natives to a series of incidents that clearly present a conflict between (a) duty toward law, and (b) duty toward a human being under condemnation of the law, whose crime has, in their eyes, been extenuated. In order to create a favorable impression that justice has been done and the external laws of humanity obeyed, Hardy utilizes the device of suspense: he thereby shows how the sympathies of the natives are favorably disposed toward humanity and the first stranger and unfavorably disposed toward a punitive law and the second stranger. As he controls the attitudes of the natives, he controls the emotions of his readers in the same way. To make his case credible Hardy extensively describes not only the natives but also the characteristics of the first two strangers. These are ambitious aims, which Hardy successfully achieves.

The opening one-fifth of the story is an introduction to the human kindness of the natives. The section moves from the big to the little—from the natural scenery surrounding Higher Crowstairs, to the general scene of humanity within the house, to the specific scene represented by Shepherd Fennel and his wife. Hardy is at great pains to show the perpetually human ways of the folk, not only in 182–, but by implication during all periods of human history. He makes the scene universal in his description of the dancing, which he describes in the words *apogee* and *perigee*. In other words, the dancing has been going on as long as the planets have been moving in their orbits. The incident the natives celebrate is the age-old one of birth and initiation into life (in this specific case, a Christening). These people, Hardy suggests, are human beings uncontaminated by anything modern, for they have an "absolute confidence" in one another that begets "perfect ease," and that makes them immune to the modern poison of allowing business interests to

[4] Thomas Hardy, "The Three Strangers," in *Short Stories for Study*, 3rd ed., Raymond W. Short and Richard B. Sewall, eds. (New York: Holt, Rinehart & Winston, Inc., 1956). Parenthetical page numbers refer to this edition.

interfere with friendship (p. 108). In short, this first section establishes contact with the folk and with their basic humanity—so strong a contact that it will not be lost during the remainder of the story. Clearly, Hardy is going to make use of these human characteristics later on. This first section is therefore an effective introduction.

Against this backdrop, the second section builds suspense and offers the possibility of a false resolution. Covering slightly more than half of the story, this section introduces suspense in the persons of the three strangers and the actions in which they are engaged. Although throughout the section a person might lose focus on the natives, it must be emphasized that Hardy's real purpose in bringing in the strangers is to illustrate his main idea that the natives are kind and human. Each of the strangers is mysterious, although Hardy resolves the mystery of the second stranger almost immediately. Of the three strangers, the first is characterized by his likeableness, his desire to remain anonymous, his lack of tobacco, and his taking a weapon when the second knock on the door is heard. The second stranger is of course the hangman, upon whom Hardy focusses dislike. The third stranger is not developed at all, except that the section closes with the idea that he is the escaped criminal. Momentarily, therefore, attention is drawn away from the mystery surrounding the first stranger, since the third is actually a red herring. The second section therefore concludes on a note of suspense.

The third section, the last part of the story, brings out the events leading up to the resolution of the suspense caused by curiosity about the identities of the first and third strangers. In a comic scene the natives search for and capture the third stranger, who then informs his captors that the first stranger, and not himself, is the escaped criminal. At this point Hardy demonstrates that his story all along has been building up to the reaction of the natives when they learn this fact. The knowledge forces them into a decision, which they tacitly make "on the side of the fugitive," since they feel that "the intended punishment was cruelly disproportioned to the transgression" (p. 131). After this climax—the human decision of the natives—the story quickly ends.

The total effect of Hardy's structure, therefore, belies the expectations aroused by the title, and a casual reader might feel that Hardy has cluttered his story with too much detail about the natives. But more consideration shows that the action concerning the three strangers exists in order to bring out the warm humanity of the natives, and that the story, just like all stories, is finally about the entire society in which it occurs. In this case, Hardy suggests, or implies, that the story is as old as the race.

His use of suspense supports my claim. He deliberately avoids saying until the very end that the first stranger is the escaped sheep-stealer, although his hints about this fact, at second reading, are obvious. In this way, he builds up sympathy for the stranger, and avoids an early, purely legal reaction against him until all the facts are in. Because of this delay in our knowledge, Hardy successfully molds opinion about the stranger *as a human being* and *not* as a criminal. And, since the reader's opinion is formed along with that of the natives, he becomes sympathetic toward their decision to neglect the strict letter of the law in favor of the more compelling human obligation, particularly in view of the obnoxious and severe character of the law as personified by the hangman. Hardy wants no enduring suspense about the harshness and injustice represented by this second, horrid figure who delights in his ghoulish work.

Hardy therefore ends his story just as he began it, on the notes of (a) the overwhelming need for human kindness and (b) the permanence of life, in which birth and death are cycles. Thereby, he has created a unified structure with a total impression similar to the one occasioned by his statement about the life of the folk, the natives, in his poem "In Time of 'The Breaking of Nations' ":

> Yet this will go onward the same
> Though Dynasties pass.

SECOND SAMPLE THEME

The Emotional Undulations
of Steinbeck's Story "The Snake" [5]

John Steinbeck's story "The Snake" is a mystery story, not in the detective sense but in the sense that it creates perplexity, bafflement, mild thrills, and final satisfaction. Before the end, the story provides a series of shocks plus a few touches of wry amusement. The principal character Dr. Phillips, the marine biologist, seems at first worthy of admiration, but then he becomes offensive; finally, however, he becomes worthy of deep commitment. At the same moments that Steinbeck redeems the doctor, he builds up repulsion and perplexity through his second major character, for the story, in keeping with its name, moves from extremes of emotion like the undulations of the rattlesnake that figures so prominently in the action.

The final section of the story, characterized by flat description,

---

[5] John Steinbeck, "The Snake," in T. Y. Greet, Charles E. Edge, and John M. Munro, eds., *The Worlds of Fiction: Stories in Context* (Boston: Houghton Mifflin Co., 1964). Parenthetical page numbers refer to this edition.

creates only mild interest concluded by mild shock. The opening two pages follow Dr. Phillips with the proper detachment from the tide pool to his commercial laboratory. His execution of the cat, however, because it is described in the same flat manner, is shocking. No matter how intellectually one can be convinced of the need for killing animals for experiments, the description of an actual killing causes shock. Steinbeck creates a hostile response to Dr. Phillips when the cat to be killed is removed from the cage:

> Dr. Phillips lifted down the milk and walked to the cat cage, but before he filled the containers he reached in the cage and gently picked out a big rangy alley tabby. He stroked her for a moment and then dropped her in a small black painted box, closed the lid and bolted it and then turned on a petcock which admitted gas into the killing chamber. While the short soft struggle went on in the black box he filled the saucers with milk. One of the cats arched against his hand and he smiled and petted her neck (p. 362).

This quiet description is devoid of any pity or repulsion, and thus produces a vacuum of emotion that the reader must, temporarily at least, fill. The emotional response is also accompanied by shock and resentment against the doctor, whose smile and whose immediate preparation of a can of beans, seems cold and unfeeling.

Having established this mood of mild repulsion, Steinbeck in the next section of the story introduces a new character, a woman who replaces the doctor as an alienated figure. Steinbeck presents wryly amusing details about her to show that she has snakelike features: her forehead is "flat": her eyes glitter; she is exceptionally silent and patient, like the snake waiting for his prey; and her chin, between her "lower lip and point," is short (p. 364). Because Steinbeck does not explicitly make the comparison but presents the details so that the reader must make the comparison for himself, the amusement of the portrait is accompanied by the thrill of discovery.

Mildly comic as the discovery is, however, the woman does not sustain amusement but becomes an object of repulsion. Steinbeck brings out this reaction against her at the same time that he elicits admiration for the doctor. He polarizes emotions between the two characters by showing the doctor as increasingly more human while the woman evinces no warm human qualities at all. He uses the omniscient point of view for the doctor but the dramatic for the woman in order to define the doctor's shock at the lady's desire to buy the rattlesnake. The story's emotional undulations reach their widest curve as Steinbeck describes the doctor's feelings about the lady's request:

> He hated people who make sport of natural processes. He was not a sportsman but a biologist. He could kill a thousand animals for

> knowledge, but not an insect for pleasure. He'd been over this in his mind before (p. 366).

Admiration for the doctor's humanitarian role is reinforced when he saves the woman from being bitten when she puts her hand into the rattlesnake's cage.

Simultaneously with admiration for the doctor, the woman's responses to the death and eating of the rat elicit disgust. It is as though the S shape taken by the snake in approaching the rat is descriptive of the responses Steinbeck wishes to effect. Although the snake's desire for the rat is natural, the woman's seems unnatural, ghoulish: Steinbeck's repeated descriptions comparing her with the snake no longer amuse; they repel. Again, however, the style influences one's responses. The flatness, the almost clinical narration, prevents repulsion from hardening into hate. Steinbeck's scene is a medical laboratory, where scientific detachment produces the attitude that people should be rescued, not condemned.

Because the doctor never sees the woman again and is therefore prevented from helping her, and also because her strange desire to see the snake eat the rat is never explained, the dominant emotion produced in the final page of the story is perplexity. Although the reader's curiosity and the wish to see things through is thus frustrated, the story's conclusion is by no means frustrating. That the woman never returns to see another rat eaten, even though she promises to do so, suggests that her desires were satisfied by the incident. There is a "Lady or the Tiger" mystery about what gave rise to her need, but at least this one episode is completed.

The emotional pattern of the story is therefore a gentle weaving from emotion to emotion, from shock to wry amusement, from sympathy to disgust, from bafflement to satisfaction. None of these states is extreme, for the flat, straightforward descriptions prevent extremes. Steinbeck so structures his development of Dr. Phillips's character to evoke the maximum sympathy; from a distant figure externally described, the doctor develops as an acquaintance and then almost as a friend, with understandable human doubts and perplexities. The woman, on the other hand, receives no such favorable treatment; her external appearance and manner reflect some internal torment that the reader is not privileged to understand. In the absence of any mitigating detail, the reader must either be repelled by her or at best must reserve judgment. In other words, although the story itself comes to an end, the subject matter touches an unknown part of human life that has not yet yielded to the researches of science. The doctor nevertheless continues to search for an answer, and this, his most admirable trait, is sufficient to produce a conclusion that satisfies emotionally.

The Theme on

IMAGERY

CHAPTER

11

Imagery is a broad term referring to the verbal comparison of one or many objects, ideas, or emotional states with something else. The use of imagery is a means by which an author relates something he wishes to express to something you yourself either have experienced or can easily imagine as your own experience. He accomplishes this end through *analogy;* thus, at the heart of communication through imagery is this assumption: "I cannot describe this idea for you, nor can I tell you how this character felt, but I can provide you with an analogy—an image—which by its similarity to your own experience or by its ability to touch your imagination will make you understand the idea or re-create his emotional state." Thus, a writer wishing to express a character's joy may say not simply "He was happy" but might write a sentence like "He felt as though he had just received a million-dollar check." It is unlikely that any of the author's readers have had such an experience themselves, but they can easily *imagine* how elated such an experience would make them feel, and therefore they can re-create the joy experienced by the literary character. The author has illustrated one thing—joy—in terms of another—the receipt of a large sum of money.

KEATS'S SONNET ON CHAPMAN'S HOMER

As a literary parallel to the million-dollar check image, let us examine Keats's poem "On First Looking Into Chapman's Homer." Keats wrote the poem after he first read Chapman's translation of Homer, and his main idea is that Chapman not only translated Homer's words but also transmitted his greatness. A fair expository restatement of the poem might be the following:

> I have read much European literature and have been told that Homer is the best writer of all, but not knowing Greek, I couldn't appreciate his works until I read them in Chapman's translation. To me, this experience was an exciting and awe-inspiring discovery with extensive implications that I only dimly realized.

It is also fair to say that this paraphrase destroys Keats's poetry. Contrast the second sentence of the paraphrase with the last six lines of the sonnet as Keats wrote them:

> Then felt I like some watcher of the skies
>   When a new planet swims into his ken;
> Or like stout Cortez when with eagle eyes
>   He stared at the Pacific—and all his men
> Looked at each other with a wild surmise—
>   Silent, upon a peak in Darien.

Notice that Keats did not say, as did the paraphrase, that he felt the excitement of a great discovery; instead he used imagery to show and to objectify his feelings, so that the reader might re-experience feelings similar to his own. The prose paraphrase does not demonstrate the feelings sufficiently, but the use of imagery allows the reader to experience and visualize exciting moments of great discovery and thereby to share the poet's attitudes. Most of us have difficulty in seeing things as others see them, and therefore we are often indifferent when someone tells us of his emotions. If Keats had said only "I felt excited," his poem would probably not cause anything but skepticism or boredom in us, because we would find no descriptions of objects from which we could reconstruct the precise degree of his emotion. But we certainly can respond to the situation that Keats's imagery causes us to visualize. Imagery, in other words, conveys a close approximation of experience itself, and it calls forth the most strenuous imaginative responses from the reader. In fact, a person cannot regard himself as a good reader until he can re-experience what the writer shows through his imagery.

Some Definitions

The word *image* refers to single literary comparisons. Keats's reference to the "watcher of the skies," for example, is an image. *Imagery* is a broader term referring to all the images within a passage ("the imagery of line 5, or of stanza 6"), an entire work ("the imagery of Eliot's 'Prufrock' "), a group of works ("the imagery of Shakespeare's Roman plays"), or an entire body of works ("the development of Shakespeares' imagery").

To describe the relationship between a writer's ideas and the images, particularly the metaphors, that he chooses to objectify them, two useful terms have been coined by I. A. Richards (in *The Philosophy of Rhetoric*). First is the *tenor,* which is the sum total of ideas and attitudes not only of the literary speaker but also of the author. Thus, the *tenor* of the million-dollar check image is joy or elation. Second is the *vehicle,* or the details that carry the tenor; the vehicle of the check image is the description of the receipt of the check. Similarly, the tenor of the sestet of Keats's sonnet on Chapman's Homer is awe and wonder; the vehicle is the reference to astronomical and geographical discovery.

Characteristics of Literary Imagery

Imagery is important in both expository and imaginative writing. In fact, it would be difficult to find any good piece of writing that does not employ imagery to at least some extent. But imagery is most vital in imaginative writing, where it promotes immediate understanding and makes suggestions and implications—nonlogical processes that are not central to expository writing.

Usually, imagery is embodied in words or descriptions that denote sense experience that leads to many associations. A single word naming a flower, say *rose,* evokes a definite response in most readers: a person might visualize a rose, recall its smell, associate it with the summer sun and pleasant days, and recall the love and respect that a bouquet of roses represents as a gift. But the word *rose* is not an image until its associations are called into play by a writer, as in these famous lines by Robert Burns:

> O, my luve's like a red, red rose
> That's newly sprung in June . . .

Once the comparison has been drawn, all the pleasant connotations of the word *rose* are evoked; these connotations become the *tenor* of the image. That a rose may have unpleasant associations, however, perhaps because of its thorns, should probably not be considered. Such an extension of meaning, although truthful, would likely represent a misreading of the lines.

It would, that is, unless the writer deliberately calls some of these less happy ideas to mind. In one of the most famous poems about a rose, by Edmund Waller ("Go Lovely Rose," in which the speaker addresses a rose that he is about to send to his reluctant sweetheart), the speaker draws attention to the fact that roses, when cut, die:

> Then die—that she
> The common fate of all things rare
> May read in thee:
> How small a part of time they share
> That are so wondrous sweet and fair.

Here the poet is directing the reader's responses to the speaker's original comparison of the rose with his sweetheart, and the structure of the poem is coextensive with the development of the image. In this poem, the tenor is an awareness that life is both lovely and fragile.

Imagery may of course become complex, and it may be found everywhere. Aristotle, in describing methods of argumentation in his *Rhetoric,* mentions that writers often will use *inductions* or *examples* in order to advance their ideas (Book II, Ch. 20). An induction is actually an image that advances the argument—it is a part of argument. The ancient Aesop composed *fables,* which were little pointed stories to which later editors have attached *morals,* or explanations of Aesop's arguments. Jesus Christ spoke constantly in *parables,* which are little narratives embodying profound religious insights. These parables, like those of the Good Samaritan and the Prodigal Son, are being interpreted today in sermons and church-school classes throughout the world. Medieval preachers utilized the *exemplum,* a little story that served as the springboard for a sermon. The medieval Englishman *Orm* wrote the *Ormulum* as a long collection of such *exempla* for use in the churches. All these types of stories today may properly be discussed as imagery.

Imagery and Language

Not only is imagery essential in all types of literature, but it is at the heart of language itself; it is ingrained in our very habits of thought and expression. As only one example out of tens of thousands, the word *channel,* with its allied word *canal,* referred originally to a large trench, ditch, or canal. Because it is a vivid term, it has been used as an image in reference to "directing or forwarding, placing within confines"; anyone familiar with bureaucratic procedures knows what it means to go through "channels." When the wide commercialization of television required the creation of new terminology, *channel* was applied to the frequencies used by the various stations. Quickly the term was applied to the stations themselves, and thus we speak of "Channel 2" and "Channel 4" without thinking about the way in which the word was fashioned in this sense. When an image loses its power to stimulate, as in this instance, we speak of it as a "dead image," or "dead metaphor." Despite the many dead metaphors in our language, the process of image-making continues, as it has in the past, to add to our word stock. New needs and situations call forth the utilization of existing words and concepts, which are usually applied as images.

Imagery and Rhetorical Devices

The vehicles of imagery have been classified rhetorically; the fable and the parable, for example, are distinctive enough to be classified as rhetorical types. The most important types you can look for are these:

SIMILE. A simile is a comparison using "like" or "as." The second line in these two lines is a simile:

> It glows and glitters in my cloudy breast
> Like stars upon some gloomy grove.

In the six lines from Keats (see p. 136) there are two similes, each conveying the excitement of discovery. In imitation of Homer and Virgil, Milton wrote "epic similes"; that is, fairly extensive similes that attempted to elevate his subject matter.

METAPHOR. A metaphor is a comparison that does not use "like" or "as." The tenor is *implied* in the vehicle and is not introduced by a preposition or a clause marker. A metaphor may consist of a single word, as in Keats's poem "To My Brothers."

> Small, busy flames *play* through the fresh-laid coals.

It may also be more extensive, as in Shakespeare's Sonnet No. 146, when the speaker compares his body to a house and his soul to a tenant in the house:

> Why so large cost, having so short a lease,
> Dost thou upon thy fading mansion spend?

CONCEIT. A conceit, specifically a "Metaphysical conceit," is a fairly long simile or metaphor that introduces an especially unusual or witty image. Frequently the development of the conceit controls the structure of the poem. Perhaps the most famous metaphysical conceit is Donne's comparison of lovers and compasses in "A Valediction: Forbidding Mourning."

SYNECDOCHE. In a synecdoche, which is a special kind of metaphor, a small part stands for a large part, as in the nautical phrase "All hands aboard," in which the word *hands* signifies all the sailors, presumably because their hands are so vital in the management of the ship.

METONYMY. A metonym, also a metaphor, is a term that stands for something with which it is closely associated. The President, for example, is closely associated with the White House, so that "news from the White House" is in effect news of actions and policies of the President. Similar to this are "the Pentagon," "Madison Avenue," "Broadway," and so on.

SYMBOL.   A symbol—a most important term—is the second half of a metaphor or simile with the first part left out. The vehicle in a symbol has its own objective reality, but it also stands for something else. Thus, the flag symbolizes the aims and aspirations of the nation. In George Herbert's poem "The Collar," the collar is, first of all, the collar of a clergyman, but second it stands for the Christian religion with all that Christianity signifies. Many objects are commonly understood as symbols; some of these are mistletoe, rings, the laurel bough, water or the sea, and many others. References to these objects as symbols usually require little emphasis or explanation by the author.[1] Quite often, however, a writer may develop his own symbols within a work or series of works. In Swift's poem "Description of the Morning," the reference to wheel ruts in the street symbolizes Swift's general idea that London life of the time was worn and grooved. Sometimes a character may become symbolic, like Figaro in Beaumarchais's plays *The Barber of Seville* and *The Marriage of Figaro*. Figaro, the barber, was taken as a symbol of the good, able man who was kept servile by the aristocratic social and political system of eighteenth-century France.

The use of symbolism has characterized a great deal of modern literature. William Butler Yeats, for example, worked constantly with symbols like the *gyre* and the city of Byzantium. James Joyce, in his fiction, developed a theory of symbolism that he employed in his works—the idea of "epiphany" or radiance. Joyce thought that certain objects, statements, actions, and details crystallized or summarized everything he wanted to say about a character or group of characters. Thus, in the story "Counterparts" from *Dubliners,* a man beats his young son after a day during which he himself has been browbeaten. His action symbolizes the human tendency to take frustrations out on others.

Closely connected with symbol is the term *controlling image,* which is an image developed so thoroughly throughout a work or which is so vital and pervasive that one may interpret the work in the light of the image. In the sample theme, attention is drawn to Shakespeare's controlling image of the prophet, or prophetic voice, which runs throughout John of Gaunt's speech.

Also merging with symbol and metaphor is intensely vivid descriptive writing. Such writing, of course, is every author's goal, and it is

---

[1] See J. E. Cirlot, *A Dictionary of Symbols,* trans. Jack Sage (New York: Philosophical Library, 1962).

usually not regarded as imagery. To the degree that an accurate and vivid description can evoke an impression that the author wishes to control, however, the effect of vivid writing is the same as that of imagery and specifically symbolism. John Masefield's poem "Cargoes" is a three-stanza poem describing three ships from three periods of history. Although Masefield does not make any comparisons, his views of the different periods are made explicitly clear by his descriptions. Similarly, a description of a natural setting that refers to colors, shapes, conditions of light, and so on, will suggest responses that are sympathetic to the author's story, and for this reason such descriptions in truth are like symbolism and metaphor.

ALLEGORY.   Allegory has been often defined as extended metaphor, or as moving symbols. An allegory is an entire story that is self-sufficient but that also signifies another series of events or a condition of life as expressed in a religion or philosophy. The most widely read allegory in our language has been Bunyan's *Pilgrim's Progress,* which at one time was almost as important as the Bible. Spenser's *The Faerie Queene* is a series of allegorical narrative poems, each one referring to separate concepts of Christian goodness. The parable and the fable without the moral attached are in effect short allegories. Ancient *myths* were also allegorical in nature.

PERSONIFICATION.   In personification, something abstract, like a season of the year, is given human attributes, as in this famous example from Tennyson's "In Memoriam":

> . . . Nature, red in tooth and claw,
> With ravine, shriek'd against his creeds.

Imagery and Attitudes

In considering the tenor of any given imagery, you ought to recognize that imagery is effective in rendering attitudes. It can elevate the subject matter or reduce it in size or ridicule it. Furthermore, it can also produce these same effects on the speaker, if the author so wishes. To see some of these effects operating in a short space, the following passage from Shakespeare's *Antony and Cleopatra* is instructive:

> The hearts
> That [spaniel'd] me at heels, to whom I gave
> Their wishes, do discandy, melt their sweets
> On blossoming Caesar; and this pine is bark'd,
> That overtopp'd them all.

—IV.xii.20–24

The word *hearts* in the first line is a synecdoche, by which hearts refers to Antony's followers. The image implies (a) that his followers seemed to be fully committed to him ("with all their hearts"), and (b) that they stayed with him through emotion and not principle, and therefore they found it easy to leave him when their emotions had shifted.[2] The images of *discandying* and *blossoming* both connote a strong attitude of disparagement on Antony's part, particularly when they are compared with the final metaphor, which is drawn from the experience of woodsmen. Antony is tall and firm as a pine, and like a pine he "overtopp'd" everyone and everything around him. But now his strength is gone, as is the strength of a tree when its bark is removed; even though he has not yet crashed to the ground and is as tall as ever, he will inevitably die. His imagery indicates that he knows the political fate of a leader without followers, and it also suggests his belief that he still is superior to those who will replace him in power and prestige. As you can see, these images convey a completeness of statement and implication that literal language could approximate only with many more words and then not as well.

Imagery can also serve as a comic device, usually by diminishing the thing being compared. The question, "Are you a man or a mouse?" suggests a metaphor of diminution if the response is the second alternative. A more extensive image of diminution is this mock-epic simile that Henry Fielding wrote in *Tom Jones* just before his description of a family battle between Mr. and Mrs. Partridge:

> As fair Grimalkin, who, though the youngest of the feline, degenerates not in ferocity from the elder branches of her house, and though inferior in strength, is equal in fierceness to the noble tiger himself, when a little mouse, whom it hath long tormented in sport, escapes from her clutches for a while, frets, scolds, growls, swears; but if the trunk, or box, behind which the mouse lay hid, be again removed, she flies like lightning on her prey, and, with envenomed wrath, bites, scratches, mumbles, and tears the little animal (Book II, Chapter 4).

Imagery and Allusions

Fielding's image becomes more meaningful when one recognizes its dependence on epic similes as they were used by Homer and Milton and also when one identifies "Grimalkin" as a witch in cat form that is referred to by the witches in *Macbeth*. In other words, a certain amount

---

[2] The word *spaniel'd* in line 21 is a conjectural emendation by one of Shakespeare's editors, but it is a powerful comparison of dogs and Antony's followers that would be worthy of Shakespeare's imaginative genius, and it is very likely the word that Shakespeare used.

of literary knowledge is required for full understanding and appreciation. Imagery is often complicated in this way by the *allusion* to other works, such as the classics or the Bible. The image in the original source, having been used in this way, then becomes a vital part of the writer's context. In Donne's sonnet "I Am a Little World Made Cunningly," for example, the concluding lines are:

> . . . burn me, O Lord, with a fiery zeal
> Of Thee and Thy house, which doth in eating heal.

The problem raised by the paradox in the last line is partially solved when you realize that the image in the metaphor is from Psalms 69, 9: "For the zeal of thine house hath eaten me up." Until the Biblical image is known, however, the line will be difficult to visualize and understand completely.

This example brings up the problem of the amount of definition necessary for the comprehension of imagery. For the most part your attempt to visualize, smell, taste, touch, and hear the experience described or suggested will suffice to convey the meaning of the imagery to you. In these cases a dictionary is superfluous. But an allusive image, like the Biblical one in Donne's poem, or an archaic image, may require a dictionary in addition to any explanatory notes supplied by the editor of the work you are reading. As an example, let us look briefly at these lines from Pope's *Essay on Criticism:*

> Some, to whom Heav'n in Wit has been profuse,
> Want as much more, to turn it to its use;
> For *Wit* and *Judgment* often are at strife,
> Tho' meant each other's Aid, like *Man* and *Wife.*
> 'Tis more to *guide* than *spur* the Muse's Steed;
> Restrain his Fury, than provoke his Speed;
> The winged Courser, like a gen'rous Horse,
> Shows most true Mettle when you *check* his Course.

> —lines 80–87

Pope has sometimes been dispraised by the assertion that he was not an imaginative poet, but instead was ratiocinative or "discursive." A close look at a passage like this one renders this assertion absurd. Pope is talking about the relationship of reason to imagination, and is stating, briefly, that judgment (the perceptive, critical, discriminating faculty) must always be in control of imagination (or *fancy,* the other common word for the faculty, which is related to the words *fanciful* and *fantastic*). Pope compares judgment to a rider on a race horse. All the strength and speed of a thoroughbred ("gen'rous Horse") are of no value, he says, unless a good jockey rides and paces it well. In line 86 Pope mentions "The winged Courser" (a flying horse) and opens the door to allusion.

By referring to a classical dictionary, you can learn that the flying horse of antiquity was Pegasus, who was ridden by Bellerophon in his fight against the monster Chimaera. Bellerophon was assisted in his fight by the gods, particularly by Athena, who was the goddess of wisdom. Other references may also apply. A dictionary tells you that the word *chimerical* (fantastically unreal) is derived from the name of the monster. The editor may tell you that in the seventeenth and eighteenth centuries pure fantasy was regarded as being akin to madness. In the context of the time when Pope wrote, this allusion to the winged horse seems to be saying this: "If you wish to avoid madness or just foolishness in your writing, and if you wish to be favored by the goddess of wisdom, you must guide your imagination by judgment." Thus Pope's imagery works in two ways, literal and allusive, to strengthen his point that judgment is necessary in works of imagination and criticism.

You can see that reference books and annotated editions can be indispensable in guiding you to an understanding of at least some of the implications of an author's imagery. You may justifiably ask how you can learn about allusions when you don't recognize them. The answer is to read a good, annotated text and to look up all words and references that are not immediately familiar to you. There are responsible, "definitive" editions of most writers either available or in process of publication. See the card catalogue in your library to find out about these editions.

Preparing Your Theme

Your job in preparing this theme, as always, is to be alert and to employ all facilities that can aid your understanding and appreciation. You must study your poem or passage word by word. Savor each word and set up a classification of what sorts of responses the words elicit. You might set up a series of lists headed by the words *Sight, Smell, Taste, Hearing, Touch,* and *Combinations* (how could you classify the image "embalmed darkness" except by this latter category?). Then check yourself: Can you visualize a word or description? Can you recall a touch or taste similar to that which the words describe?

With images that cause visual responses you might aid your imagination by drawing sketches. Some people might object to sketching images on the grounds that it tends to limit your responses too narrowly, but if it aids you in responding to a work, it is not despicable. The following line from Shakespeare's Sonnet No. 146, for example, offers an interesting challenge to the imagination that might be aided by a sketch:

> So shalt thou [the speaker's Soul] feed on
> Death that feeds on men, . . .

—line 13

Just how far does the image invite complete visualization? That is one problem faced by the student with a theme to write about this poem. Do the metaphors *feed* and *feeds* invite a response visualizing an eater, while eating, being eaten, or should the words be read without the reader's attempting to imagine specific feeders? One student responded to these lines with the following drawing:

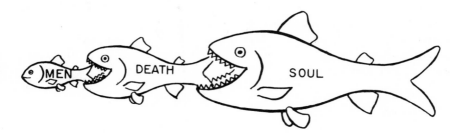

This drawing vividly shows the relationships involved, though it tends to demean Soul, Death, and Men (perhaps the student was thinking that men, in this case, are "poor fish"). Whether or not you carry your visualization this far, it is clear that Shakespeare's speaker is calling Death voracious because it seizes men for prey. But he is also asserting that the Soul can be equally voracious and more powerful than Death, even though it is also dependent on Death for its sustenance.

Whether you make a drawing or use your ability to visualize the impressions suggested by the words, you are concerned in your analysis to see the effect of imagery in the work. How does the imagery convey meaning? What particular attitudes does it communicate or suggest? (That is, how do you feel about Death and the Soul after reading the line from Shakespeare? Or how do you feel about Keat's excitement presented in "On First Looking into Chapman's Homer"?) How fully developed are the images? Do they stem from single words, or are they developed at greater length throughout a line or several lines, or perhaps even throughout the entire work? Is there a controlling image, and what is its effect? Are there many images, few images? Do the images in the work make the work particularly powerful, feeble? Why? Are there symbols? Is the story allegorical? Does the imagery at one point in the work create any special effect on other parts of the work? Does the imagery seem to develop in any special pattern? (For example, Robert Frost's poem "Out, Out—" develops a pattern of sound beginning with the noisy, snarling buzz saw and ending with the feeble heartbeat of the dying boy; after the boy's death, Frost's description of the people turning away contains no words describing sound. The references to sound and silence within the poem therefore create an image of what happens to the boy's heart.) These are the questions that you should try to answer in your theme.

Organizing Your Theme

INTRODUCTION

In your introduction you should make a brief statement about the nature of the work you are analyzing. Related to this will be your central idea, which is the statement of the main point you wish to illustrate about the imagery (i.e., that it is mainly visual, or that it makes the poem powerful, or that it is ineffective, or some other point that your analysis has uncovered).

BODY

There are a number of approaches to discussing imagery, and you may choose whatever method, or combination of methods, you wish. Here are some possible choices:

1. Discussion of the meaning and effect of the imagery. In effect, here you would be explaining in prose your interpretation of the various images. In Eve Merriam's poem "Robin Hood," for example, Robin Hood comes back to Sherwood Forest to establish the forest as a preserve next to the "Hood enterprises / for Sherwood Homesites." In explaining this action as a metaphor or symbol, you would say that modern commercialism has pre-empted the sense of adventure, romance, and justice that may have existed in earlier times. In determining the effect of the metaphor you would probably draw attention to its combination of cynicism, derision, and amusement.

2. Discussion of the frequency and the types of images in the work. Does the writer characteristically express himself in imagery? How many images are there? How often do they occur? Can any of the images be elevated to the status of symbol? How applicable is the symbol to the rest of the work? to life generally? Does the writer use images appealing to one particular sense (e.g., sight, hearing) rather than to the others? Does he record colors, sounds, and shapes? How well? Can you draw any conclusions about the author's—or his persona's—taste or sensibility as a result of your conclusions?

3. Discussion of the frames of reference of the imagery, and of the appropriateness of the imagery to the subject matter. Here you might show the locations from which the images are derived. Does the writer favor images from Nature, high society, low society, banking and industry, science, warfare, politics, reading, and so on? Are these images appropriate to the subject matter? If the subject is the dreariness of a 9 to 5 office routine, for example, would an image of paper clips and commas be appropriate (see Theodore Roethke's poem "Dolor")? Similarly, in a tragedy, would it be appropriate or not to draw images from joyous rituals of springtime? What other conclusions can you draw?

4. Discussion of the effect of one image, or series of images, on the other images and ideas in the poem. Usually you would pick an image that occurs early in the work and ask if this image acts as a controlling image over the ideas or mood (tone) of the work. Thus, the first paragraph of Swift's *Battle of the Books* (a prose work) contains an uncomplimentary image pertaining to the behavior of hungry dogs; in this way Swift conveys the impression that the whole battle between the "Ancients" and "Moderns" has a physiological origin that is anything but flattering. In an analysis of this sort, you would try to show the importance of the controlling image throughout the work.

5. Discussion of the extent to which the imagery points a work outward, toward those virtually indefinable areas of implication and suggestion that make literature an enduring art. For example, in a poem entitled "All Watched Over by Machines of Loving Grace," Richard Brautigan describes a vision in which "deer stroll peacefully / past computers." This symbol pushes the imagination through a cynical exposé of mindless naïveté into a region of general hope, but the mind is never quite freed from Brautigan's gentle smile at both his speaker and reader. As for most symbols, the vehicle is not complex; it associates Nature and machine. But the tenor becomes exceedingly complex and suggestive. In carrying on a discussion of imagery along such lines, you would be in fact refining the type of discussion suggested in types 1 and 3. Your emphasis here, however, is not so much on explanation as on the richness and suggestiveness of the writer's images.

CONCLUSION

In your conclusion you should describe your general impressions. You might briefly refer to images that you did not discuss in the body of your theme, with the idea of showing that there is much that could still be uncovered. Or you might try to describe the general relationship of the imagery to some of the various ideas made in the work you have been discussing. You might also state how the imagery deepened your experience of the work or your insight into the nature of literature itself (if you have been working with type 5 exclusively, however, you will already have been concentrating on this aspect of imagery in the body of your theme). In a more comprehensive analysis you might compare the imagery in the work you have analyzed with imagery employed by the same writer in other works written earlier or later in his career. Conclusions of this kind can reveal a great deal about a writer's development.

Hints

Instead of trying to discuss every single image in the work, concentrate on typical, unusual, and particularly important images.

Be prepared to relate the imagery to conclusions the author apparently expected you to reach. Always emphasize the ways in which the imagery—the vehicle—brings out conclusions and attitudes—the tenor.

It is desirable and helpful to reproduce your poem or passage, double-spaced, and to number its lines. As with the theme on a specific problem, utilize the editor's line numbers when you are reproducing a passage from an extensive work. Otherwise, number from *1* to the end. Refer to these line numbers in your theme. If you are asked to analyze the imagery in an extensive passage or in a story or novel, you might reproduce several short examples from the work to be cited in your discussion.

SAMPLE THEME

A Study of the Imagery
in Shakespeare's Richard II,
II.i, 33–70 [3]

GAUNT [*speaks*]

Methinks I am a prophet new inspired,	33
And thus expiring, do foretell of him,	34
His rash fierce blaze of riot cannot last,	35
For violent fires soon burn out themselves,	36
Small showers last long, but sudden storms are short,	37
He tires betimes, that spurs too fast betimes;	38
With eager feeding, food doth choke the feeder;	39
Light vanity, insatiate cormorant,	40
Consuming means soon preys upon itself.	41
This royal throne of kings, this sceptered isle,	42
This earth of majesty, this seat of Mars,	43
This other Eden, demi paradise,	44
This fortress built by Nature for herself,	45
Against infection, and the hand of war;	46
This happy breed of men, this little world,	47
This precious stone, set in the silver sea,	48
Which serves it in the office of a wall,	49
Or as a moat defensive to a house,	50
Against the envy of less happier lands,	51
This blessed plot, this earth, this realm, this England,	52
This nurse, this teeming womb of royal kings,	53
Feared by their breed, and famous for their birth,	54
Renowned for their deeds, as far from home,	55
For Christian service, and true chivalry,	56

3 Matthew W. Black, ed., *The Life and Death of King Richard the Second*, A New Variorum Edition of Shakespeare, James McManaway, ed. (Philadelphia and London; J. B. Lippincott Co., 1955), pp. 101–105. The spelling is here modernized.

As is the sepulchre in stubborn Jewry	57
Of the world's ransom, blessed Mary's son,	58
This land of such dear souls, this dear-dear land,	59
Dear for her reputation through the world,	60
Is now leased out (I die pronouncing it)	61
Like to a tenement or pelting farm.	62
England bound in with the triumphant sea,	63
Whose rocky shore beats back the envious siege	64
Of watery Neptune, is now bound in with shame,	65
With inky blots, and rotten parchment bonds.	66
That England, that was wont to conquer others,	67
Hath made a shameful conquest of itself.	68
Ah! would the scandal vanish with my life,	69
How happy then were my ensuing death?	70

This image-studded speech is above all dramatic; it is spoken by the dying John of Gaunt to the Duke of York, his brother. Gaunt's aim is to praise England and to show the impending danger of the profligate rule of Richard II and also to imply—but only to imply—to York that Richard, although ruling legally, could be removed. The remarkable speech also demonstrates the fertility of the dying Gaunt's mind, the alienation and death of which does not bode well for Richard, particularly because he has also alienated Bolingbroke, Gaunt's son.

The passage consists of three major sections, characterized first by imagery suggesting Richard's profligacy, second, by imagery pointing out England's greatness, and third, by imagery asserting that Richard's effect on England is destructive. Dominating the entire speech are two images that are announced in the first two lines: Gaunt is dying and he expresses this fact as a metaphor of expiring—breathing the last. This image in fact controls the passage like a symbol, directing the visual imagery in the first section and also that in the third. A second image is that of the prophet, the role Shakespeare gives Gaunt on his deathbed to provide an analogical basis for the Biblical imagery in the second section.

In the first section the imagery reflects Richard's prodigality—prodigality, that is, in Gaunt's eyes. Metaphorically, Gaunt compares Richard first to a blazing fire (lines 35, 36). The basis for the image is this: the king is like a fire to his subjects, providing them with heat and light, and he should assume this role constantly. To this end, the king needs a slow, steady, life-giving supply of fuel and draft. But Richard is a blaze, and although he now is brilliant, he will soon deplete the fuel and die, perhaps after having burned or scorched his country.

This notion of dying down and tiring is pursued in the remaining images in the passage, drawn from water, travel, and food. Richard is thus compared with a destructive storm, not a life-giving small shower (37). He is like a horseman who spurs his horse too strongly and who will thus tire himself and his horse and not reach his destination (38). He is choking himself with food and is so greedy that, like a cormorant, he is actually devouring himself (40, 41). These images connote a progression from natural prodigality to human foolishness and ultimately to suicidal gluttony. Both suicide and gluttony were, in Renaissance Christian values, sinful. Gaunt's condemnation of Richard as a person could not, therefore, be more emphatic.

In abrupt contrast to these images of waste are the images in the second section, which is a virtuoso piece of imagery in praise of England and one that is often excerpted. The section consists of a nineteen-line noun group with eighteen nouns in apposition, with their modifiers but with no principal verb. There is no grammatical movement, but there is a brilliant progression of images. Primary is the resumption of the prophetic image from line 33, which suggests the metaphorical comparison of England and the Old-Testament Eden (44). In the latter part of the section, the image from the New Testament alludes to Christ, Mary, and the doctrine of vicarious atonement (56–58). Clearly, to Gaunt, England is a Holy Land, and England should be a fulfillment of history the way the New Testament was a fulfillment of the Old Testament. Just as Christ was born to save the world, English kings should be born to a similar role. Through suggestion and implication, Gaunt's imagery here raises England to about as high a plane of estimation as one could imagine a country could reach.

In addition, the many other images in the second section attribute other glowing, noble qualities to England. The images progress from the large, majestic, and masculine to the small, domestic and feminine. The "sceptered isle" in line 42 and the "seat of Mars" in line 43 become the "blessed plot" in line 52. This garden image hearkens back to the small-shower image of line 37 and certainly to the Eden reference in line 44: the water of life should fall gently on the land and render her fertile. From this generally feminine image, Gaunt metaphorically equates England with both a nurse and a mother (the reference to "womb" is a synecdoche) of noble sons who defend the Christian faith. Ultimately, as has been shown, he makes the comparison of England and Mary. The full weight of all these images in this second section is that England is father, lord, protector, redeemer, and mother— all things to all men.

Grammatically, the third section completes the noun group in the second section by providing a principal verb for it. This final section puts the first two sections together by associating Richard and England and asserting that the association is hurting England. The verbal metaphor in line 61 is a powerful condemnation of Richard's financial manipulations: he has now leased the country itself as security for his borrowing to fight foolish wars, and the English people now are no better than tenants in their native land. The land itself has been made a "tenement or pelting farm" (62). This image of a legal stranglehold is continued in lines 65 and 66, where Richard's financial commitments (and perhaps even Richard's control of the Crown itself) is equated with "inky blots, and rotten parchment bonds." Constantly in this final section, Gaunt's speech is filled with images that contrast his idea of the naturally powerful and wealthy condition of England (it has even made the sea "triumphant") with his idea that Richard's kingship has sickened the country. He concludes by taking up, once again, the cormorant image of line 40; this time he states that England has "made a shameful conquest of itself" (68). His implication is that the condition should be removed, and if he cannot remove it by his death, someone who is still alive should remove it. Although the speech is not an incitement to rebellion, it leaves the door open to rebellion.

Gaunt's speech is a vital part of the play. The images Shakespeare gives him—more than thirty in these heavily packed lines—appeal to ideal standards in religion, government, patriotism, economics, husbandry, horsemanship, eating habits, and housekeeping. Implicit in the second section, and clearly stated in the first and third, is the idea that Richard has fallen short in all these areas. The speech is heard by York, who during much of the play stays with Richard because he believes that the King rules legally; but it offers to York an ultimate reason for switching allegiance when the good of the country demands it. When York goes, symbolically, Richard is lost, and Shakespeare may well be showing here why York was persuaded to go.

Beyond this dramatic function, Shakespeare seems to have another aim in his selection of fertile images. He implies that the support of men like Gaunt is necessary for any ruler; men with such patriotic fervor, moral strength, and analytical insight can prove deadly foes, just as they can be stalwart friends. To lose their support, as Richard has, is disastrous. Therefore the imagery in the speech, which prefigures the actual deposition later in the play, produces a paean to England, a cause of important dramatic action, and a lesson in political leadership.

The Theme Analyzing

TONE

CHAPTER

12

Tone is one of the most important concepts to understand and describe in the study of literature. Ideally, tone refers to the means by which a writer conveys attitudes. Although it is a technical subject, in practice the discussion of tone becomes focused on the attitudes themselves. For this reason, the terms *tone* and *attitude* are sometimes used synonymously. You should remember, however, that tone refers not to attitudes but to that quality of a writer's style that reveals—or creates—these attitudes. If you preserve this distinction you should be able to handle a theme about tone and should quickly appreciate all its implications for literary study.

Studying and describing tone requires the greatest alertness and subtlety, because your understanding of tone will depend largely on your ability to make inferences from the work you are reading (sometimes this process is called "reading between the lines"). Your analysis of tone is, in effect, your analysis of the author's mind at work, and through this analysis you can become aware of the vitality of literature— the profound, alive creativity of the author's mind as seen in his words. Reading a work of literature without perceiving its tone is like watching a speaker on television with the sound turned off; without tone you can guess at meaning, but cannot understand it fully.

Tone in Operation

Tone in literature has been borrowed from the phrase *tone of voice* in speech. You have certainly heard this phrase and may even have been criticized at one time or another for having said something in a certain tone of voice or for having indicated an attitude that has displeased a parent, friend, customer, or teacher. Tone of voice, in other words, is a reflection of your attitude toward the person or persons whom you are addressing and also toward the subject matter of your discussion. In the personal circumstances of speech, tone of voice is made up of many elements: the speed with which you utter your words, the enthusiasm—or lack of it—that you project into what you say, the pitch and loudness of your speech, your facial expressions, the way you hold your body, and your distance from the person to whom you are speaking.

Your attitudes are always basic to your opinions, friendships, activities, and even your deepest personal philosophy. Think briefly about the tone of these statements, which you may have heard or said: "Don't call me; I'll call you." "Oh, yes, I would be absolutely overjoyed to make the beds, do this morning's dishes, and sweep and mop the floor." Or imagine that before an examination a good friend tells you, "I hope you get the grade you deserve on the test." You may wonder about his exact meaning. To make it clear, he may accompany his words with a roguish smile, which makes you see that your friendship is not without a certain degree of antagonism. He wishes you to do well, yet he would probably not grieve uncontrollably if you did not. But perhaps you realize that your friendship is sound if he feels safe in expressing his complexity of attitudes toward you. All these situations, and many more that you could supply yourself, require a consideration of tone.

As a literary comparison, let us look briefly at this passage from *Gulliver's Travels,* written by one of the great masters of tone in English literature:

> Imagine with thy self, courteous Reader, how often I then wished for the Tongue of *Demosthenes* or *Cicero,* that might have enabled me to celebrate the Praise of my own dear native Country in a Style equal to its Merits and Felicity.[1]

You have here a passage in which Gulliver is perfectly sincere about praising England, whereas Swift the satirist, behind the scenes, is just about to deliver a satiric condemnation of his England. The control of tone makes these contrasting attitudes evident and makes this passage comic. Swift controls the tone by causing Gulliver to refer to the two most famous ancient orators who were known for their ability to speak well but who were also known for their powers to condemn. He also makes Gulliver use the ambiguous phrase "equal to its Merits and Felicity" and the possibly sarcastic word "celebrate." The tone here is quite similar to that in the previously mentioned banter with the imaginary friend, with this difference: in the literary work you are not aided by

[1] Robert A. Greenberg, ed., *Gulliver's Travels: An Annotated Text With Critical Essays* (New York: W. W. Norton & Co., Inc., 1961), II, vi, 103.

the physical, conversational context of the interchange. All you have is the printed page; to interpret it properly you have only a dictionary, other reference works, and, above all, your intelligence.

Tone, of course, may be described in many ways, as there are many human moods. Here is a partial list of words that might describe tone in particular passages.

> simple, straightforward, direct, unambiguous
> complicated, complex, difficult
> forceful, powerful
> ironic, sardonic, sarcastic
> indirect, understated, evasive
> bitter, grim
> sympathetic, interested
> indifferent, unconcerned, apathetic
> antagonistic, hostile
> violent, outraged, indignant, angry
> elevated, grand, lofty
> serious, solemn, sepulchral, ghoulish
> comic, jovial, easy, friendly

A thesaurus would supply you with many more words, and it is conceivable that there are, somewhere, literary works to which all the words you discover might be applied.

Problems in Describing Tone

The study of tone is the study of the ways in which attitudes are manifested in a particular literary work. Therefore, when you write a theme about tone, you must attempt to name and describe these attitudes and analyze the means by which they are expressed. Your statements will be based on inferences that you make from the text.

You must also attempt to describe the intensity, the force with which the attitudes are expressed. This task is difficult, but necessary, and it is one of the ways by which you can amplify your statements about the nature of the attitudes. The force of the tone depends on the intrinsic seriousness of the situation, the speaker's degree of involvement in it, and his control over his expression. You would recognize the differences in intensity between the statements in the two columns:

1	2
"This report is not what we expected."	"This report is terrible."
"Mr. Student, your paper shows promise, but it is not, as yet, up to passing standards."	"Mr. Student, your paper is a slovenly disgrace."

In describing the difference, you would necessarily concentrate on the differing *intensities* of the tones expressed in the quotations. Or, compare the intensities of tone implicit in these two quotations:

(1) Written on a wall in Saigon: "Yankee, go home."
(2) Written on a wall in Paris: "Yankee, go home—via Air France."

These last quotations bring up another, closely related, element in the consideration of tone—namely, that of control. A writer may feel deeply about a subject, but if he gives vent to his feelings completely he is likely to create not a literary work but only an emotional display. He must always control the expression of sentiment, because his appeal must be not only to his readers' sympathies but also to their understanding. A fine example of the control of attitude is *Antony and Cleopatra* (V. ii, 241–281). Cleopatra is about to commit suicide. Just before she does, Shakespeare introduces a rustic on stage to bring her the asp. The resulting interchange between Cleopatra, serious and about to die, and the stupid but concerned clown is clearly designed to arouse laughter.

Enter Guardsman and Clown [with Basket].

GUARD   This is the man.

CLEOPATRA   Avoid, and leave him.

Exit Guardsman.

Hast thou the pretty worm of Nilus there
That kills and pains not?

CLOWN   Truly I have him. But I would not be the party that should desire you to touch him, for his biting is immortal. Those that do die of it do seldom or never recover.

CLEOPATRA   Remember'st thou any that have died on't?

CLOWN   Very many, men and women too. I heard of one of them no longer than yesterday; a very honest woman, but something given to lie, as a woman should not do but in the way of honesty—how she died of the biting of it, what pain she felt. Truly, she makes a very good report o' the worm; but he that will believe all that they say shall never be saved by half that they do. But this is most falliable, the worm's an odd worm.

CLEOPATRA   Get thee hence; farewell.

CLOWN   I wish you all joy of the worm.

[Sets down his basket].

CLEOPATRA   Farewell. . . .

—lines 241–260

The problem in interpreting this scene involves Shakespeare's attitude toward Cleopatra and toward his audience. It is likely that Shakespeare introduced the comic scene in order to keep his treatment of Cleopatra from becoming purely sentimental. He knew that one way to produce laughter is to heap misfortune upon misfortune, so that an audience will ultimately respond to additional misfortunes with laughter, not with sympathy. Cleopatra's suicide is the final misfortune, and lest his audience not respond with sorrow, Shakespeare provides the clown to siphon off, as it were, his audience's tension by giving it a legitimate release in laughter. In this way he directs a proper amount of sympathy toward Cleopatra and deepens our concern for her. The situation is complex, but Shakespeare's handling of it indicates the control of the master.

Irony

The greatest skill of the writer is often his courage to treat a serious problem in a light or comic way. By doing so he maintains proportion, shows control, and makes his work generally effective. Shakespeare must have had great confidence in his own ability to evaluate dramatic situations to succeed with this comic scene. You may remember similar situations in your own life. Have you ever had the impulse to insult a friend, parent, or a "steady" date? In friendly banter, however, you always assume that your friend will be able to see through your "insult" into your genuine fondness. Treatment like this is usually called *irony,* a term describing ambiguity or indirection. In literature, as in friendship, irony implies a compliment by the writer to the reader, for it indicates that the writer assumes skill and intelligence on his reader's part sufficient to see through the surface statement into the seriousness or levity beneath. Irony implies that the writer has great control over his material and much confidence in his readers. Sir Winston Churchill, for example, has been quoted as saying, "Democracy is the worst type of government, except all the rest." His ironic statement implies great understanding of human imperfections; it implies that man is in a process of evolving and endeavoring to perfect his political institutions; but it also implies respect for democracy and for those who love it. The statement shows great control over tone.

The major types of irony are *verbal, situational,* and *dramatic. Verbal irony* is a form of indirection or ambiguity by which the opposite of what is said is usually intended. Often, verbal irony may be described as *understatement* or *overstatement.* Thus, a soldier may describe a fierce battle by saying "We had a bit of a go at it." This is understatement.

Overstatement, or hyperbole, may be seen in this description of a bad situation: "Everything is just absolutely dandy."

The term *situational irony,* or irony of situation, is usually employed to describe misguided hopes or misinterpreted motives about a given situation. Thomas Hardy was adept at creating situational irony, as in *The Return of the Native,* when Eustacia appears at the window of her home briefly and glances at the visiting Mrs. Yeobright outside. Because a former suitor is visiting Eustacia, and also because she believes that her husband Clym will answer the door, she does not admit Mrs. Yeobright. Mrs. Yeobright has seen Eustacia at the window and misinterprets Eustacia's motives; she is disheartened and leaves for home, only to meet death on the heath. All subsequent disasters in the novel stem from this incident, and their effect on the tone of the novel is that the ill consequences are much more pathetic because they could have been easily avoided.

Dramatic irony applies when a character in a drama or fictional work perceives a situation in a limited way while the audience sees it in greater perspective. The audience sees double meaning whereas the character sees only one. Perhaps the classic example of dramatic irony is found in *Oedipus Rex,* where Oedipus thinks he is about to discover that someone else murdered his father, while the audience knows all along that he himself is the murderer and that as he condemns the murderer he condemns himself. In Hemingway's story "My Old Man," dramatic irony is utilized skillfully. This story is told by a son about his father who is a jockey but who also becomes involved in deals to fix horse races. During the first part of the story the narrator does not know the significance of the events he is describing, while the reader can see that the father is guilty of fixing races. During the latter half of the story, Hemingway subtly employs dramatic irony to focus on the son's attempts to mask from himself the significance of the father's actions and also to avoid the realization that his father has undergone physical and moral deterioration. The father's death at the end of the story, and the comments by the two "guys" about the father, finally and brutally force the boy to face the truth. Hemingway thus creates a poignant account of a loss of innocence, and he does so by using dramatic irony to show that the boy possessed innocence that could be lost.

Identifying Tone in Literature

As you have undoubtedly concluded, the study of tone is quite general. It requires studying everything in a literary work that might contribute more than just the denotative statement. To perceive tone you must be completely alert. You must be constantly aware of the general impression that a passage leaves with you, but you must also be analytical enough to study the particular ways by which this effect is achieved. You must understand all the words; you must read the work carefully, then study the passages you select for discussion in order to determine the connotations of the words and the rhythms of the cadence groups. Anything might present an illustration of tone, and to understand the tone you must respond to everything.

Look at this passage from Lytton Strachey's biography of Florence Nightingale in *Eminent Victorian*, a work known for its tone:

> Eventually the whole business of purveying to the hospitals was, in effect, carried out by Miss Nightingale. She alone, it seemed, whatever the contingency, knew where to lay her hands on what was wanted; she alone could dispense her stores with readiness; above all, she alone possessed the art of circumventing the pernicious influences of official etiquette. This was her greatest enemy, and sometimes even she was baffled by it. On one occasion 27,000 shirts, sent out at her instance by the Home Government, arrived, were landed, and were only waiting to be unpacked. But the official "Purveyor" intervened; "he could not unpack them," he said, "without a Board." Miss Nightingale pleaded in vain; the sick and wounded lay half-naked, shivering for want of clothing; and three weeks elapsed before the Board released the shirts. A little later, however, on a similar occasion, Miss Nightingale felt that she could assert her own authority. She ordered a Government consignment to be forcibly opened, while the "Purveyor" stood by, wringing his hands in departmental agony.[2]

The tone here conveys admiration and respect for Miss Nightingale, as contrasted with contempt for the official incompetence against which she had to work. Notice the diction Lytton Strachey employs in conveying his attitude toward her: "she alone," "readiness," "even she," "pleaded," "felt that she could assert," "ordered." These words are to be contrasted with those used in description of the officialdom: "pernicious influences," "baffled," "official 'Purveyor'," "three weeks elapsed before the Board released the shirts," "wringing his hands in departmental agony." When these opposite series of words are placed in the context of "the sick and wounded lay half-naked, shivering for want of clothing," their opposition is made even more apparent. Lytton Strachey does not say directly that Florence Nightingale was heroic, yet his *tone* clearly indicates that he thought she was. Diction is the principal way by which he has communicated his tone, which is clear and unambiguous.

Take another instance, this time from the Old English poem "The Wanderer," in a modern prose translation by Professor R. K. Gordon:

> Whither has gone the horse? Whither has gone the man? Whither has gone the giver of treasure? Whither has gone the place of feasting? Where

2 (New York: Harcourt, Brace & World, Inc., 1918), pp. 146–47.

are the joys of hall? Alas, the bright cup! Alas, the warrior in his corslet! Alas, the glory of the prince! How that time has passed away, has grown dark under the shadow of night, as if it had never been! Now in the place of the dear warriors stands a wall, wondrous high, covered with serpent shapes; the might of the ash-wood spears has carried off the earls, the weapon greedy for slaughter—a glorious fate; and storms beat upon these rocky slopes; the falling storm binds the earth, the terror of winter. Then comes darkness, the night shadow casts gloom, sends from the north fierce hailstorms to the terror of men. Everything is full of hardship in the kingdom of earth; the decree of fate changes the world under the heavens. Here possessions are transient, here friends are transient, here man is transient, here woman is transient; all this firm-set earth becomes empty.[3]

The details here indicate the tone—one of despair for the prosperity of man in his earthly state. Complementing the details is a series of abstractions that indicate the effect of the hailstorms and darkness on the minds of men. This semantic interpretation is augmented by the rhythms of the original (faithfully preserved in the translation). The statements are short, even abrupt at the end. The impression is given that the earth definitely holds terror for mankind. There are no subordinate clauses in which the poet might express any qualifications or exceptions to the examples he has given. Thus, the diction, sentence structure, and rhythm contribute to the tone of despair.

Unlike the passage from *Gulliver's Travels*, which is ironic and ambiguous, the tone in these last two examples is straightforward and positive.

Our analysis of these examples was largely concerned with style, but tone may also be caused by the sheer weight of accumulated evidence. The multiplication of examples in support of a claim effects a tone of certainty, and the constant insistence on some attitudes produces a tone of solid conviction. As an example, look at the sermon on hell by Father Arnall in Chapter III of Joyce's *A Portrait of the Artist as a Young Man,* in which the tone is firm, solid, and inescapable. Few persons can read this section without being emotionally shaken by the sheer weight of the evidence presented by Father Arnall. Or think briefly about Thoreau's assertions throughout *Walden* that our industrial civilization is lifeless and artificial. Upon reading this book, one is swayed by the tone either to assent to Thoreau's position or else to question his own position thoroughly. It is difficult to imagine that a reader could be unaffected in any way by Thoreau's tone.

It is fair to conclude that tone is an integral part of meaning and literary excellence. Tone controls responses, and your responses are essential in your literary experience. Control over tone distinguishes plain statement from artistic statement. As you analyze the tone of a work

---

[3] *Anglo-Saxon Poetry,* rev. ed., Everyman's Library No. 794 (New York: E. P. Dutton & Co., Inc., 1954), pp. 74–75.

you will realize that the degree of a writer's control over tone provides a strong basis for evaluating his stature as a writer.

Your Approach to Tone

Your main problem in reading the work assigned is to determine to your satisfaction what the dominant tone is. You must therefore carefully examine not only what is said but the context in which it is said. In order to support your claim about tone, you will need to study those factors (style, structure, idea) that cause the particular tone that you have noted.

The amount of analysis you do will depend on the length of the work you are discussing. In a long work you might analyze representative passages that support your central idea. If the work is short, perhaps a short poem, you might very well attempt to analyze the entire work.

Once you have determined your interpretation of the tone, you should state that as your central idea. Then, without making distortions, you should gather material that will support your central idea. Let the material produce the idea. Do not neglect material that opposes your idea. So long as what you analyze has bearing on your central idea, you might bring in considerations of style, ambiguity, accumulation of evidence—all at one time. Just remember to point your discussion toward your basic argument.

Beyond the single statement (your central idea) about tone, you might very well discover that the tone in your literary work is made up of a complexity of moods, a progression of tones. An excellent critical article has been written describing a progression of tone in the poetry of Pope,[4] and an entire book has been written to show that a typical poem by John Donne is structurally dependent on a complex progression of attitudes.[5] In your theme, if your central idea is that there is a complexity of tone or progression of attitudes, you would construct your argument to demonstrate the validity of your claim.

Organizing Your Theme

The main problem in your discussion of tone is that your remarks are based on inferences. You cannot, therefore, state absolutely that your

[4] Maynard Mack, "The Muse of Satire," *Yale Review* (1951), XLI, 80–92.
[5] Leonard Unger, *Donne's Poetry and Modern Criticism* (Chicago: Henry Regnery Co., 1950).

author actually *held* a certain attitude; you can instead only *infer* that he held that attitude. Your theme is not biographical, but interpretive. Be aware that your inferences might result as much from your own attitudes as from those of the author. For example, recent attempts to interpret the tone of Chaucer's *The Prioress's Tale* have implied that because Chaucer treats the Prioress with gentle irony in the *General Prologue,* he was hostile to the anti-Jewish sentiment expressed in her story. It would seem that in their attempt to make Chaucer as tolerant of the Jewish faith as a modern intelligent person should be, many readers have read their own enlightenment into Chaucer's work. But if you remember that great writers generally held views that were current at their times and that their attitudes may not coincide exactly with your own, you will be properly cautious in making remarks about tone.

One further caution: keep your central idea uppermost in your reader's mind. You must inevitably talk about what has happened in the work you have read, but bring in these references *only* to illustrate and amplify your remarks about tone. Never forget your point; never descend to mere synopsis.

INTRODUCTION

State your central idea. You should not only define the tone briefly but also describe the force and conviction of the tone. Your thesis sentence should be a statement about the areas in which you plan to develop your discussion. If there are any particular obstacles to the proper determination of the tone, either in the work or in your personal attitudes, you should state these in your introduction also.

BODY

This should be a pointed discussion of the major elements in the work that caused you to arrive at your central idea. You are free to organize this section in any way you wish. Two suggested methods are: (1) If there is a unity of tone throughout the work, you should organize the body in order to show the scope of the tone; that is, you would show that various sections of the work are similar in tone. Or you might wish to illustrate the depth of the attitudes. In this plan, you would analyze a few passages (be sure that they are representative) in order to show the characteristic methods by which the author conveyed his depth of attitude. (2) If there is a shift of tone, or if there is complexity or plurality of attitudes within the work, you might organize the body of your theme in order to mirror the shift or complexity. For example, the eighteenth-century satirist Jonathan Swift would often mildly defend things he was bitterly attacking. The modern reader must therefore be constantly alert for this complexity of attitude. The sample theme, on Stephen Crane's tone in "The Open Boat," asserts that two major attitudes exist simultaneously in the work, even though these attitudes are not contradictory. The theme is organized to show how the attitudes are essential to the meaning of the story. Just as human values are often complex, so is the tone in most good writing.

CONCLUSION

The principal object of your conclusion is to relate the question of tone to your understanding and evaluation of the work. Elements to consider in evaluation are (1) the intensity and (2) the control over attitudes.

SAMPLE THEME

Tone in Stephen Crane's "The Open Boat" [1]

In "The Open Boat" Stephen Crane shows a tone of admiration and sympathy for four men cast adrift in a small boat (and, symbolically, for the plight of mankind generally), and he also exhibits a tone of bafflement and mild scorn at the apparent indifference, hostility, and arbitrariness of the universe. The story is divided into seven sections that mark the developing action but have little to do with the tone except that Crane's admiration for the characters and arguments against Nature are stronger at the end of the story than at the beginning. The two attitudes exist simultaneously throughout the story, just as the essential conflict in the story is between the men in the boat and the natural forces preventing them from reaching land easily. Crane renders his admiration and scorn through his descriptions of the men, his running commentary on the situation in the boat, and his descriptions and evaluations of Nature.

Crane's descriptions of the men emphasize their admirable, cooperative spirit. Every reference made to Billie the oiler, for example, is cast in language of approval. When Billie is asked by the correspondent to spell him at the oars, Billie's response is a quick "Sure," even though he has been doing more than his share already (p. 45). On other occasions Billie is shown as a man who is "busy"

---

[1] Stephen Crane, "The Open Boat," in Harold Simonson, ed., *Trio*, 3rd ed. (New York: Harper & Row, 1970). All parenthetical page numbers in this theme refer to this edition.

with the affairs of the boat (p. 31) and also as a "wily surfman" (p. 37) and a shrewd judge of human nature (p. 35). Crane does not make a big case for Billie's selflessness, but when the men leave the boat for shore it is the correspondent who takes the piece of life preserver that had been at the bottom of the boat. It is clear that Crane invites us to see that Billie left it for the correspondent, in a spirit of selfless cooperation. Although Crane focuses his admiration on Billie, he also surrounds his descriptions of the other men with the same explicit fondness. He shows that the Captain is always awake and in command, and that even the cook does his share during the long night by warming the tired rowers after they have been spelled from their back-breaking duty. Similarly, the correspondent works along with the others despite the fact that a man of his profession would probably not be accustomed to hard labor. The tone is that of admiration for all the men.

Superimposed upon these descriptions of the men is Crane's running commentary on the action, which indicates sympathy for the men and a shared set of values with them. Crane verbalizes what could have been expressed by the men had they been more articulate, emphasizing their spiritual kinship, for example, at the beginning of section III:

> It would be difficult to describe the subtle brotherhood of men that was here established on the seas. No one said that it was so. No one mentioned it. But it dwelt in the boat, and each man felt it warm him (p. 33).

Throughout the story such commentaries suggest the closeness of the narrator and the men. It is as though the speaker has become so much a part of the situation that he moves from his own stance as narrator into the language and speech patterns of the men. The teeth of the shivering correspondent, for example, play "all the popular airs" (p. 45). Such an ironic overstatement would be more typical of the men than of an uninvolved narrator. Similar also are the commentaries (a) comparing moving in the boat to the difficulties of stealing eggs from under a hen (p. 32), (b) claiming that the coldness of the water was "tragic" (p. 48), (c) complaining that the backaches of a man rowing are more numerous than the aches that might befall a regiment of men (p. 37), and others. These commentaries, wry and almost comic as they are, fit right in with the pattern of Crane's admiration for the men.

To be contrasted with this admiration are Crane's descriptions and evaluations of Nature, which emphasize that the sea is uncertain, hostile, sinister, and arbitrary. Crane spends much time describing the "ugly brute" of a seagull early in the story (p. 32), and later he devotes more attention to a circling shark, which is cutting the water with its fins as it presumably waits to claim the men. These are physical manifestations of the sea's hostility, and Crane goes beyond them into a larger, cosmic fabric illustrating the helpless lot of mankind in a bleak, indifferent universe. Crane's commentary about throwing "bricks at the temple" (p. 43) in anger and frustration, his frequent interjections about the unfairness of drowning within view of sand and trees (pp. 36, 40, 43), the reference to the "ninny-woman, Fate" (p. 36), together with the claim that "the whole affair is absurd" (p. 36), are at once a function of his admiration for the men and his derision and deepening scorn for the seemingly arbitrary universe in which the strongest man, Billie the oiler, can drown. This commentary is more in the style of the contemplative, rather than the closely involved, narrator. It thus serves to broaden Crane's attitudes in the story by emphasizing the symbolic value of the boat and the men and by making the attitudes seem applicable to human beings in general.

The boat tossing on the waves and our earth speeding through inscrutable space are thus similar, and it is evident that Crane uses "The Open Boat" as an illustration of his own assessment of man's fate and his attitudes toward this fate. Bafflement, helplessness, anger, disillusion, bitterness, despair, scorn—all these attitudes seem to be suggested by the arbitrary death of Billie. Crane expresses nothing positive when he considers the sea and the universe. But when he looks inwardly toward mankind, he finds hope. It is, at the end, the man who performs the act of rescue who has the halo "about his head" (p. 49). Crane seems to be in the position of asking questions but receiving no answers that lead to any orderly purpose. In the absence of answers from without, he seeks them from within, and therefore "The Open Boat" shows that admiration is deserved only by those who promote our survival through assistance and cooperation. The author's attitudes show that he is not removed from the plight of the men and of mankind generally, but is an integral part of it.

The Theme Analyzing
PROSODY

CHAPTER

13

Prosody is the word commonly used to refer to the study of sound and rhythm in poetry. Although sound and rhythm are the primary concern of prosodic study, these elements are never to be discussed in a vacuum; they are always an integral part of every good poem and are important only as they are related to the other parts. *Prosody* is the general word referring to sound and rhythm, but other, equally descriptive, words are *metrics, versification, mechanics of verse,* and *numbers.* (*Numbers* is not common at present, but it was current in Pope's time. Longfellow also used it.) Some persons call sound and rhythm the *music* of poetry. Whatever term your instructor might use, then, he means the study of sound and rhythm in poetry.

Your instructor will usually ask you to write a theme about prosody in order to give you the opportunity (1) to develop your sensitivity to the poet's language *as sound,* and (2) to become aware of the relationship of sound and rhythm to content. You will realize, as you make your analysis and write your theme, that the poet devoted much of his creative energy not only to the content of his poem but equally to the manner of conveying his content. This assignment will help you to become a more skilled reader, better equipped to define poetry and analyze sounds. You should also have an additional standard by which to measure the quality of poems. In short, this assignment should deepen your appreciation of a poet's achievement.

Many students, having accustomed themselves to pay attention only to the ideas and events in prose works, approach a theme on prosody with much apprehension. They feel either that the study of prosody is barren and devoid of content or that they cannot handle the assignment because they have never done it before. But the study of prosody is not barren, and there is no more reason for timidity about this assignment than about any other. With knowledge of a few terms and concepts, together with close attention to a poem, you can do a good job. There is much pleasure to be gained from analyzing a poem like Donne's "Batter My Heart" and from seeing that his style is in complete accord with his meaning. When you come to this realization you have actually encountered the living mind of the poet at work, selecting words and arranging rhythms not just by accident but by premeditated design and masterly control. You cannot appreciate poetry fully until you know something about prosody.

Your main problem in this assignment is to develop the vocabulary for discussing what you and every sensitive reader can perceive. In essence, your job is to translate the written poem into the spoken poem and then to describe the noteworthy and outstanding characteristics of the sounds. Fortunately, the study of metrics has provided you with a ready-made vocabulary for discussing what you hear. Much of your preparation for this assignment will be simply to learn the vocabulary and apply it.

Poetry and Prose: Rhythm

Poetry is difficult to define exactly. It is like prose because it employs words to convey thoughts and impressions and to tell stories, but prose is expansive—its content is characterized by the use of examples that are usually developed at some length. In addition, prose is comparatively less intense than poetry in its presentation of emotions. As a result, when you read a prose passage, your voice tends to remain within a rather narrow range of pitch; the accents and lengths of the individual words are submerged. Poetry is usually more demanding. It is more compact and more intense in its expression, and the poet consequently devotes special care to the sounds and rhythms of words and lines. When you read poetry, therefore, you must give particular attention to individual words; your units of expression will be shorter; your voice will go through a wider range of pitch. The reading of poetry generally requires more vocal activity than the reading of prose; this additional activity is a direct result of poetry's greater compactness and intensity.

Poetry and Prose: Segments

Just as poetry involves particular attention to rhythm, it requires special emphasis on the sounds of individual words and also on individual sounds composing these words. These individual sounds have been classified by modern students of language as "segments." For example, in the word *soft* there are four segments, or individual meaningful sounds, that make up the word; these segments are formed by the letters *s, o, f,* and *t.* In this word, each letter that spells (*graphs*) the word also indicates a *segment* of sound. But this is not always the case. In the word *enough,* for example, there are only four segments, formed by *e, n, ou,* and *gh;* the last two segments require two letters each.

In prose, you are likely to read by sentence lengths, minimizing the segments as you emphasize the ideas in the text. But in reading poetry you might frequently linger over various segments, if they seem to have been intended for that purpose by the poet. Imagine reading these lines without making your listeners conscious of the *s, l, m,* and *w* consonant sounds and of the *short ĭ, short ŏ,* and *short ŭ* vowel sounds:

> And more, to lulle him in his slumber soft,
> A trickling streame from high rocke tumbling downe
> And ever-drizling raine upon the loft,
> Mixt with a murmuring winde, much like the sowne
> Of swarming Bees, did cast him in a swowne:
>
> —Spenser, *The Faerie Queene,* Canto I, Stanza 41

Try reading aloud the passage of prose you are now looking at; linger over some of the sounds; give your voice a similarly wide range of pitch. Perhaps the effect of this overreading will make you aware of some of the differences between poetry and prose. Poetry—unlike prose—invites intensive, energetic reading because of its compact, intense nature. If you can perceive these facts, you must realize that poets also have this objective in mind. You can see that a study of rhythm and segments is an integral part of poetic study.

Various Demands on the Sound of Poetry

From the discussion thus far, you can realize that there are three main elements that must be considered in prosodic analysis. These are *rhetoric and emotion, sound,* and *rhythm.* All are equally important, and all act at the same moment in any given poem.

RHETORIC AND EMOTION

First and foremost is the rhetorical and emotional demand. Because poetry is an art of communicating through words, the poet will necessarily wish to create emphasis by arranging his phrases, sentences, and paragraphs in the most effective way. As this arrangement must affect the levels of pitch and stress and will affect the placement of pauses, the rhetorical demand is sometimes in agreement with, and sometimes at odds with, the formal rhythm of the poem, depending on the poet's will.

The term used to describe the arrangement of words in groups according to rhetorical demand is *cadence group* (also discussed in Chapter 14, pp. 202–204). Words do not exist independently, but have meaning only as they form a part of phrases and clauses. The word *in,* for example, is a preposition, but is not very meaningful alone. In phrases like *in the dooryard* and *in the night,* however, it becomes part of an indissoluble unit of meaning—prepositional phrases that are also cadence groups. The word *star* conveys a certain amount of meaning, but *the great star* forms a syntactic and rhythmical unit, a cadence group. The following lines by Walt Whitman are spaced according to such cadence groups:

When lilacs last   in the dooryard bloom'd,
And the great star   early droop'd   in the western sky   in the night.

Such groups may or may not correspond to regularly rhythmical demands in poetry. Here is an example of poetry in which the cadence groups are contained within a rhythmical norm:

What passing-bells   for these who die as cattle?
Only the monstrous anger   of the guns.
Only the stuttering rifles   rapid rattle
Can patter out   their hasty orisons.

—Wilfred Owen, "Anthem for Doomed Youth"[1]

You may perceive a rhythmical similarity between the groups *What passing bells* and *can patter out;* the second and fourth syllables are more heavily pronounced (stressed) than the first and third. You may also perceive the rhythmical similarity (augmented by verbal repetition) of *Only the monstrous anger* and *Only the stuttering rifles.* This kind of poetry, in which cadence groups form part of a recurring pattern, is loosely called *traditional.* Poetry like Whitman's, however, in which cadence groups behave more or less arbitrarily according to meaning and the poet's apparent wishes rather than to rhythmical regularity, is called *free verse.* Poets of both free and traditional verse share the desire to create effective, moving ideas through the manipulation of cadence groups. The difference between them is that the free-verse poet allows rhetoric to govern his verse completely, while the traditional poet allows both rhetoric and rhythmical regularity to govern his.

The role of emotions in poetry deserves special consideration in

[1] Wilfred Owen, *Collected Poems.* Copyright Chatto & Windus, Ltd., 1946, © 1963. Reprinted by permission of New Directions Publishing Corporation, the Estate of Harold Owen, and Chatto & Windus, Ltd.

your study of prosody. Depending on the emotions demanded by a poem, you may raise or lower your voice, increase or decrease the speed of your pronunciation, accentuate or minimize certain sounds, and pause heavily or lightly after certain words. Emotion, in short, affects the expression with which you read a poem or passage. You can describe the effect of emotion in prosody to the extent that it affects pitch, stress, length, and pause, but you will probably find that the various tones of voice and the subtle shades of spoken expression are very difficult to describe in your theme.

SOUND

You must consider the sounds of the words themselves, both independently and as they influence one another in their order in the lines. The good poet puts words together so that their sounds will augment his meaning, not contradict it; he can use the *sounds* of his words as a form of expression. In addition to the dictionary meanings of the words within lines, and from line to line, he may use words that contain identical segments; in this way, he unifies his poem not only by developing his ideas, but also by echoing earlier sounds. Sometimes he may even use words containing sounds that are actually reminiscent of the things he is describing, as in the conclusion of the passage from Tennyson analyzed in the sample theme.

RHYTHM

Another important element is the rhythm of the words when arranged into lines of poetry. The rhythm of English is usually determined by the relationship of heavily stressed to less heavily stressed syllables.[2] In pronouncing words you give some syllables more force (loudness) than others. For convenience, you may call the syllables to which you give more force *heavily stressed,* and those to which you give less force *lightly stressed.* In most English poetry the poet has regularized the heavily and lightly stressed syllables into patterns called *feet.* He usually fills his lines with a specific number of the same feet, and that number determines the *meter* of the line. Frequently, rhetorical needs lead him to substitute other feet for the regular feet. Whether there is *substitution* or not, the

---

[2] Martin Halpern has challenged this traditional view by claiming that in iambic verse, for example, stress alone is not the only element determining feet, but that pitch and length are equally important. If one holds this position he will discover less substitution in English poetry than if he maintains the traditional view, but he will also discover greater variety within the limits of the foot. See "On the Two Chief Metrical Modes in English," *PMLA,* LXXVII (1962), 177–86.

number and kind of feet in each line constitute the meter of that line. Notice that the major influence here is number; that is, you measure English verse by dividing syllables according to degrees of stress.

The complex interaction of all these various demands produces what we commonly call the sounds and rhythms of a poem, and the prosodic interest created by any poem depends on the degrees of tension produced by the various demands. If all the demands were perfectly in accord, the result would be perfect regularity, and soon, perfect boredom. In most poetry, however, each element has a certain degree of independence, thereby producing effects of variation and tension. Variation is a strong cause of interest and beauty, and tension promotes interest and emotional involvement in a poem. An understanding of prosody is important in evaluating poetry because sound and rhythm are important in the structural and emotional complex that is poetry.

Minimum Requirements for Considering Sounds in Poetry

Although you have been speaking the language for many years, the chances are great that you have not systematically studied the sounds that you utter daily. For this reason you must be sure, before you undertake a prosodic analysis, that you have a basic approach to the analysis of sound.

The segments of words are usually divided into *vowel sounds* (including *semivowels*) and *consonant sounds*. It is important to emphasize the word *sound* as distinguished from the letters of the alphabet, for, as will be seen below, the same letters often represent different sounds. You should have some acceptable notational system for indicating sounds. Perhaps the most readily available systems of pronunciation are in the collegiate dictionaries; these systems, which have won fairly wide acceptance, take into account regional differences in pronunciation. If you have questions about syllabication and the position of stresses, you can use the dictionary as an authority. Two other systems of indicating sounds are based upon more recent scientific analyses. The first is the *International Phonetic Alphabet* as adapted for use in English, and the second is a system called *phonemic*.[3] The great virtue of these notational systems

---

[3] For a lucid discussion of English phonetics, see W. Nelson Francis, *The Structure of American English* (New York: Ronald Press Co., 1958), pp. 51–118. For the phonemic system, see Francis, pp. 119–61, and Donald J. Lloyd and Harry R. Warfel, *American English in its Cultural Setting* (New York: Alfred A. Knopf, 1956), pp. 294–318. For a discussion of the contributions that linguistic study can make to the study of prosody, see Ronald Sutherland, "Structural Linguistics and English Prosody," *College English*, XX (1958), 12–17, reprinted in Harold B. Allen, ed., *Readings in Applied English Linguistics*, 2nd ed. (New York: Appleton-Century-Crofts, 1964), pp. 492–99.

is that they are more descriptive than those in the dictionaries. The phonemic system is especially useful because it presents a satisfactory method of analyzing not only sounds but also *stress, pitch,* and *juncture.* These are the so-called "suprasegmental phonemes"; that is, they are those elements of speech production other than segments that contribute to meaning. Because both the phonetic and phonemic systems would require chapter-length explanation and because the dictionary systems are readily available, the dictionaries will be the guide in the following discussion and sample theme.

VOWEL SOUNDS AND THEIR QUALITIES

Vowel sounds are produced by vocal vibrations resonating in the space between the tongue and the top of the mouth. The tongue is held in one position during the entire production of the sound. It is possible to hold a vowel sound for a considerable length of time (e.g., *whee-e-e-e-e*) and for a short time (e.g., *whit*). There are two systems operating in the pronunciation of vowel sounds: first is *front-central-back;* second is *high-mid-low.* These terms are derived from the position of the tongue during the pronunciation of a vowel sound. For most purposes in your analysis of prosody, you need to consider only the extremes of *high-front* and *low-back.* Observe that the vowel sound *ē, ĭ, ā,* are all produced in a narrow space between the tongue and the hard palate. These sounds are both *front* and *high.* By contrast, pronounce the *ä* in *arm.* Notice that your tongue is still in a front position, but that it has dropped far down in your mouth. This *ä,* in other words, is a *low front* vowel sound. Now pronounce the vowel sound *ō* as in *coal.* Notice that your tongue has stayed high, but has dropped *back* in your throat. The *ō* sound is a *high, back,* and *rounded* sound. Now pronounce the *ô* in *orphan,* and the *o͞o* in *troop.* Notice that these are both *back* and *low rounded* sounds.

To a considerable degree, the context in which a word appears governs the pitch and intensity of the sounds in that word. Briefly, however, the low, back sounds tend to be lower in pitch than the front, high sounds. For this reason, although the sounds themselves are neutral in meaning, they can be used by poets to augment light (high-front) or heavy (low-back) effects. A remarkable example of the combination of high-front and low-back vowel sounds is this couplet from Pope, which demonstrates an interweaving of front *ā* and *ē* sounds through back *ō, ä,* and *o͞o* sounds, just as the river that Pope describes would weave through the cold wasteland:

> Lo where Maotis sleeps, and hardly flows
> The freezing Thanais through a waste of snows.
>
> —*The Dunciad,* III, 87–88

SEMIVOWEL SOUNDS

The semivowels are *w, y,* and *h.* These are segments that (1) begin in a vowel position but glide into a following vowel, thus performing the function of a consonant, as in *w*ind, *u*nion, *y*es, or (2) begin the central vowel of a syllable but glide into a new position, thus in effect forming the second part of a diphthong, as in *go* (go*w*) and weigh (wa*y*, or (3) begin in the position for a following or preceding vowel sound but add aspiration (breathy air) to the sound, as in *h*earty and a*h*em (but notice that the *h* is frequently silent, as in *h*onor).

CONSONANT SOUNDS

There are two kinds of consonant sounds. *Stop sounds* are made either by the momentary stoppage and release of sound when the lips touch each other or when the tongue touches the teeth or palate (i.e., *p, b, t, d, k, g*). Spirant or continuant sounds are made by the introduction of the voice or a stream of air in conjunction with the careful positioning of the tongue in relation to the teeth and palate (i.e., *n, l, th* [*th*orn], *th* [*th*e], *s, z, ch* [*ch*ew], *j* [*j*aw], *sh* [*sh*arp], *zh* [plea*s*ure], and *ng*), or in conjunction with a touching of lower lip and upper teeth (i.e., *f* and *v*). Some consonant sounds are *voiced;* that is, produced by the use of the voice (e.g., *b, d, v, z*). Others are *voiceless;* that is, produced by air alone without the assistance of the voice (e.g., *p, t, f, s*). Consonant sounds themselves are meaningless unless they are put into a context. The *s,* for example, in a context of rage, can augment the rage, but in a quiet context it can produce a drowsy, sleepy effect (see the earlier example from Spenser).

When discussing consonant sounds, you must be especially aware of the differences between the letters themselves and the sounds they represent. There is often a difference between spelling or *graphics,* and pronunciation or *phonetics.* Thus the letter *s* is used in spelling the words *s*weet, *s*hrove, and flow*s*, but the sounds produced are not all the same. *Sweet* produces *s;* the *s* in *shrove* is bound with an *h* to yield *sh;* and *flows* produces *z.* It would be wrong to say that these sounds are the same. Similarly, the words *shape, ocean, nation, sugar,* and *machine* all possess in common the sound *sh,* but each word uses different letters to spell the sound. *Shape* uses *sh; ocean* uses *ce; nation* uses *ti; sugar* uses *s;* and *machine* uses *ch.* Despite the spelling differences, the sounds are identical, and it would be wrong not to group them together.

Meter and Rhyme

Once you have acquired a method for analyzing and describing sounds, you can go ahead to the analysis of meter and rhyme.

METER

Meter is the systematic regulation of poetic rhythm. In order to discover the prevailing metrical system in any poem, you *scan* that poem. The act of scanning is called *scansion*.

Your first problem in scansion is to recognize where syllables are and to distinguish one syllable from another. Experience has shown that students who in the early grades have been taught to read by the "word-recognition" method, as contrasted with the "syllable" method, often find it hard to distinguish syllables. This difficulty is unfortunate, because an understanding of syllables is the first requirement in developing feeling for rhythms in poetry. You must therefore be especially cautious and realize that words like *merrier* and *terrier,* for example, are three-syllable words, as is *solitude;* another three-syllable combination is *dial hand.* If you find difficulty in perceiving the syllables in lines of poetry, a good idea is to read each word aloud separately, pronouncing every syllable, before reading the words in poetic context. The practice of reading poetry aloud is good in any event. If you have been encouraged to read for speed, you must abandon this approach when you read poetry.

The next step in preparation for your theme is to interpret *stress* or *accent.* You are concerned to show the syllables that receive major and light stress, and you need a system for showing these syllables. In scansion a heavy or primary accent is commonly indicated by an acute accent mark (') or slash (/), whereas a light accent may be indicated by a circle or zero (°). There is no reason for absoluteness in this system, however, for your instructor might direct you to indicate heavy accents by an upright line (|) or a horizontal (−) and weak or light syllables by a horizontal (−), a cross (×), or a half circle (◡). As with the determination of the number of syllables in a line you must, when you read aloud, listen carefully to hear which syllables are heavily stressed and which are lightly stressed. If you are ever in doubt, use the dictionary and the stress given there. For example, the pronunciation of the word *indeciduous* is shown as follows in *Webster's New World Dictionary:*

in´di sij´oo wəs

A light accent mark is placed over *in*, whereas *sij* receives a heavier accent mark. The other syllables are lightly stressed. If you found a line of poetry in which this word appeared, then, you would scan it as follows:

The ĭn - / dĕ - cíd / ŭ-oŭs treés / spring forth.

Although the demands of the poetic line may lessen the force of a heavily stressed syllable in relation to other words in the line, you will seldom be mistaken if you rely on the dictionary.

There is a problem in determining accent because some stresses are stronger than others, and some lightly accented syllables are stressed more than others. In fact, modern linguists have recognized three degrees of major stress. The first is *primary, major,* or *heavy,* indicated by an acute accent (/). The second is *secondary* or *medium,* shown by a circumflex accent (∧). The third is *tertiary* or *light,* marked by a grave accent (\).[4] It seems obvious that you should recognize these differences when you scan poetry. A line like the following, by Ben Jonson, can be scanned as regular iambic pentameter:

If thŏu / woŭldst knów / thĕ vír - / tŭes óf / măn-kínd.

The syllables *wouldst, tues,* and *man* are all lightly stressed according to the demands of meter (see below), yet you can feel that these syllables should receive heavier emphasis than *the* and even the word *of* (*of* is a major stress according to the meter). Similarly, *thou, know,* and *virtues* accumulate stress, so that the heaviest accent of the three falls on *vir,* just as *virtues* contains the climax of the idea of the line. Yet by what the acute accent indicates, *thou, know,* and *vir* all seem to receive the same emphasis as *of.* How can you indicate these differences when you make your scansion?

If you feel confident enough of your perceptions, you might attempt to use the acute, circumflex, and grave accents to show differences among the various heavily-stressed syllables. If your ear is not highly trained, however, a more likely compromise is to use the acute accent for the heaviest major stresses, and the grave accent for less heavy major stresses. Thus, the line by Johnson might be scanned as follows:

Ĭf thŏu / woŭldst knŏw / thĕ vír - / tŭes òf / măn-kínd.

Let us see how the opening line of Shakespeare's *Henry V* might be marked:

Ó! fŏr / ă Muse / of fire / that would / ăs - cénd . . .

If you do not use this system but employ only the acute accent and the

4 See Lloyd and Warfel, p. 315, or Francis, p. 153.

circle, be sure in your theme to show your awareness that not all heavy stresses are equal.

Since discussion of rhythm could be endless, you should know at least the following. Rhythm in poetry is usually considered in terms of metrical *feet,* and the names of the feet are derived from Greek poetry. In English, the most important feet are the two-syllable foot, the three-syllable foot, and the imperfect foot.

Feet Consisting of Two Syllables

1. IAMB. A light stress followed by a heavy stress (be̯ - háve). The iamb is the most common foot in English poetry because it is capable of great variation. Within the same line of five iambic feet, as in the examples from Jonson and Shakespeare, each foot can be slightly different in intensity from the others. In this line from Wordsworth, each foot is unique:

The winds / that will / be howl - / ing at / all hours.

Such variability, approximating the rhythms of actual speech, makes the foot suitable for just about any purpose, serious or light. The iambic foot therefore assists the poet in focusing attention on his ideas and emotions. If he uses it with skill, it never becomes monotonous.

2. TROCHEE. A heavy accent followed by a light (ú - nit).

These two feet deserve special attention. Most English words of two syllables are trochaic (e.g., région, doctrine, author, willow, morning, early). Words of two syllables having an iambic pattern usually have prefixes (e.g., control, because, despair, sublime), or else they are borrowed from a foreign language and their pronunciation is unchanged in English (e.g., machine, garage, technique). Because trochaic rhythm is often called *falling, dying, anticlimactic,* and *feminine* (this term was in use before the advent of the women's liberation movement), and because iambic rhythm is usually called *rising, elevating, climactic,* and *masculine,* a major problem in English poetry has been to fit many trochaic words into iambic patterns. A common way to solve the problem—and a way consistent with the natural word order of the language—is to place a definite or indefinite article or a possessive pronoun, or some other single-syllable word, before a trochaic word (e.g., the building; a framework; their number; nice ladies). The result is an iamb followed by the light stress needed for the next iamb. For example, Thomas Gray, in the third line of his "Elegy Written in a Country Churchyard," introduced an article before the word *ploughman* (*The ploug - | man*). Next he introduced a two-syllable adverb *homeward,* which is also trochaic (*The plough - | man home - | ward*). After this he placed a verb *plods,* a word of only one syllable which thus completed three iambs (*The plough - | man home - | ward plods*). Gray completed the line with a three-word phrase *his weary way.* Notice that he used a single-syllable pronoun before the trochaic word *weary* in order to fit this word into the iambic pattern. The final line is a perfectly regular iambic line of five feet (iambic pentameter):

The plough - | man home - | ward plods / his wear - | y way.

Shakespeare did virtually the same thing in this line, from his sonnet "Let Me Not to the Marriage of True Minds":

With - in / his bend - | ing sick - | le's com - | pass come./

Notice that Shakespeare began the second foot with the possessive pronoun *his,* a one-syllable word that enabled him to include three successive trochaic words within the iambic pattern. The inclusion of the single syllable *come* at the end of the line completed the pattern and made the line perfectly regular iambic pentameter.

Another obvious means of using trochaic words is to substitute them for iambs, a device often used at the beginning of a line, as Yeats did here:

Turn - ing / and turn - | ing in / a wid - | en - ing gyre.

Often poets avoid the problem entirely by reducing the number of polysyllabic words in their lines and by relying heavily on one-syllable words, as Oliver Goldsmith did in this line:

A breath / can make / them as / a breath / has made.

In studying prosody, you might attempt to consider the number of polysyllabic words, as has been done here, and observe the methods by which the poet has arranged them to fit or conflict with a basic metrical pattern.

3. PYRRHIC. Two unstressed syllables, as in *on their* in Pope's line *Now sleep - | ing flocks | on their | soft fleec - | es lie.* The pyrrhic is usually substituted for an iamb or trochee and usually consists of

weakly accented words like prepositions and articles. For this reason it would be impossible in English for an entire poem to consist of pyrrhics.

4. SPONDEE. Two heavy accents, as in *rough winds* in Shakespeare's line *Rough winds / do shake / the dar - ling buds / of May*. Like the pyrrhic, the spondee is primarily a substitute foot in English. An acceptable way to draw attention to a spondee is to connect the two syllables with a mark like a corporal's chevrons, as is done here. Spondees seem to create special difficulty in prosodic analysis. A principal reason is that quite often *pitch* is confused with *stress,* as in the following example:

Such seems / your beau - / ty still.

Although *beauty still* may easily be spoken at one pitch, there is a definite weakening of stress over the *y*, so that *beauty* is definitely not a spondee. Similarly, in *Three winters cold,* the syllables *three* and *win* are of equally heavy stress, and should therefore be marked as a spondee; but *ters* and *cold* are not equal, since *ters,* as a part of *winters,* receives a weak stress.

Another problem with spondees occurs if they are mistaken for pyrrhic feet. A spondee is the juxtaposition of two syllables of equally *heavy* stress, not of equally *light* stress.

Feet Consisting of Three Syllables

1. ANAPAEST. Two light stresses followed by a heavy *(ear - ly light)*.

2. DACTYL. A heavy stress followed by two lights *(might - i - est)*.

The Imperfect Foot

This consists of a single syllable; (°) by itself, or (/) by itself. The imperfect foot is a variant or substitute occurring in a poem in which one of the major feet forms the metrical pattern. The second line of "The Star-Spangled Banner," for example, is anapaestic, but it contains an imperfect foot at the end:

What so proud - / ly we hailed / at the twi - / light's last gleam - / ing.

Most scansion of English verse can be carried out with reference to these feet. The following nonce lines, for example, utilize all the feet listed:

TROCHEE   IAMB   IAMB   ANAPAEST   SPONDEE

How in / my thoughts / those hap - / pi - est days / shine forth—

TROCHEE   DACTYL   IAMB   PYRRHIC   SPONDEE

Days of / mel - o - dy / and love / and a / great dream.

UNCOMMON METERS.   In many poems, however, you might encounter
variants that have not been listed above. Poets like Browning, Tennyson,
Poe, and Swinburne experimented with uncommon meters. Other poets
manipulated pauses or *caesurae* (see below, p. 182) to create the effects of
uncommon meters. For these reasons, you might need to refer to other
metrical feet, such as the following:

1. AMPHIBRACH.   A light, heavy, and light, as in *Forever* in Browning's

line *Man has | For - ev - er*. Amphibrachs may be seen in a full line
from Swinburne's "Dolores":

Ah, feed me / and fill me / with plea - sure.

The amphibrach is the major foot in Browning's "How They
Brought the Good News from Ghent to Aix"; e.g.,

And in - to / the mid - night / we gal - loped / a - breast.

2. AMPHIMACER or CRETIC.   A heavy, light, and heavy, as in Browning's
Love is best and *praise and pray*. The amphimacer occurs mainly in
short lines or refrains, and also may be seen as a substitute foot, as in
the last foot of this line from Tennyson's "Locksley Hall":

In the / spring a / young man's / fan - cy / light - ly / turns to /
thoughts of love.

3. BACCHIUS or BACCHIC.   A light followed by two heavy stresses, as in
Some late lark in W. E. Henley's line *Some late lark | sing - ing*, or as
in *Till good day* in Swinburne's line *Till good day | shall smile |
a - way | good night*. The bacchius often occurs as a substitute for an
anapaest, as in the last foot of this line from Browning's "Saul":

Where the long / grass - es sti - /fle the wat - /ter with - in /
the stream's bed.

Note: In scanning a poem to determine its formal meter, always try to explain the lines simply, by reference to the more common feet, before turning to the less common ones. If a line can be analyzed as iambic, for example, do not attempt to fit the bacchius or the amphibrach to it unless these feet are unmistakably indicated. The following line is iambic:

The file / of men // rode forth / a - mong / the rills. ///

It would be a mistake to scan it thus:

The / file of men // rode / forth a - mong / the rills. ///

This incorrect analysis correctly accents *file of men* and *forth a-mong,* but by describing these phrases as two amphimacers, respectively, it must resort to the explanation that *The* and *rode* are imperfect feet. Such an analysis creates unnecessary complications.

RHYME

Rhyme, which refers to the recurrence of syllables that sound alike —usually in words ending lines (e.g., t*ime* and ch*ime*)—is the most easily recognized characteristic of poetry. When you describe a rhyme scheme, you should use letters (i.e., *a, b, c,* etc.). Each new letter indicates a new sound; a repeated letter indicates a rhyme. In a Shakespearean sonnet, for example, the rhyme scheme is *abab cdcd efef gg.* The rhyme scheme of an Italian or Petrarchan sonnet is *abba abba cd cd cd.*

Whenever rhyme occurs you should analyze its effects and the way these are achieved. Observe the grammatical forms of the rhyming words. If a poet rhymes only nouns, for example, his rhymes are likely to be monotonous, for he should show some variety in the grammatical forms. Another area of study is whether the rhymes are unusual or surprising. If a poet relied on "sure returns of still expected rhymes" (like the *breeze* blowing through the *trees*), his rhymes would be obvious and dull. Observe that in the following couplet by Byron the rhyming words are verbs, and that wit and surprise result from the riddle in the first line and the meaning of the final word:

> 'Tis strange—the Hebrew noun which means "I am,"
> The English always use to govern d–n.

> —*Don Juan,* I, xiv, 111–112

Although few rhymes will provide the humor of this one, you should observe the method of rhyming in the poems you study. As you make further analyses you will be impressed with the way in which your under-standing of the craft of poetry will grow.

In connection with rhyme, the following terms are important. In *eye rhyme* or *sight rhyme* the rhyming words look the same but are pro-nounced differently (e.g., "Broken is the clock I *wind*" and "I am frozen by the *wind*"). In *slant rhyme* the rhyming vowel sounds are different in quality whereas the consonant sounds are identical (e.g., *could* and *solitude*). Rhymes falling on a strong accent are commonly called *mascu-line,* though perhaps you would prefer to use terms like *heavy-stress rhyme* or *single-syllable rhyme* instead. Heavy-stress rhyme may be seen in these lines from Robert Frost's "Stopping by Woods on a Snowy Evening":

Whose woods / these are / I think / I know.

His house / is in / the vil - / lage though.

Rhymes falling on a light stress, either on a trochee or a dactyl or an amphibrach, are called *feminine,* though you could as conveniently refer to *falling rhyme, dying rhyme, trochaic rhyme, dactyllic rhyme* (or *triple rhyme*). The second and fourth lines of the first stanza of "Miniver Cheevy" by Edwin Arlington Robinson conclude with a falling rhyme:

Miniver Cheevy, child of scorn,
Grew lean while he assailed the *seasons;*

He wept that he was ever born
And he had *reasons.*

Dactyllic or triple rhyme is scarce, though it may be seen in these lines from Browning's "The Piper of Hamelin":

Small feet were *pattering*, wooden shoes *clattering*,
Little hands clapping and little tongues *chattering*.
And, like fowls in a farm-yard when barley is *scattering*, . . .

Usually, but not necessarily, heavy-stress rhyme is appropriate to serious purposes, while falling and triple rhymes lend themselves easily to comic effects.

Segmental Poetic Devices

After you have finished your scansion, you should study the poem in order to discover any segmental poetic devices employed by the poet. The common ones follow.

ASSONANCE

In connection with vowel sounds you should become familiar with *assonance,* which is the employment in close quarters of identical vowel sounds in different words (e.g., sw*i*ft Cam*i*lla sk*i*ms). Be cautious, however, about equating sounds like the *e* in d*e*ceived with the *ē* in tr*ee;* the *e* in d*e*ceived is not a true long *ē,* but rather a half-long *e,* and some would maintain that it is a *schwa* (a sound like the *a* in s*o*fa). Also, you should not select isolated instances of a sound in your description of assonance. If, for example, you find three words in the same line that include a long *ā* sound, these form a pattern and are worthy of mention as an instance of assonance; *but,* if you find a word six lines later that includes a long *ā,* this word should not be mentioned as part of the pattern. The word is too far away from the pattern to be significant.

DEVICES USING CONSONANT SOUNDS

Two common poetic devices employ consonant sounds:

1. ALLITERATION.   There are three kinds of alliteration. (a) Most commonly, alliteration is regarded as the repetition of identical consonant sounds beginning syllables in relatively close patterns—for example, "La*b*orious, heavy, *b*usy, *b*old, and *b*lind," and "While *p*ensive *p*oets *p*ainful vigils keep." Used sparingly, alliteration gives strength to a poem by emphasizing key words, but too much *c*an *c*ause *c*omic consequences. (b) A special kind of alliteration is *consonance,* whereby words are repeated that contain the exact patterns of two or more identical consonant sounds—for example, *live, leave; groaned, ground; terror, terrier; top, tip; grab, grub,* and so on. This device does not occur very often in most of the poems you will encounter, for it calls attention to itself and might detract from an important idea. (c) Another form of alliteration occurs when a poet repeats identical or similar consonant sounds that do not begin syllables but that create a pattern and thereby have prosodic importance—for example, "In the*s*e place*s* freezing breeze*s* ea*s*ily cau*s*e snee*z*e*s.*" (In this example both *s* and *z* are sounded as *z;* such a pattern is hard to overlook.) In "The *p*e*bb*les in the *b*u*bb*ling *p*ool," both *p* and *b* are *labial* consonant sounds (i.e., they are made by a momentary stoppage of breath at the lips); *p* is a *voiceless* stopped sound, whereas *b* is a *voiced* stopped sound. Because of the similarity, the two sounds should be mentioned as part of a pattern of alliteration.

2. ONOMATOPOEIA.   Onomatopoeia is a blend of consonant and vowel sounds with rhythm to create the effect of imitating the sound of

the thing being described. Onomatopoeia is technically difficult to achieve because it depends almost entirely on context (some rare instances of onomatopoeic words like *buzz* being excepted), but it is powerful when it occurs. For example, at the end of the passage from Tennyson's "Morte D'Arthur," which is analyzed in the sample theme, a lake is mentioned. Because our minds are directed toward the image of a lake, the *l* sounds (which, along with *r* sounds, are frequently called "liquids") may be taken to suggest the sounds of waves lapping against a shore. This combination of sense and sound is onomatopoeia.

Pause and Emphasis: Other Means of Poetic Effect

PAUSE (CAESURA)

Spoken speech is composed of groups of syllables forming intelligible units, separated by pauses that add to the intelligibility. In linguistics, these pauses are called *junctures*.[5] In poetry, the pause is called a *caesura* or *cut*. In this line by Ben Jonson, for example, there are two pauses, or *caesurae*:

> Thou art not, *Penshurst*, built to envious show.

The first caesura follows *not* and the second follows *Penshurst*. In the following line by Pope there are three caesurae:

> His actions', passions', being's, use and end.

You can see that poets arrange pauses judiciously in order to make their lines interesting, varied, and emphatic. In your prosodic analysis, you should make observations about the use of caesura in the poem you analyze.

For scansion, the caesura is best indicated by two diagonal lines (//) in order to distinguish it from the single diagonal lines separating feet. For most purposes these two diagonals are all you need. However, there are subtle distinctions among caesurae, and as you develop your ear you will perceive these distinctions. A pause before which the voice is not raised, such as the one between *Penshurst* and *built*, might best be shown by the two diagonal bars (//). The pause between *O* and *for* in *O! for a Muse* is also of this nature, because the pause indicates that there is more to follow immediately. But the pause at the end of a declarative sentence is different, as it usually follows a lowering of *pitch* and is therefore a

---

[5] For a brief and lucid account of junctures, see John Nist, *A Structural History of English* (New York: St. Martin's Press, 1966), pp. 46–48.

definite means by which the end of a statement is indicated. Perhaps these caesurae, usually marked by a period or semicolon in the poem, could be marked by three diagonals (///). Then too, there is still a different caesura that immediately follows the elevation of pitch that usually indicates a question. This type might conveniently be marked with a reverse double diagonal (\\).

EMPHASIS

PITCH AND LENGTH.   Pitch and length are two of the most important elements in effective expression. So far as pitch indicates meaning through the raising and lowering of the voice before pauses, it can be fairly well analyzed and discussed. More difficult, however, and far more subtle, is the raising and lowering of the voice that occurs because of the dramatic requirements of a poem, or because of the need for keeping the voice interestingly modulated. This variation is subjective to the extent that it is not properly a part of essential, denotative meaning, but for the most part the poetry you read will demand various levels of pitch. If a reader is at all sensitive, he cannot read poetry at the same vocal level.

Demanding similar alertness is the perception of length or *quantity*. Length is in an anomalous position in the scansion of English poetry because it does not determine the formation of metrical feet. But length is certainly important in the sensitive reading of poetry, and you should be aware of it.

Length is inherent in the long vowel sounds, as in the words *all, raid, reed, red, road, broad, food* and *bird.* Any of these words preceded by a word containing a short vowel sound forms an iamb (e.g., *the road*), but if two of them are together, they cause a spondee (e.g., *broad road*). Shorter vowels can be seen in the words *bat, bet, bit, bought, but, foot,* and *the.*

Although the lengths of vowels in particular words are relatively fixed, the poet can create greater or lesser lengths by the ways in which he uses words in context. Notice, for example, how Shakespeare controls length in these lines by the careful selection of words:

> . . . and then my state,
> Like to the lark at break of day arising
> From sullen earth, sings hymns at heaven's gate.

> —Sonnet No. 29, lines 10–12

As contrasted with the lengthened *ā* of *day,* the vowel sounds in *like, lark,* and *break* are restrained by the voiceless consonant stop *k.* The greatest skill, however, is shown in the way the passage (and the entire sonnet) builds toward the phrase *sings hymns,* which contains short *i* vowel sounds lengthened by the nasal consonants sounds *ng* and *m* (both of which are lengthened by the voiced continuous consonant sound *z*). As the poem reaches its climax in the image, the sound also reaches its climax. There are few more glorious experiences in English poetry than reading these lines, and the cause cannot be explained only by stress. The principal cause, in the context, is length.

Needless to say, the most skillful prosodists are able to make the matters of pitch and length infallibly right, whereas lesser poets cannot control them. As you read more and more good poetry, your awareness of pitch and length will improve. A good way to hasten this improvement is to read poetry aloud, and read it aloud frequently. If it helps you, try to act out the situation of the poem as you read.

When you make your first prosodic analysis, your instructor will probably not expect much from you in the analysis of pitch and length, but as you progress in your study of poetry you should be able to indicate your perceptions in your themes. One of the marks of your increasing understanding and appreciation of poetry (and also of your ability to write about it) will be your growing awareness of pitch and length.

EMPHASIS ACHIEVED BY METRICAL VARIATION, FORMAL AND RHETORI-CAL.   Most poems are written in a pattern that can readily be perceived. Thus Shakespeare's plays usually follow the pattern of *blank verse* (un-rhymed iambic pentameter) and Milton's *Paradise Lost* follows this same pattern. Such a pattern is no more than a rhythmical norm, however. For interest and emphasis (and perhaps because of the very nature of the English language) the norm is varied by *substituting* other feet for the normal feet and also by the rhetorical effect of such substitution.

The following line is from the "January" eclogue of Spenser's *Shepherd's Calendar.* Although the abstract pattern of the line is iambic pentameter, it is varied by the substitution of two other feet:

All in / a sun - / shine day, / as did / be - fall.

In the first foot, *All in* is a trochee, and *shine day* is a spondee. This line shows formal substitution; that is, a separate, formally structured foot is substituted for one of the original feet.

Many poets, however, create the effect of substitution by a means that we shall call *rhetorical* variation. An outstanding example of this variation in an iambic pentameter line is this one by Pope:

His ac - / tions', // pas - / sions', // be - / ing's, // use / and end;

Ordinarily there is one caesura in a line of this type, but in this one there are three, each one producing a strong pause. The line is regularly iambic and should be scanned as regular. But in reading, the effect is different.

Because of the pauses, that occur in the middles of the second, third, and fourth feet, the line is actually read as an amphibrach, a trochee, a trochee, and an amphimacer, thus:

$$\overset{\circ}{\text{His}} \overset{/}{\text{ac}} \text{ - } \overset{\circ}{\text{tions'}}, // \overset{/}{\text{pas}} \text{ - } \overset{\circ}{\text{sions'}}, // \overset{/}{\text{be}} \text{ - } \overset{\circ}{\text{ing's}}, // \overset{/}{\text{use}} \overset{\circ}{\text{and}} \overset{/}{\text{end}};$$

Although lines like this one are regular, the practical effect—the rhetorical effect—is of variation and tension. In the following well-known line from Shakespeare's *Twelfth Night*, rhetorical variation may also be seen:

If music be the food of love, play on!

This line is regularly iambic except, perhaps, for a spondee in *play on*, but the reading of the line conflicts with the formal pattern. Thus, *If music* may be read as an amphibrach and *be the food* is in practice an anapaest. Because of the subordinate clause, the caesura does not come until after the eighth syllable. These rhetorical variations produce the effect of natural, ordinary speech, because Shakespeare has lavished a good deal of his art on the line.

In whatever poetry you study, your main concern in noting variation is to observe the abstract metrical pattern and then to note the variations on this pattern—formal and rhetorical—and the principal causes for these variations. By analyzing these causes you will greatly enhance your understanding of the poet's craft.

EMPHASIS CAUSED BY TENSION BETWEEN SENTENCE STRUCTURE AND LINES. The basic working units of expression in prose are phrases, clauses, and sentences. The same applies to poetry, with the added complexity that metrical demands frequently conflict with these units. Some poets (e.g., Milton, Chaucer, Wordsworth) create emphasis and tension in their poetry by making strong demands for sentence structure over and against an established metrical pattern. Here, for example, is a short passage from Wordsworth, laid out as prose:

> And I have felt a presence that disturbs me with the joy of elevated thoughts; a sense sublime of something far more deeply interfused, whose dwelling is the light of setting suns, and the round ocean and the living air, and the blue sky, and in the mind of man.
>
> —"Tintern Abbey," lines 93–99

It is difficult, yet not impossible, to perceive the actual line divisions in this example. Wordsworth is superimposing an extended sentence structure on the metrical structure, a characteristic habit that is perfectly in keeping with meditative or philosophic poetry. Similarly, Milton is famous for his extended verse paragraphs in blank verse.

Other poets, by contrast, blend their sentence structure almost completely into their rhythmical pattern. Take, for example, this passage from Pope, which is also laid out as prose:

> Nor public flame, nor private, dares to shine; nor human spark is left,
> nor glimpse divine! Lo! thy dread empire, Chaos, is restored; light dies be-
> fore thy uncreating word: thy hand, great Anarch! lets the curtain fall; and
> universal darkness buries all.

> —*The Dunciad,* IV, 651–656

The sentences are perfectly fitted to the lines, making the counting of
feet comparatively easy, and we could determine the length of each line
easily, without the aid of the rhyme. As a result, Pope and poets like him
have frequently been accused of too much "boring regularity," whereas
poets like Wordsworth and Milton have been praised for their greater
"freedom." In actuality, the principles of variation are used by all these
poets, with Wordsworth and Milton adding extensive syntactic variation
to metrical variations.

You should know the technical terms connected with these variations. If a pause occurs at the end of the line, that line is called *end-
stopped:*

> A thing of beauty is a joy forever:

But if the line has no punctuation mark and runs over into the next line,
it is called *run-on.* The term used to describe run-on lines is *enjambment:*

> Its loveliness increases; it will never
> Pass into nothingness; but still will keep
> A bower quiet for us, and a sleep
> Full of sweet dreams, . . .

> —Keats, "Endymion," lines 1–5

Organizing Your Theme

You should attempt to show the operation of all these component elements of poetry. Your theme should contain the following parts.

INTRODUCTION

This section should include a brief discussion of the rhetorical or
dramatic situation of the poem as it leads into a consideration of prosody.
That is, is the poem narrative or expository in structure? Is there a
speaker? Who is he? What are his characteristics? What situation is described? What special poetic theories are apparently being exemplified in
the passage? What is the principal idea of the passage? What is the
dominant mood of the poem? The object of answering questions like

these (you do not need to answer all of them, and may want to ask others) is to make possible the evaluation of how well the prosody of the passage lives up to the expectation aroused by the rhetorical or dramatic situation. Discussion of these questions is therefore very important. As a structural device in your themes, the discussion will give more purpose and logic to the technical discussion to follow (the introductory discussion will also help you in your prosodic analysis of the poem or passage).

BODY

Here you should discuss the rhythmical and segmental techniques of the passage or poem. You should describe the formal metrical pattern first. Does the poet seem to move naturally and effectively within the confines of poetic meter, or does his thought seem at war with the meter? How successful is he in placing important words or syllables in positions of stress? Is he successful in shaping meter and subject matter into suitable climaxes? How effectively does he control caesurae? Do the pauses seem to occur haphazardly, or as part of a controlled pattern of variation? What formal substitutions occur in the pattern of verse? What rhetorical variations occur? How are they achieved, and what end do they serve?

In discussing segmental aspects you will be referring mainly to assonance, alliteration, consonance, and onomatopoeia. Is assonance or alliteration used with any apparent design to emphasize certain important words? Or is it used without such a design? Can you perceive any continually recurring segments throughout the passage? Does this recurrence seem part of any plan? You should also consider whether any closely related sounds are used, such as the s and the z, or the p and the b. It would also be relevant to observe whether certain types of sounds are used as a means of achieving emphasis (for example, a passage containing a number of b, t, and k sounds might deserve mention as an instance of poetic strength).

CONCLUSION

Here you should evaluate the success of the passage. Did the prosody seem appropriate to the rhetorical situation? Did it conflict, and if so, does that conflict provide grounds for an adverse judgment? Did the prosody augment the idea of the passage? Did it give the passage more power than the idea alone would give it? In short, answer the question of how well the sounds and the rhythms succeeded in being an instrument of communication and a device by which the poet may evoke the proper emotions in the reader.

Hints

1. At the beginning of your paper you should provide a triple-spaced version of the passage under analysis. Make at least two carbon copies in order to employ them for various analytical purposes, as in the sample following, where one copy shows metrics and the others show alliteration and assonance.

2. Number each line in your example, beginning with *1*, regardless of the length of the passage.

3. In preparing your material, you should follow this procedure:
   a. Establish the formal pattern of the verse and note all the positions of formal substitutions.
      (1) Indicate the separate feet by a diagonal line (/). Indicate caesurae by a double diagonal (//). If you wish to make refinements, reserve the double diagonal for caesurae that do not affect the pitch of the voice; use a triple diagonal (///) for voice-lowering caesurae and a reverse double diagonal (\\) for voice-raising caesurae.
      (2) Indicate lightly stressed syllables by the circle (o), or, if your instructor prefers, by the half circle (ᵕ) or cross (x). Show heavily stressed syllables by the acute accent (´) or slash (/) and by the grave accent (`).
   b. Read the passage for rhetorical substitutions; make notes about where they occur and about how the poet creates them.
   c. Discover the various segmental poetic devices. Circle letters indicating a pattern of alliteration and assonance, and draw lines indicating the connection. Different colored pencils are effective in distingushing the various patterns, or, if you use only one pencil or pen, you might set up a system of dotted, wavy, cross-hatched, or double-cross-hatched lines in order to distinguish the patterns. The sample theme uses a system numbering the various metrical variations, though on your own work sheets you would do better to use colored pencils. Any easily recognized system that is convenient for you, however, is acceptable. It is also a good idea to circle the metrical variations (thus, anapaests and trochees might be circled to help you identify them easily when you begin to write).

4. At the bottom of your pages, provide a key to your circles and lines.

5. It is best to use a standard pronunciation guide for your discussion of sounds. You may employ one of the standard collegiate dictionaries. If you have had formal linguistic study, use the phonemic or phonetic systems; otherwise you will probably find the dictionary system more convenient.

6. Underline all sounds to which you are calling attention. If you refer to a sound within a word (e.g., the *l* sound in *calling*), underline only that sound.

7. If you prepare these versions with care, half your job is over. All you need do after this preparation is to describe what you have analyzed

and noted. Here your connecting lines of the same types or colors can help you immeasurably, for the lines and colors are obvious and will help you remember important variations and devices of sound.

SAMPLE THEME

*A Prosodic Analysis of Lines 232–243
of Tennyson's "Morte D'Arthur"* [6]

METRICAL VARIATION

But the o- / ther swift- / ly strode // from ridge / to ridge, //   1

Clothed with / his breath, // and look- / ing, // as / he walk'd, //   2

Lar-ger / than hu- / man // on / the fro- / zen hills. ///   3

He heard / the deep / be-hind / him, // and / a cry   4

Be-fore. /// His own / thought drove / him // like / a goad. ///   5

Dry clash'd / his har- / ness // in / the i- / cy caves   6

And bar- ren/chasms, // and all / to left / and right   7

The bare / black cliff / clang'd round / him, // as / he based   8

His feet / on juts / of slip- / pe-ry crag // that rang   9

---

[6] *The Complete Poetical Works of Tennyson,* W. J. Rolfe, ed. (Cambridge, Mass.: Houghton Mifflin Co., 1898), p. 66.

Sharp- smit- / ten // with / the dint / of ar- / med heels— ///   10
——3—— —4— ———1———

And on / a sud- / den, // lo! // the lev- / el lake, //   11
———2——— —4—

And the / long glor- / ies // of / the win- / ter moon. ///   12
——5—— ——3—— —4— ———1———

¹ = Anapaest, or effect of anapaest.   ⁴ = Effect of imperfect feet.
² = Amphibrach, or the effect of   ⁵ = Pyrrhic.
    amphibrach.   ⁶ = Trochee, or the effect
³ = Spondee.   of trochee.

ALLITERATION

But the other swiftly strode from ridge to ridge,   1

Clothed with his breath, and looking, as he walk'd,   2

Larger than human on the frozen hills.   3

He heard the deep behind him, and a cry   4

Before. His own thought drove him like a goad.   5

Dry clash'd his harness in the icy caves   6

And barren chasms, and all to left and right   7

The bare black cliff clang'd round him, as he based   8

His feet on juts of slippery crag that rang   9

Sharp-smitten with the dint of armed heels—   10

And on a sudden, lo! the level lake,   11

And the long glories of the winter moon.   12

‒ ‒ ‒ ‒ ‒ ‒ ‒ = S   ——————— = B

‒ ‒ ‒ ‒ ‒ ‒ = H aspirate   ············· = L

‒ —‒ —‒ = K

ASSONANCE

But the other swiftly strode from ridge to ridge,   1

Clothed with his breath, and looking, as he walk'd,   2

Larger than human on the frozen hills.   3

He heard the deep behind him, and a cry   4

Before. His own thought drove him like a goad.   5

Dry clash'd his harness in the icy caves   6

And barren chasms, and all to left and right   7

The bare black cliff clang'd round him, as he based   8

His feet on juts of slippery crag that rang   9

Sharp-smitten with the dint of armed heels—   10

And on a sudden, lo! the level lake,   11

And the long glories of the winter moon.   12

——————— = $\bar{O}$ ‒ ‒ ‒ ‒ ‒ ‒ = $\breve{A}$

—— ‒‒ —— = $\bar{I}$ ‒ ‒ ‒ ‒ ‒ = $\ddot{A}$

The poem itself is a dramatic tale within a tale. The poet Hall tells the story; the narrator, Tennyson's speaker, who relates what Hall tells, has been dozing before the story, while the parson sleeps through the telling. Slightly comic as it is, this sleep also lends a dreamlike quality to the poem and enables Tennyson to achieve his "high" purpose. For the poem is about the passing of the old order (symbolized by the death of Arthur), and the old order does not pass without the regret of those who are left behind, who magnify and elevate the order to unparalleled heights. Tennyson's technique of removing the story from his own voice to Hall's makes this elevation possible and actually justifies the claim that the story is a "Homeric" echo. In short, the poem captures the magic of the old order, and also its heroic, brave, undaunted ruggedness.

The passage selected for prosodic analysis moves in sympathy with this passing of the heroic age. The motion described is from the mountainous heights where Arthur was wounded to the level lake on which he will travel to his final rest—from the elevated to the low. It is reasonable to expect, therefore, that the passage should convey the impression of Sir Bedivere's exertion as he performs his last service for his dying monarch. The passage should be strong just as Bedivere is strong; it should uncompromisingly support the elevated and magical evocation of the poem itself; it should end on an emotional key similar to that experienced by Bedivere as he reaches his goal.

The rhythm of the passage is everywhere alive to this dramatic situation. The basic metrical pattern is iambic pentameter, but this pattern is highly varied. Any description of Tennyson's metrical variations is arbitrary, but with this reservation I will try to describe them.

The passage opens with an anapaest (*But the ó-*), and there is another anapaest in line 9. Tennyson seems to like anapaests, for he creates their effect in many other lines by inserting a pause within an iamb and then making the heavy stress of the iamb fall onto a preposition or a conjunction that must then fit into the next iamb (which usually contains the object of the preposition), as follows:

$$\overset{\circ}{\text{and}} \ \overset{/}{\text{look}}\overset{\circ}{\text{ing}} \ // \ \overset{\circ}{\text{as}} \ \overset{\circ}{\text{he}} \ \overset{/}{\text{walked}}$$

$$\overset{\circ}{\text{than}} \ \overset{/}{\text{hu}}\overset{\circ}{\text{man}} \ // \ \overset{\circ}{\text{on}} \ \overset{\circ}{\text{the}} \ \overset{/}{\text{frozen hills}}$$

$$\overset{\circ}{\text{be}}\overset{/}{\text{hind}} \ \overset{\circ}{\text{him}} \ // \ \overset{\circ}{\text{and}} \ \overset{\circ}{\text{a}} \ \overset{/}{\text{cry}}$$

He creates this type of rhetorical anapaestic variation in lines 2 (twice), 4, 5, 6, 8, 10, and 12. A related variation is the frequent appearance of an amphibrachic rhythm, which is produced in lines 2, 3, 4, 6, 7, and 11. In line 11 for example, the first five syllables precede the caesura:

> ° ` ° ` ° /
> And on / a sud- / den, // lo! // . . .

Because *And on* forms a regular iambic foot, *a sudden* seems to be a unit too, since there is no other syllable to go with *sudden*. Thereby a rhetorical amphibrachic rhythm is formed. Still another related variation is that of the apparently imperfect feet in lines 2, 5, 8, 10, 11, and 12. These imperfect feet are usually produced by their closeness to a caesura, as in the following:

> ° / ⌢ ⌢ °
> The bare / black cliff / clang'd round / him //

> ` ° ⁄
> as / he based . . . .

In this line *him* is in effect all by itself, though in theory it is the unstressed syllable in the iamb *him // as*. But a theoretical foot does not an actual make, and I submit that the two words do not belong together.

Perhaps the most effective metrical variation in the passage is the frequent use of spondees, which appear in lines 5, 6, 8 (twice), 10 and 12. These substitutions, occurring mainly in the section in which Sir Bedivere is forcing his way down the frozen hills, permit the lines to ring out, as in:

> ° / ⌢ ⌢
> The bare / black cliff / clang'd round /

and

> ⌢ ° / °
> Dry clash'd / his harness . . . .

Other, less significant, substitutions are the trochees in lines 3 and 7, and the pyrrhic in line 12. The total effect of these variations is to support the grand, free conception of the heroic action described in the lines.

Many of the variations I have described are produced by Tennyson's free handling of his sentence structure, which results in a free placement of the caesurae and in a free use of end-stopping and enjambment. It is interesting that four of the first five lines are end-stopped (two by commas, two by periods). Bedivere is walking but exerting himself during these lines and apparently he is making short tests to gather strength for his ordeal. The ordeal comes during the next four lines, when he makes his precarious descent; none of the lines containing this description is end-stopped. Bedivere is disturbed (being goaded by "his own thought"), but he must keep going, and we may presume that the free sentence structure and the free metrical variation enforce the difficulty and mental disturbance he is experiencing. But in the last two lines, when he has reached the lake and therefore his goal, the lines "relax" with feminine caesurae exactly following the fifth syllables. In other words, the sentence structure of the last two lines is fairly regular, an effect designed perhaps to indicate the return to order and beauty after the previous, rugged chaos.

This rhythmical virtuosity is accompanied by a similar brilliance of sound. Alliteration is an obvious and startling device in these lines; some notable examples are the recurrent aspirate *h*'s in lines 3–6 (*h*uman, *h*e, *h*eard, be*h*ind, *h*im, *h*is, *h*arness), the *b*'s in lines 7 and 8 (*b*arren, *b*are, *b*lack), the *s*'s in line 1 (*s*wiftly *s*trode,) the *k*'s in lines 6–9 (*c*lash'd, *c*aves, *c*hasms, *c*liff, *c*lang'd, *c*rag), and the *l*'s in lines 11 and 12 (*l*o, *l*evel, *l*ake, *l*ong, g*l*ories). Assonance is also working throughout as a unifying device, as in the $\bar{o}$ pattern of lines 1, 2, 3, and 5 (str*o*de, cl*o*thed, fr*o*zen, *o*wn, dr*o*ve, g*o*ad),

the $\breve{a}$ pattern of lines 7, 8, and 9 (ch*a*sms, cl*a*ng'd, bl*a*ck, cr*a*g, r*a*ng), the $\ddot{a}$ pattern of line 10 (sh*a*rp, *a*rmed), the $\bar{\imath}$ pattern of lines 4–7 (l*i*ke, dr*y*, *i*cy, r*i*ght). One might also remark that there are many

high-front vowel sounds (i.e., $\bar{e}$, $\bar{a}$, $\breve{\imath}$, $\breve{a}$) in the first ten lines. But in the last two lines, which describe the level lake and the moon,

Tennyson introduces a number of low, back vowels(i.e., $\breve{o}$, $\breve{u}$, $\bar{o}$,

$\overset{\psi}{o}$, $\tilde{o}$, $\breve{u}$, $\overline{oo}$). The striking effect of the vowels in these last two lines can be pointed out only when they are heard immediately after the two preceding lines:

> . . . as he based
> His feet on juts of slippery crag that rang
> Sharp-smitten with the dint of armed heels—
> And on a sudden, lo! the level lake,
> And the long glories of the winter moon.

> —lines 8–12

As these last two lines are read, their back, low vowels make possible a lowering of vocal pitch and a certain relaxation of vocal tension, and thereby they are eminently appropriate at this point in the poem, when Sir Bedivere has attained his goal.

The last two lines are, in fact, almost totally onomatopoeic, since the liquid *l* sounds are definitely imitative of the gentle lapping of lake waves on a shore and in the line of the moon. There are other examples of onomatopoeia in this short passage, too. In line 2 Tennyson brings out the detail of Sir Bedivere's walking in the presumably cold air "Clothed with his breath," and in the following five lines Tennyson employs many words with the aspirate *h* (e.g., *h*is *h*arness); in this context, these sounds suggest Sir Bedivere's labored breath as he carries his royal burden. Similarly, the explosive stops *b* and *k*, *d* and *t* in lines 6–10 seems to be imitative of the sounds of Sir Bedivere's feet as he places them on the "juts of slippery crag."

This short passage is a mine of prosodic skill—a virtuoso piece that I do not expect to find on every page I shall read of English poetry. The sounds and the rhythms of the words and lines themselves, put into this context by Tennyson, actually speak along with the meaning; they emphasize the grandeur of Arthur and his faithful follower, and for one brief moment bring out the magic that Tennyson associated with the fading past. In the poem, the outright glory of this passage makes understandable Sir Bedivere's previous reluctance to cast away King Arthur's sword. Such glory is not to be thrown away easily; but now it is gone, and we can regain it only in our imagination, or in Tennyson's poem.

The Theme Analyzing

PROSE STYLE

CHAPTER Style is usually understood to mean the way in which a
14 writer employs his words, phrases, and sentences to achieve
his desired effects. It should be distinguished from *structure,*
which is concerned with the organization and arrangement
of the work as a whole. Although *style* may be used loosely to comprise
the writer's entire craft, for this theme you will be concerned with the
word in its narrow sense. As you read a work of literature you become
aware of its style, even though you may not be able to describe the style
accurately after you have finished reading. The main obstacle to discussing style is usually that you do not have the descriptive vocabulary for
embodying your perceptions, and so the best you can say is that the style
is simply "good," "bad," "crisp," "elegant," "formal," "brilliant," or the
like, with an uneasy hope that no one will ask what you mean. Perhaps
your previous experience with literature and with composition has been
concerned not so much with style as with content. The result is that
analyzing style is like experiencing weightlessness for the first time.

Let us grant, then, that style is difficult to describe and analyze.
You may have discovered, however, that critics and reviewers in the
Sunday papers and elsewhere are constantly praising or condemning
writers for their style. You can see the desirability of being familiar with
an approach to style, for how else can you formulate your own opinions?
What do the critics look for? What criteria do they use as a basis of
judgment? Is it possible, in short, for a student to be let in on the
"mysteries" of discussing style, or should these matters remain in the
hands of the critics, forever out of reach?

Purpose of Stylistic Analysis

The object of your theme is to make you aware of style: what it is, how to discuss it, how to evaluate it, how to relate it to the achievement of the literary work as a whole, how to define the characteristics of each writer's style. Because style is concerned with diction, phrases, sentences, and sound and rhythm—together with the relation of all these matters to the entire work under consideration—you will have to wrestle with sentences and words, and from time to time you may be thrown on your ear. But if you persist you will develop the ability to make some accurate and useful observations about a writer's style. You will learn much and will be well on the way toward a dependable means of evaluating literature.

Limitations

In your analysis you will not be able to make observations about an entire work because of limited space. To write this assignment, you need only to take a short passage—a single paragraph is best, although a passage of dialogue is also satisfactory—and use it as the basis of your observations. As with the prosodic analysis, it is usually best to select a well-written passage or else one that conveys a good deal of the writer's argument, for the author will have devoted his best skill and energy to such passages. You must be aware of the limitations in this selection, for the discussion of one paragraph does not necessarily apply to the whole work in which the paragraph appears. But if you make these points—that your method of analysis would be the same for any passage in the whole book and that the paragraph is important in the book—the generalization you make will have implications for the entire work. The authenticity of your remarks will depend on the skill and knowledge you show in your analysis. Always beware, however, of making hasty generalizations. With these reservations, your theme about style will be of great value to you.

Main Problem

The main problem you will encounter in this assignment is how to discover your writer's style. Suppose, for example, you choose to analyze a piece of dramatic prose or a passage of dialogue from a novel; or suppose you select a passage from a novel that is told from the first-person point of view. When you speak about the style of these passages, are you describing the *writer's* style or the *speaker's* style? Suppose that you analyze, in the same work, two passages that are dissimilar in style? Did the writer's style change, or did he adapt it to fit the different places or speakers? And if he did so adapt it, what are you trying to discover by an analysis of style?

The answer seems obvious. In your analysis you are trying to determine the degree of the writer's *control* over his subject matter. Control is what matters. If you discover that your writer adheres to the same style throughout his work, that fact might lead you to conclude that he has inadequate control over his subject matter. But you should ask some further questions. Does he have some definite end in view in using this one style? If so, what is it? Is he successful? The aim of your analysis is always to describe specific characteristics and to make at least partial judgments of why these characteristics appear and what they contribute to the work.

To see how this aim might be fulfilled, look at the following example, from *The Merchant of Venice,* Act I, Scene ii:

> If to do were as easy as to know what were good to do, chapels had been churches and poor men's cottages princes' palaces. It is a good divine that follows his own instructions: I can easier teach twenty what were good to be done, than to be one of the twenty to follow mine own teaching. . . .

From the style of this passage, it seems clear that Portia (the speaker) is a woman with a rapid mind, well befitting her masquerade as an intelligent lawyer-judge later in the play. Her first sentence uses simple diction in a complex structure. Of her first fourteen words, six compose infinitives and two are verbs; a total of eight words out of fourteen, or over 55 per cent serve as verbs or verbals. Her mind, in other words, is active. The first fourteen words are also part of an if-clause, dependent on the verb in the following main clause. The ability to use subordination in sentences is regarded as the mark of a good mind and a good style. Portia, too, shows an ability to use rhetoric—in this sentence the rhetorical device called *zeugma* (the use of a single word with double grammatical weight).[1] The main clause of the first sentence is equivalent to two clauses, but the verb is used only once: "chapels had been churches and poor men's cottages [had been] princes' palaces." Portia's language is

---

[1] This definition pertains to zeugma in its simplest sense. When a word works doubly grammatically, however, it frequently takes on two meanings, so that many people regard the double meaning as essential to a definition of zeugma. Thus, in Pope's line "Or stain her honor or her new brocade," *stain* carries double weight grammatically, and also double meaning, first as a metaphoric stain on honor, and second as a literal stain on a brocade. In this line, therefore, *stain* works as a zeugma, a metaphor, and a pun. Complications like these are not unusual, but are not essential.

exceedingly simple, but she shows a fine sense of rhetorical and logical balance.

To be contrasted with Portia's speech is this one by Ophelia in *Hamlet,* Act IV, Scene v:

> Well, God 'ild you! They say, the owl was a baker's daughter. Lord! we know what we are, but know not what we may be. God be at your table!

Ophelia makes this speech after she has become insane. Her words are simple, and her sentences are disconnected. Just when she seems to become coherent (in sentence three) her thought is swiftly broken, and her last sentence seems as random as her first. Had Shakespeare introduced the intellectual toughness of Portia's speech here, he would not have shown a broken mind but an alert one in all its powers. Thus he gave Ophelia these disconnected sentences, so unlike her coherent speeches in poetry earlier in the play.

The point about these two passages is that although they differ in style, Shakespeare's control and artistry do not. In fact, the passages show his mastery of dramatic prose. The study of style should aim toward a description of the writer's ability to control his words to serve his needs.

Approaches to Style

The three chief ways to describe style are (a) the analysis of the grammar in a passage, (b) the analysis of the rhythm and sound, and (c) the analysis of the words, their denotation and connotation, their influences on each other in context, their symbolic values, their functions in similes, metaphors, and other rhetorical figures.

ANALYSIS OF GRAMMAR

The nomenclature of grammar is a useful tool in describing a writer's sentences. As you have been taught grammar, you should not have trouble undertaking the analysis of grammar in your passage. For example, the following sentences from the beginning of Hemingway's *A Farewell to Arms* have been justly praised by critics:

> [1] In the late summer of that year we lived in a house in a village that looked across the river and the plain to the mountains. [2] In the bed of the river there were pebbles and boulders, dry and white in the sun, and the water was clear and swiftly moving and blue in the channels. [3] Troops went by the house and down the road and the dust they raised powdered the leaves of the trees. [4] The trunks of the trees too were dusty and the leaves fell early that year and we saw the troops marching along the road and the dust rising and leaves, stirred by the breeze, falling

and the soldiers marching and afterward the road bare and white except for the leaves.[2]

You will observe that in this paragraph Hemingway employs the word *and* many times. Of the four sentences, the last three are all compound sentences (independent clauses joined by *and*), whereas the first one is complex. Usually compound sentences do not demonstrate cause-and-effect or other relations and so are best used in narrative description. A number of compound sentences tend to declare, rather than to analyze (similarities between Hemingway's passage and parts of the King James Bible have been noticed in this connection). Also, compound sentences strung together may, under some circumstances, suggest resignation on the speaker's part. These remarks apply here.

In this passage there are also many prepositional phrases. There are sixteen phrases, to be exact (one with a compound object). Of these sixteen, twelve are adverbial, and of these twelve, eight modify verbs. This number is to be contrasted with the number of single-word adverbs —three. The proportion of phrases is so high that you might justifiably conclude that the characteristic method of modification in the passage is the use of phrases. Prepositional phrases usually require many *in*'s, *of*'s, and *the*'s; so a passage with many phrases would likely contain many monosyllabic words. In this passage, there are 126 words; 103 have one syllable; twenty-two have two syllables; and one has three syllables. The method of modification thus has a close relationship to the simple, rather stark diction of the passage, for if Hemingway had relied on single-word adverbs he would necessarily have used more polysyllabic words. (Notice that the three single-word adverbs are all polysyllabic: *swiftly, early, afterward*. The longest word in the passage is an adverb.)

You can see that a knowledge of grammatical terms (in this example, a knowledge of conjunctions, compound sentences, complex sentences, adverbs, phrases, nouns) aids in the analysis, description, and evaluation of style. Without this knowledge you are handicapped in discussing style.

Let us take a sentence from another writer. The following is from Theodore Dreiser's *The Titan*. It has probably never been praised by anyone:

> From New York, Vermont, New Hampshire, Maine had come a strange company, earnest, patient, determined, unschooled in even the primer of refinement, hungry for something the significance of which, when they had it, they could not even guess, anxious to be called great, determined so to be without ever knowing how.[3]

2 Reprinted with the permission of Charles Scribner's Sons and Jonathan Cape Ltd. from *A Farewell to Arms* by Ernest Hemingway, p. 3. Copyright 1929 Charles Scribner's Sons; renewal copyright © 1957 Ernest Hemingway.

3 New York: Dell Publishing Co., Inc. (Copyright World Publishing Co.), 1959, p. 25.

This sentence begins with a prepositional phrase used adverbially, with four objects of the preposition. Then Dreiser introduces the verb (*had come*), and then the subject of the verb (*strange company*). Immediately after the subject there are three adjectives that modify it. There is then a fourth adjective (*unschooled*) modified by an adverb phrase (*in even the primer*), and the object of the preposition is modified by an adjective phrase (*of refinement*). Then there is a fifth adjective (*hungry*) modifying the subject of the sentence. This fifth adjective has complex modification; first there is an adverb phrase (*for something*), and then the noun *something* is modified by an adjective clause, which in turn has with it an adverb clause (*the significance of which, when they had it, they could not even guess*). The original series of adjectives is resumed with *anxious*, which is modified by the adverbial infinitive *to be called great*. The adjective series ends with the seventh, *determined*, which is modified by the adverbial infinitive phrase *so to be*, which is modified by the adverbial *without ever knowing how*.

If you have been confused by this grammatical description, you will readily agree that the sentence begins simply but unusually and becomes difficult and involved. It is inverted and rhetorically dramatic; it depends for its full effect on close study in its context on the printed page, whereas the example from Hemingway could be readily followed if someone read it aloud. In Dreiser's defense, you might say that the sentence explores a difficult avenue of thought: Dreiser is describing the makeup of a giant, a *titan,* and theoretically his language should therefore be grand and sweeping. In fact, this sentence fits into his design, for its seven adjectives build up to a cumulative impression of bigness. In its way, this sentence is quite effective.

Among other things, grammatical analysis reveals the complexity or simplicity of a writer's style. You should observe whether the sentences fall into patterns. Are most of the sentences simple, compound, or complex? Why? Is there a recurrence of any rhetorical devices that can be described grammatically (e.g., parallelism, zeugma, chiasmus)? Are the sentences mainly *loose* or *periodic,* and why? Always be alert to the special characteristics of your passage. For example, you might notice that its sentences are filled with many adjectives, or with subordinate clauses. Your grammatical study should conclude by trying to answer the question of why the elements are as they are. In this way you will see the usefulness of analyzing grammar when you discuss style, for the two are inseparably identified.

A word of caution is perhaps needed. The description of grammar can become deadly and sterile if it leads to no generalizations. It is not an end in itself. But the labor of grammatical analysis can produce stimulating and sometimes startling results.

RHYTHM AND SOUND

RHYTHM.   Some analysts of style become vague or rapturous when they speak about the rhythm of prose. The reason is not far to seek, for prose rhythm is difficult to analyze and still more difficult to describe. If you keep your ear alert and if you combine the results of your hearing with the analysis of grammar in a passage, you can arrive at accurate and useful generalizations about prose rhythms. The rhythm of prose can seldom be accurately described by iambs, trochees, dactyls, and so on, for words that could be measured neatly by feet in poetry are actually part of some larger rhythmic pattern in prose. The rhythm of prose, in short, is generally vaster than that of poetry, in keeping with the prose writer's general intention to develop his thoughts extensively. To feel prose rhythm, read this passage, which opens Nathaniel Hawthorne's story "The Hollow of the Three Hills."

> [1] In those strange old times when fantastic dreams and madmen's reveries were realized among the actual circumstances of life, two persons met together at an appointed hour and place.   [2] One was a lady, graceful in form and fair of feature, though pale and troubled, and smitten with an untimely blight in what should have been the fullest bloom of her years; the other was an ancient and meanly dressed woman, of ill-favored aspect, and so withered, shrunken and decrepit that even the space since she began to decay must have exceeded the ordinary term of human existence.   [3] In the spot where they encountered no mortal could observe them.   [4] Three little hills stood by each other, and down in the midst of them sunk a hollow basin, almost mathematically circular, two or three hundred feet in breadth, and of such depth that a stately cedar might but just be visible above the sides. . . .[4]

Although these sentences could easily be scanned as iambs, anapaests, and the other poetical feet, you will notice that it is more accurate to submerge many of the accents in larger prose rhythms; that is:

Thŕee líttle hílls stood bý each other,

and dówn in the mìdst of them sunk a hòllow bàsin.

In hearing the rhythm of these fragments, notice that stresses are placed on fewer syllables than in a verse passage of comparable lentgh. There is less stress because in prose the individual *cadence groups,* or *phraseological groups,* are the basic developmental and rhythmical units. A typical sentence is usually made up of two or more cadence groups.[5]

A cadence group is an intelligible word group that a speaker fits

---

4 In Myron Matlaw and Leonard Lief, eds., *Story and Critic* (New York: Harper & Row, 1963), p. 64.

5 Cadence groups are also discussed in the chapter on Prosody (Chapter 13), p. 168.

together rhythmically when speaking, and that a reader takes in at one "eyeful" when reading. Thus, for example, the phrase *those times* is a meaningful unit. In reading the two words, you consider them together. If you add the preposition *in* at the beginning, you make a prepositional phrase, and then consider *in those times* as a three-syllable rhythmical unit. If, as Hawthorne has done, you add the two adjectives *strange old* as modifiers of *times,* you then have a five-syllable rhythmical unit, *In those strange old times* (sentence 1). Having begun with a short cadence group, we have seen it lengthened.

What you should do in analyzing prose style for rhythm is to mark the cadence groups in order to observe whether they range from short and rapid to long and leisurely or to something in between. Rely on your own vocal pauses as you read, being careful to mark the ends and beginnings of groups as suggested by punctuation marks, and the natural, if slight, pauses (*junctures*) between subjects and predicates, compound subjects, and so on. As you analyze the various groups you might arrange them schematically by putting a noun phrase on one side of the page, and the corresponding verb phrase on the other, or by alternately arranging various dependent clauses. Thus, the first sentence of "The Hollow of the Three Hills" might be laid out as follows:

In those strange old times	when fantastic dreams and madmen's reveries were realized among the actual circumstances of life,
two persons met together	at an appointed hour and place.

With this scheme may be contrasted a rhythmic analysis of two sentences from Katherine Anne Porter's story "He":

He did grow	and he never got hurt.

A plank blew off the chicken house and struck him on the head and he never seemed to know it.[6]

While it is unwise to make generalizations from only these sentences, it is possible to observe in Hawthorne a tendency toward longer sentences, resulting in rhythmical units that are not self-contained clauses. Hawthorne's rhythmical units are embodied in phrases like the beginning prepositional-adverb phrase ("In those strange old times"), and the sentence is so extensive that it is made up out of six units. The rhythmical units in Katherine Anne Porter's sentences, by contrast, are coincidental with complete sentence structures. It is also possible to see in Hawthorne a tendency to arrange his diction and his stresses in patterns of two (e.g., *strange old; dreams . . . reveries;* and *hour and place*). Only an analysis

    [6] In Sean O'Faolain, ed., *Short Stories: A Study in Pleasure* (Boston: Little, Brown and Co., 1961), p. 255.

of a greater number of sentences, however, would confirm whether these tentative conclusions have any validity. Your job in analyzing a prose passage is to make a similar attempt to discover and to characterize its rhythms. As a means of self assistance, you should read the passage aloud and listen for its rises and falls, its lengths of utterance. It is also helpful to have a fellow student read the pasage aloud to you, so that you will be better able to observe its rhythms.

SOUND. Despite the differences between poetry and prose, the various "poetic" devices such as alliteration, assonance, and onomatopoeia may also be at work in prose (see pp. 180–82). You should be alert for them. Look at the example from Hemingway again. If you listen, you will hear that Hemingway employs assonance in sentence 2 (moving, blue); in sentence 3 (house, down, powdered); sentences 3 and 4 (leaves, breeze, we, trees). The passage from Hawthorne's "The Hollow of the Three Hills" utilizes assonance and also a good deal of alliteration. In sentence 1, for example, you may notice "met together" and "reveries were realized." In sentence 2 there is "graceful in form and fair of feature," and "blight" and "bloom." A closer study would reveal a number of other segmental devices. The effect of this attention to sound should be to make the reader stop and listen, and to concentrate on the suggestions and the connotations of the prose. In commenting on passages like these you should certainly establish their similarity to poetry and should also include this fact in your evaluation of the style.

DICTION—MEANING OF WORDS IN CONTEXT

This phrase of stylistic study is the one in which you will probably feel most at home, for you have always been aware of the problems of meaning. You should observe, however, that a study of diction does not simply rely on dictionary definitions but goes beyond the meanings of the words to a study of their relationships in context. Words rarely exist by themselves but are in a context in which one word affects another, and your interest here should be to observe and record these relationships.

Look at the words in your passage and see where they take you. You are on an exploration and may or may not discover something valuable. Some guidelines for your itinerary might be the following questions: Are any important words repeated? Why? Are there any unusual words? Surprising words? Why? Do the words have common etymologies? (E.g., are most of the words Anglo-Saxon in origin, or are there many of Latin or Greek derivation? Consult your dictionaries for etymologies.) Does the author use many adjectives before a noun? After a noun? Why? What is the effect? Are the words in the passage mainly specific or general? Concrete or abstract? Why? (Observe in the passage from Hemingway that the words are mainly specific and concrete, whereas in that from

Dreiser there are many abstract words; what is the difference in effect caused by this difference in diction?) Are any of the words allusive; that is, do they suggest other contexts, literary, historical, scientific, or whatever? What are the connotations of the words as distinguished from the denotations? Does the passage rely on these connotations? How? Is there dialect in the passage? What is its effect? You can see that your understanding of point of view is relevant here, for the persona of the piece will create the nature of the diction (characterize as narrators: Huckleberry Finn, Holden Caulfield, Jane Eyre, or the speaker of "Only the Dead Know Brooklyn" by Thomas Wolfe).

These are the main questions you will attempt to answer in your analysis of diction, though there may be others that will come naturally out of the passage you select. Your principal tools here are a dictionary, your reading experience, and your alertness. Be on the lookout for relationships, but do not invent them if they do not exist. Be ready to take the hints provided you by the author.

Organizing Your Theme

Your theme should have the following points. In the body you may arrange your analysis into any order you wish. Please recognize that even though the theme is a general one on style, any one of the points in the body could easily be developed into an extensive theme in its own right.

INTRODUCTION

A brief description of the work from which you have selected the passage you will analyze, followed by a brief discussion of the purpose and intent of the passage you have selected, will suffice. Many of the questions you need to answer are in the opening section of the prosodic analysis (see pp. 186–87). The main point to answer here, however, is "What is the relationship of my passage to the work as a whole? What was the passage trying to do, and how well did it succeed?"

BODY

In this section you should consider three points.

1. The grammar of your passage. You should also observe the lengths of the sentences, but try to make your count point toward worthwhile conclusions. By modern standards, an average sentence is about twenty words long. If you have five sentences of, say, a ten-word aver-

age, with lengths from five to fifteen words, you may say that the sentences are short, terse, sparse, laconic, brief. If, on the other hand, the sentences average fifty words, you can say that they are full, round, rotund, or perhaps wordy or rambling.

2. The rhythm and sound of the passage. You may wish to integrate this discussion with your consideration of grammar and punctuation, as grammatical and phraseological units dictate rhythms. Perhaps you might be observing a long sentence characterized by many extensive rhythmical units, as in the following by Edmund Burke:

> I am convinced we have a degree of delight, and that no small one, in the real misfortunes and pains of others; for let the affection be what it will in appearance, if it does not make us shun such objects, if on the contrary it induces us to approach them, if it makes us dwell upon them, in this I conceive we must have a delight or pleasure of some species or other in contemplating objects of this kind.
>
> —*A Philosophical Enquiry Into The Origin Of Our Ideas Of The Sublime And Beautiful,* Section XIV

Or perhaps you are reading short sentences and rhythms, as in this passage from John Webster:

> Now you're brave fellows. Caesar's fortune was harder than Pompey's: Caesar died in the arms of prosperity, Pompey at the feet of disgrace.
>
> —*The Duchess of Malfi,* V, v, 57–61

Study your passage carefully and observe not only the rhythms but the sounds. The sample theme, analyzing a passage from Faulkner, points out instances of alliteration and assonance. If you study your passage carefully you should make worthwhile and interesting conclusions.

3. The diction. This section might well be the longest, for you are always aware of problems of meaning. Discuss the diction in context and try to make observations about its relationship to the thought and intent of the passage.

CONCLUSION

Make a concluding evaluation of the style—a summary of your findings. How well did the passage contribute to the entire work? If it did not contribute much, did it detract?

Hints

1. This theme is designed to increase your perceptions, sensitivity, and appreciation. Listen carefully; read carefully; try to feel the full force of the passage you select.

2. Make a copy of your passage and place it at the start of your theme.

3. Number each sentence in your passage.

4. When you write, use quotations to illustrate your points. Do not just quote in a vacuum, however, but explain your point and make your analysis before or immediately after your quotation.

5. *Underline* all elements to which you wish to draw attention.

6. Always indicate the sentence numbers of your quotations.

SAMPLE THEME

An Analysis of the Prose Style in the
Last Paragraph of Chapter 20 in
William Faulkner's Light in August [7]

> [1] It is as though they had merely waited until he could find something to pant with, to be reaffirmed in trumph and desire with, with this last left of honor and pride and life. [2] He hears above his heart the thunder increase, myriad and drumming. [3] Like a long sighing of wind in trees it begins, then they sweep into sight, borne now upon a cloud of phantom dust. [4] They rush past, forward-leaning in the saddles, with brandished arms, beneath whipping ribbons from slanted and eager lances; with tumult and soundless yelling they sweep past like a tide whose crest is jagged with the wild heads of horses and the brandished arms of men like the crater of the world in explosion. [5] They rush past, are gone; the dust swirls skyward sucking, fades away into the night which has fully come. [6] Yet, leaning forward in the window, his bandaged head huge and without depth upon the twin blobs of his hands upon the ledge, it seems to him that he still hears them: the wild bugles and the clashing sabres and the dying thunder of hooves.

The passage I have selected is the concluding paragraph of the Joe Christmas-Gail Hightower story in Faulkner's *Light in August*. The paragraph, in the present tense, describes Hightower's dying thoughts, which are passing from consideration of the apotheosis of Joe Christmas to the galloping cavalry. This vision of the cavalry had earlier been Hightower's plague, but here it indicates his mental "triumph and desire." Previously vague and by some thought to be sacrilegious, the men and horses now illustrate Hightower's final vision of truth—namely, that all men are brothers and that human life at any moment is on a grand crest rushing toward a final, glorious shore. Just as Hightower's vision is affirmative and grand, so should Faulkner's style be affirmative and bold. It should illustrate the power of language, and my belief is that it does.

---

[7] From *Light in August,* by William Faulkner (New York: The Modern Library, 1950), pp. 431–32. Copyright 1932 and renewed 1959 by William Faulkner. Reprinted by permission of Random House, Inc.

The grammar, for example, is carefully controlled. None of the six sentences is exactly like any of the others, although sentences 4 and 5 begin in the same way. The entire passage is framed by two complex sentences (1 and 6), and sentence 5 is a long compound-complex sentence. Sentence 2 is simple, and sentences 3 and 5 are compound (although neither of these compound sentences has a conjunction joining the two independent clauses). All the sentences show care, skill, variety, and boldness. The first sentence, for example, is unusual and interesting. At the end of the adverb clause in this sentence Faulkner uses the word *with*, ordinarily a preposition, and then repeats it at the end of the infinitive phrase, as though to emphasize his boldness:

> until he could find something to pant *with*, to be reaffirmed in triumph and desire *with*, ...

Then he uses *with* again immediately, but now in its ordinary position as a preposition:

> *with* this last left of honor and pride and life.

This usage gives the passage both weight and emphasis.

Another strong device in the paragraph is the use of single and parallel modifiers following the word they modify. Thus, we have

> the thunder . . . , *myriad* and *drumming* . . . .

When the galloping cavalry comes by,

> They rush past, (1) *forwardleaning in the saddles,* (2) *with brandished arms,* (3) *beneath whipping ribbons* . . . (sentence 4).

This pattern of "back" modifiers is one of the most characteristic in Faulkner, as is also another pattern (also shown in the quotation from sentence 4), that of grammatical units appearing in three, frequently connected by the conjunction *and*, as in:

> honor *and* pride *and* life

and

> the wild bugles *and* the clashing sabres *and* the dying thunder of hooves.

One might notice that in this paragraph, of six sentences, these two patterns of three occur at the beginning and the end, as though Faulkner were making a neatly balanced frame.

Balance and control, in fact, are also characteristic of the rhythms in the paragraph. The passage is full, and the pauses are correctly and judiciously placed; the voice is therefore measured into fairly full but varied cadence groups. The fullest group is the second part of sentence 4. This segment is breathtaking, perfectly in keeping with the massive advance of the galloping cavalry. With the last pause of the voice falling after *past,* there are twenty-seven words that must be spoken without a significant pause—an extremely long and full rhythmical development giving an almost panoramic sweep of the cavalry:

> like a tide whose crest is jagged with the wild heads of horses and the brandished arms of men like the crater of the world in explosion.

To be contrasted with his long, broad rhythm is the almost abrupt rhythm in the next sentence:

> They rush past,
>   are gone;
>   the dust swirls skyward sucking,
>   fades away into the night
>   which has fully come.

Also, since Hightower feels that he is dying, it is interesting to note the many falling (i.e., dying) rhythms in the concluding words;

that is: *wild bugles, dashing sabres, dying thunder.* But the passage concludes on an up-beat, a note of resurrection, well in keeping with the movement of apotheosis developed by Faulkner throughout the entire chapter:

the dying thunder of hooves.

In accord with this almost poetic control over rhythm, the sounds of the passage have many poetic characteristics. Faulkner uses assonance and alliteration in almost every line. Assonance appears in the long $\bar{i}$ of f*i*nd, tr*i*umph, des*i*re, pr*i*de, l*i*fe (sentence 1); the short $\breve{u}$ in th*u*nder, dr*u*mming, r*u*st, d*u*st, s*u*cking, c*o*me (2 and 5); the *ou* diphthong in n*ow,* and cl*ou*d (3); and the short $\breve{a}$ in s*a*ddles, br*a*ndished, and sl*a*nted (4). Alliteration appears in *l*ast *l*eft (1); *h*ears, *h*eart, *h*eard, *h*uge, *h*ands, *h*ears (2 and 6); and *s*ighing, *s*weep, *s*ight, *s*wirls, *s*kyward, *s*ucking (3 and 5). These patterns cannot be overlooked, and coming as they do in this climactic paragraph, they greatly emphasize the grand, "poetic" vision of the expiring Hightower.

The mastery already described is also apparent in the diction, which leads from mainly abstract words in the first two sentences to mainly concrete words in the last four. Yet amid the concreteness of Hightower's vision of the cavalry, Faulkner puts words that stress its abstractness. The dust is *phantom dust,* and the yelling of the cavalrymen is *soundless*. In addition, the parallel verbs describing the movement of the horses are rather muffled and for this reason permit the suggestion that they are phantom-like to work:

they *sweep* into sight (3)
They *rush* past (4)
they *sweep* past (4)
They *rush* past (5)
        are gone (5)

The greatest virtue of Faulkner's diction in the paragraph is its active, bold vividness, however. The language is virtually fearless in these phrases:

the crater of the world in explosion (4)
this last left of honor and pride and life (1)
the dust swirls skyward sucking (5)
forwardleaning in the saddles (4)

It takes bold, original thinking, and much confidence, to use language in this way. All the phrases are new, accurate, and fresh. Other phrases are remarkably vivid. My favorites are:

the dying thunder of hooves (6)
beneath whipping ribbons from slanted and eager lances (4).

It takes something great to think of *eager* lances. But my comments are superfluous here.

All in all, this paragraph gleams out of the page. When I first read it for this theme I perhaps *sensed* this quality, but after having analyzed the grammar, rhythm, sound, and diction, I am amazed at how well the paragraph wears. Each time I re-read it, I recognize more and more of the real scope of a master prose stylist, and Faulkner is that. The paragraph is alive, quick. It is a fitting and brilliant conclusion to the Joe Christmas strand of *Light in August*.

The Theme Analyzing
HISTORICAL PERIOD

CHAPTER

15

Everything written, spoken, painted, or composed reflects to some degree the historical period of its composition. Indeed, we cannot open our mouths without showing attitudes, idioms, and customs of our time and place. Everything belongs in its era, whether as a revolutionary idea, reaction, or synthesis; and a major job of the disciplined reader is to understand the relationship of historical movements and artistic works. On the professional level, the record of this relationship is literary history, which is in effect the chronicling of the interaction of ideas, events, and literary modes. To study a work of literature in historical perspective is to determine the degree to which the work belongs in, and transcends, its period.

In order to carry out such a study it is necessary to have some philosophy of how literature is related to its era. You might consider first the obvious fact that as circumstances change, writers express attitudes toward these changes in literary works. One aspect of the historical approach to literature is to chronicle events and literary responses to them. In addition, you might also assume that artists themselves desire to create new ideas from existing ones and to press for improvement and reform in society. A permanent standard of judging art is its newness; that is, its status of being different, and artists are always trying to meet this standard. To the degree that writers of the past (and present) have been successful, it becomes possible to place their works in historical perspective, in the light of change at least, if not of definite progress.

Analyzing a literary work as it reflects its historical period, then, becomes the task first of determining what can be clearly deducible as coming directly out of its time, and second of deciding what is new and permanent—that is, of determining what has been created by the author of the work from ideas prevalent at the time of composition. The concern is to see both the similarity and dissimilarity of a work and its period.

Such a study of literature is valuable because it promotes the realization that ideas and ways of seeing the universe change with time and place. Too often it is easy to read texts as though they were all written last week and to attribute to writers ideas that they never had. Shakespeare as well as Swift and Pope, for example, had a number of political ideas, but they did not know about representative government as we know it today. Therefore, in considering works of theirs that touch the subject of politics, you should understand why they emphasize the importance of a just and strong monarch or the necessity of a moral aristocracy. We can enthusiastically accept their ideas that wise rulers and moral people are necessary for monarchical or aristocratic forms of government, even though we today reject these forms in favor of democracy.

The idea of reading works in historical perspective is not, however, to file them away in a historical pigeon-hole but to improve understanding of the entire work in its context. The aim is to produce accuracy of reading and of judgments and to avoid errors that result from failure to see that artists respond to their own times and frequently are bound to these times. As an example, some people have objected to Plato's ideas about an ideal republic because Plato does not rule out the custom of slavery. Therefore, they say, his ideas are invalid. Aside from the logical impossibility of this argument, simple historical consideration makes one realize that Plato had not known and did not envisage any other society but one containing slavery (this aspect of his society is, to us, dated). Once this judgment is made, most of Plato's thought assumes great relevance and importance. Historical analysis, in other words, permits you to concentrate on the more vital aspects of a work and to distinguish these from others that are imprisoned within their historical moments.

Preparing for Your Theme

The first part of your task is to read the assigned work and settle any difficulties that you may encounter in it. Next you decide what is topical about the work. Making such a decision is easy for some works, particularly those written recently. *The Grapes of Wrath,* for example, is readily seen in relation to problems of the rural, unskilled poor in America in the 1930's. Walter Van Tilburg Clark's story "The Portable Phonograph," although set under circumstances that have not come to pass, may be easily related to modern apprehensions about the disastrous effects of nuclear war.

Some modern works, however, may offer special difficulties because of their topicality; that is, some works are so closely connected with ideas and assumptions of your own that you may not readily see them in historical perspective. It is difficult to realize that our own country and age may not embody all the goals of human history. Katherine Mansfield's short story "Bliss," for example, is a searching analysis of the causes for the deterioration of a marriage. If this story seems more concerned with permanent than topical aspects of human life, you might consider that the main female character is drawn as a person who has received a certain kind of education and a certain set of values about sexual relationships. You might also consider that the institution of marriage itself is a custom that at one time was enforced by sacramental power that within this century has been losing absolute influence. Furthermore, marriage has not always been accepted by all societies at all times as the principal form of relationship between men and women. Therefore, even in such a story, which at first seems difficult to analyze in relation to history, there are materials on which to base a theme.

Other problems might arise when the work assigned is remote either in history or in place. There is a view, for example, which holds that Shakespeare's history plays were created at least partially as a defense of the Tudor monarchs' claims on the English throne. Certainly an analysis of *Henry V* in relation to its historical period would have to take this view into account.

To the degree that works like Shakespeare's history plays are written to describe and frequently to romanticize past times, they bring up another problem; namely, that of determining the relationship of noncontemporary materials to contemporary times. Browning's poem "My Last Duchess" is such a work. It was published in 1842, but its subject is a Renaissance Italian nobleman. In such works, however, the subject matter brings out ideals and attitudes of the writer, and these can then be related to the time in which the work was written, which is the only relevant time for the purpose of this theme. Thus, from the character of Browning's duke, who is callous and self-centered and who wields despotic power, it is apparent that Browning is suggesting that absolute power produces destructive results on both the individual wielding it and those around him. Specifically, Browning was writing this poem for an age that had produced Napoleon and that a year before "My Last Duchess" had seen the publication of Thomas Carlyle's lectures on *Heroes, Hero Worship, and the Heroic in History.* Browning's presentation of the duke can therefore be analyzed as something more than a dramatic study of a powerful eccentric of past times, although because of the developing concerns during the period with psychology, one could also make a good case for the poem simply as a psychological study.

Acquiring the Necessary
Background Information

A question naturally arises about the assignment to relate a work to its historical period. This is: "How do I acquire the necessary information to write the theme?"

In response to this question, it is important to realize that the major source of your information is the work itself. In your reading you can discover a great deal about the period of the author and more important about the place of the work in that period. You need to ask, and answer, a number of questions such as: Are historical circumstances specifically mentioned? What are they? What does the author say about them? Does the writer describe conditions with photographic detail, or is he less concerned with details and more with human problems? To what social class do the principal characters belong? What is their social and educational background? What values do they hold or represent? Are the characters religious or not? Is the principal character (or any character) an important part of the prevailing social and economic system as outlined in the work, or is he an outsider? If he is outside the system, what conditions have put and now keep him there? Are you made to feel pleased or angry with these conditions? Does the character eventually win a place in the system, or is he broken by it? What assumptions do you think the author had about the literary interests of his audience? That is, does it seem that the author wrote for a sophisticated audience, a simple-minded one, or a sensation-seeking one? What conclusions can you draw, on the basis of your answers to these and like questions, about the author's attitudes toward his times? Does he attempt to give a complete view or a partial view? Does he seem to be recommending values that are similar, or contrary, to those held during his era?

From questions such as these you will soon discover a suitable topic, for there is need here as always for narrowing the focus of your discussion. For example, a question about the fortunes of a particular character can lead to an avenue of inquiry like the following: Does the successful termination of Oliver Twist's difficulties reflect an optimistic or romantic idea about opportunities presented by nineteenth-century English society? Similarly, how can the misfortune of Tom Joad in *The Grapes of Wrath* be shown to reflect Steinbeck's views about American politics in the 1930's? Events or situations themselves can be focused in the same way. The details about Stephen's homelife in Joyce's *A Portrait of the Artist as a Young Man* might suggest a topic like "The Deleterious Effect of Dublin Homelife on the Individual." Franz Kafka's description of the machine in "In the Penal Colony" might lead you to pursue a topic of how the story reflects a disillusionment with the increasing technology and bureaucracy of the twentieth century. Your following through on questions like these should enable you to develop an interesting and relevant topic.

This use of the work of literature itself as an authority for your remarks in the theme may seem open to the objection that literary works are often not reliable as actual source material for history. Sometimes works contain exaggerations made for comic or satiric effect, and sometimes they develop out of improbable circumstances. As history therefore the close study of a literary work is a weak substitute for more accurate documentation.

The answer to this objection—and an important realization for you to make—is that the focus of this assignment *is* the work itself. Your theme is about the historical period only as it is reflected in the work. Your concern is not to use the work for evidence in writing history but rather as evidence of a literary reaction to historical circumstances. Even if there are exaggerations and caricature or if conditions reported are brighter or blacker than life, these very aspects of the work become an important part of the material you bring to your theme. Your aim should not be to use the work as a filter through which you attempt to acquire historical data but to determine to what use such observable data have been put within the work.

To see how this approach might operate, let us take the example of the character Hurstwood in Theodore Dreiser's novel *Sister Carrie* (1900). Hurstwood is first seen as a successful restaurateur, but in the course of the novel he slides down hill, eventually committing suicide after existing for a time on the Bowery. His decline is caused and aided by a number of accidental occurrences, mistakes in judgment, an unforgiving wife, and just bad luck. From these circumstances it seems clear that Dreiser's portrait of a soul in twilight is his attempt to show that human character, as manifested in high social position and apparent economic success, is a product of chance happenings, including those of birth and social class; remove the external props from a character and you in effect destroy him. From this observation, it can be seen that this aspect of the novel reflects a period of history in which the social sciences were beginning to grow and in which character was seen as a variable, shifting with economic and psychological circumstances. By contrast, in Shakespeare's *The Tempest,* the character Prospero has been cast out of society for many years but is portrayed as having lost none of his kindness and benevolence. The same is true of Perdita in *The Winter's Tale;* brought up amid shepherds, her nobility comes to the front, her bucolic background having no harmful effect on her character. From this comparison, it seems clear that Shakespeare took for granted assumptions about character that Dreiser questioned, and that the ages that produced these two writers were influential in these differences. A comparison of this type should by no means be construed as inviting the claim that one age is superior to another or one writer to another; rather, it should serve to account for differences that can be seen in literary works.

Some types of literature are more readily approached from the historical point of view than others. Usually novels, short stories, narrative poems, dramas, and essays are fairly obviously rooted in customs and ideas of their time. Many of these works can be discussed without extensive reading in secondary historical sources. By contrast, many short lyric poems are not obviously connected with their respective periods, and to write about these works you must prepare yourself with research. In any event, a certain amount of research is helpful in making your remarks about a period more authoritative, and it follows that as you acquire more knowledge about a period, the more inventive and original will be your topics.

Thus, your own previous work with American history has probably familiarized you with the fact that the beginning of the present century witnesses the intellectual as well as economic growth of our nation. This much you could bring to a study of the previously mentioned decline of Hurstwood in *Sister Carrie*. But a reading of background information about Theodore Dreiser might disclose the fact that Dreiser was embodying in his novel a concept of "Social Darwinism"; that is, a belief that the principles governing both nature and society were similar. On another topic, one might find in reading literary history that the early twentieth century was an age in which authors, in responding to new ways of looking at the universe and new theories about it, wanted to create new idioms and new forms in literature. Such knowledge might interest you sufficiently to work out a topic like "The Age of Experimentation in Literature as Reflected in *A Portrait of the Artist as a Young Man.*"

So it is necessary to carry out a certain amount of research, although this research should be limited to finding more material about the topic you have selected for your theme. The first guide should be your instructor, who will be happy to answer whatever questions you may ask about the relevant period or who will direct you to books that will give you answers. Much of the knowledge you will apply for this theme will have been provided you by your instructor, through classroom discussion and lectures.

Of the books, the place to start is the introductory material provided in your text. Then you might go on to consult literary histories. For American works, start with Robert E. Spiller, Willard Thorp, Thomas H. Johnson, and Henry Seidel Canby, eds., *Literary History of the United States;* for British, see Albert C. Baugh, ed., *A Literary History of England.* Further work might be done in histories of the country and period of the author, and in general background works like J. H. Randall's

Making of the Modern Mind, E. M. W. Tillyard's *Elizabethan World Pictures,* Basil Willey's four books giving background on the seventeenth, eighteenth, and nineteenth centuries, Perry Miller's *The New England Mind,* and W. J. Cash's *The Mind of the South.* Still more can be done by consulting works listed in the selected bibliography of the edition you are using. If you need still more research, you might consult the *International Bibliography* published each spring in the *Publications of the Modern Language Association.* Further research can be carried out, but this theme, which is not primarily a research assignment, will usually not require it.[1]

Indeed, it is important once again to emphasize that the text itself is a major source of your knowledge of the period. Even if the reliability of the text as a source of information has been attacked (as with James Fenimore Cooper's *Leatherstocking Saga,* which was ridiculed by Mark Twain) that should not create a problem; your concern is to determine a relation of period to work that does not depend on the absolute reportorial accuracy in the work. Such inaccuracy, in fact, could form the basis for one of the ideas in your paper.

Organizing Your Theme

In the following plan the introduction will be proportionately longer than introductions usually are, because of the need for presenting detailed information about the work and its historical period. It is possible, of course, to merge the presentation of the historical data with the discussion of the work.

INTRODUCTION

In addition to defining your central idea and thesis sentence, your aim here is to place the work in its historical period. You should identify the work, state the time of its publication, and if known, its composition. If the work, say a poem or story, was included in a collection, you should mention this fact and should also describe, briefly, the nature of the collection in order to determine whether the work is typical of the author's work. You should also include any biographical data relevant to an understanding of the work. You should also state whether there are any special problems in discussing the work, such as that it is a historical novel, or a work remote in time, or that there is some controversy about the work.

[1] For a fuller discussion of research methods, consult Appendix C.

Next, you should state the pertinent historical facts concerning the events and ideas that you have selected for discussion. There is no need for extensive explanation, but only for those details that are relevant. If the body of your theme is to contain references to many events, you need not detail them here but should emphasize instead the general attitudes held at the time about the events. If your work was written during or shortly after a recent war, for example, you may assume that your reader knows as much generally about this war as you do and needs only those details that will remind him of his knowledge. Thus, if you are discussing *For Whom the Bell Tolls,* you might state that the book is set in Spain during the Spanish Civil War; you might then go on to state that this war was not only a civil war, but was also seen as an ideological one involving other world powers; that many people felt idealistically committed to what they considered the cause of freedom supported by the Loyalists; that these idealists were sometimes used cynically; that the war highlighted for many the idea that life and love were impermanent and fleeting; and that the war was wasteful and destructive. There is nothing unusual about these conclusions: the point about them is that they are general statements about the period rather than detailed descriptions. The risk you run with such statements is that they can easily become platitudes; the best defense against this danger is that you express the ideas as clearly and as accurately as you are able and that you select only those details that are relevant to your topic.

BODY

After presenting historical facts, you should apply them in the following way. Of the parts listed, you may include both or one or the other.

1. A discussion of how the work embodies the facts, or of how the facts shape the work. Thus, *For Whom the Bell Tolls* not only demonstrates the idealism and fears of Jordan but is also a narrative that tests his ideals and the ideals of those like him in real life. The novel can be seen as an assertion that such ideals are needed at the present historical moment, even though they are engaged in a losing action. Similarly, in discussing "My Last Duchess," you might show that the duke's conversational manners (his pre-empting the discussion of marriage details by reflecting on the portrait of his former duchess and his stating that his "just pretense" for a dowry will be acceptable) can be related to the assertion that the poem is an effective counter-argument to contemporary claims about the need for "great men" in political life. Browning's "great man" is so preoccupied with his own greatness that he listens to no one and loses all sense of human kindness.

2. As the first part of the body is concerned with ideas, the second is devoted to a discussion of literary matters (i.e., style, structure, tone, point of view, imagery, etc.) that can be related to the period. Thus, ideas about the need for personal freedom may be related to poems written in free verse. An awareness of the changeability of human emotions and the shrinking of the significance of the individual may be related to the unusual line-formation in the poetry of E. E. Cummings and to his use of the small *i* as a personal pronoun. The modern stress on psychoanalysis may account for the stream-of-consciousness novel, and the development of the camera and the newsreel movie may be related to the chapters entitled "The Camera Eye" and "Newsreel" in the novels of John Dos Passos. What is important here is to apply the facts that you have acquired to the literary characteristics of the text.

CONCLUSION

To conclude you should try to determine which elements that you have discussed are out of date and which ones are still relevant and important. For purposes of your conclusion, you may assume that your own point of view is modern and up to date, although you should assert yourself humbly and emphasize your broadmindedness. Thus, in this section you might attempt to determine how relevant or desirable is Hemingway's assertion that the world still needs heroic character and action. Has the world bypassed the need for a military demolition expert and gone on to a need for a conversational and diplomatic expert? Is there still a need for both? Are Hemingway's values timely or out of date? Do the techniques of Dos Passos help or hinder your reading of, say, *The Big Money?* Is the manner of E. E. Cummings effective, or does it now seem eccentric? These are like the questions you might ask and attempt to answer in your conclusion.

SAMPLE THEME

A View of Nature and Individualism:
The Relationship of Wordsworth's
"Tintern Abbey Lines" and Its Time [2]

"Lines Composed a Few Miles Above Tintern Abbey, On Revisiting the Banks of the Wye During a Tour, July 13, 1798," by

---

[2] *The Complete Poetical Works of Wordsworth*, A. J. George, ed. (Boston: Houghton Mifflin Co., 1932), pp. 91–93. Parenthetical page numbers and line numbers refer to this edition.

William Wordsworth, was first published in *Lyrical Ballads,* the collection of poems by Wordsworth and Coleridge that marked the Romantic revolution against eighteenth-century poetry. The poem itself is religious but nonsectarian: it speaks about the relationship of past, present, and future and also about the origin of the good and moral forces that influence the individual. Wordsworth says that the occasion of his writing was a visit he paid to Tintern Abbey while on a walking trip across England (p. 91). As he continued his journey, he composed and finished the poem, committing it to paper only after he reached Bristol. The poem is thus a reflection on a highly personal experience. The expression of the idea that such individual experience leads to the highest moral good is the principal idea tying the poem to its period, which was a time of great emphasis on individual worth and on the importance of individual effort to attain truth.

At the time the poem was written, the trend in thought had been more and more focused on the importance of the individual. Philosophy, religion, politics, science, and historical events had all converged to produce the idea that individual human beings were important. Democracy in America and the revolution in France were based on the notion that the individual should have as much liberty as possible. "Inner light" theories, about how the individual could directly apprehend the mysteries of the universe, had been common in some religious faiths for more than a century. Science had opened the book of Nature and had been reading its mysteries with the aid of the physical and mathematical theories of Newton, and also with the aid of the discoveries of chemical elements. It was natural to conclude that truth could thus be found by men directly through their own inquiries and that the avenues to truth were still open both scientifically and religiously. The modern studies of psychology, sociology, and anthropology had not yet been developed, so that the mood of optimism about breaking with the past, and thereby giving man an opportunity to flower, had not yet been attacked. Generally, many people in the age when Wordsworth wrote his poem would subscribe to the notion that a single human being, standing alone, could apprehend the truths of the universe. Science of course emphasized scientific methods of attaining truth, but religion was strong, and it emphasized prophetic, nonrational means.

It is the nonrational avenue to truth and morality that is explored fully by Wordsworth in the poem. He uses himself, or perhaps rather a noble concept of himself, as the basis of his assertions. Assuming that truth and morality are necessary qualities, and also assuming that he, the speaker, is a good individual, he proceeds to inquire into the causes for his goodness. In keeping with the general recognition of the need for independence and change during the revolutionary period, he does not mention the many cultural elements that influence character for the good, but isolates only one; namely, his immediate experiences, and specifically experiences like seeing the banks of the Wye at Tintern Abbey. He concludes that his experience has improved him in two ways, first by giving him immediate pleasure, and second by providing him with retrospective pleasure.

The really major idea in the poem, and the idea that Wordsworth felt deeply and proclaimed with eloquence, is that this retrospective pleasure is a cause of restorative, creative power within the individual. Much of the first part of the poem is given over to a description of the speaker when in the state of tranquillity that produces this pleasure. Wordsworth describes it as a condition in which the "affections gently lead us on,"

> Until, the breath of this corporeal frame
> And even the motion of our human blood
> Almost suspended, we are laid asleep
> In body, and become a living soul:
> While with an eye made quiet by the power
> Of harmony, and the deep power of joy
> We see into the life of things.

—lines 42–49

To the degree that Wordsworth describes his own physical state during such moments of prophetic insight, the poem is purely individual and nonhistorical. But his idea of what takes place in these moments is not personal but is in keeping with many ideas of the time; it is akin to theories of divine inspiration—inner light—and is also like the ideas of inspiration that gave the books of the Bible their authority. Then, too, Wordsworth's fellow romantic poet, Keats, described the idea that beauty struck the individual from a "penetralium of mystery"; that is, through a process that was nonrational and mysterious. Wordsworth's poem thus reflects the contemporary thinking that the individual was not alone; forces were acting on him that were inherent in, and simultaneous with, experience of Nature. The moral effect of this force, however, could be felt only through reflection and free association, not through scientific processes.

This attempt to interpret his own experience makes Wordsworth's poem particularly timely in his own day. He wrote from the point of view of a person highly aware of the connection between himself and the universe—the type of individual who could test the revolutionary theories. It is natural then that Wordsworth would avoid mentioning all the external influences that had been previously thought to act on a person, and would emphasize the idea that goodness could best be gained through direct experience with nature and the forces transcending nature. Wordsworth is not so revolutionary that he denies the need for faith, but his faith results from a belief in the need for a spontaneous, original, unique realignment of the individual with the universe—a faith in "nature and the language of the sense" as the "nurse,/The guide, the guardian of . . . [his] heart, and soul / Of all . . . [his] moral being" (ll. 108–111). Each man must make his own faith, and must not accept formalized, ready-made answers as codified in tradition.

Wordsworth's diction is rooted in these individual ideas. In the "Preface to the Lyrical Ballads" he stated that the language of poetry and prose should be the same. That is, poetic diction should be as clear and as close to the objects described as the nature of language permitted (pp. 791–93). Accordingly, his perception in the "Tintern Abbey Lines" of the transcendent presence in the universe is couched in simple words: "setting suns," "round ocean," "living air," "blue sky," and "mind of man." His verse patterns, too, are the result of an attempt to create a medium in which a free voice could explore the effects of experience. He avoided the couplet, which had been a favorite form in the eighteenth century. The idea was to write about present issues without hindrances either of the thought or of the poetic conventions created by men of previous ages.

Wordsworth's "Tintern Abbey Lines" can thus be seen as part of a revolutionary and individualistic set of ideas that came about at the end of the eighteenth century. The principal shortcoming of the ideas, which time has exposed, is the optimism about the ease with which the individual may become moral. The poem, however, is fresh and powerful, and by no means dated. Although Wordsworth's theory that the individual could directly experience the Spirit of the Universe is not easily confirmed today, there are many persons who believe that such experience may be gained through prayer, if not through any other means. Many people in our present age of science and technology tend to be skeptical of nonrational processes of learning and therefore admire Wordsworth's poem principally for its natural descriptions and secondarily for its hints about divine power. The full theological implications of the poem may be easily ignored. The poetic practice and the theory of language behind it, fortunately, are still in the highest repute because they adhere so successfully to common sense. The strength of the poem may yet give it greater acceptance in some future age less committed to scientific method than our own. It is not the poem that is dated, but perhaps ourselves.

The Theme of
EVALUATION

CHAPTER

16

The ultimate goal of all literary study is evaluation. Evaluation is closely allied with *judgment,* which is the faculty by which we can distinguish between good and bad, right and wrong, plausibility and implausibility, and so on. *Evaluation,* as used here, means the act of deciding what is good, bad, or mediocre. It requires a steady pursuit of the best—to be satisfied with less is to deny the best efforts of our greatest writers. Evaluation implies that there are ideal standards of excellence by which decisions about quality can be made, but it must be remembered that these standards are flexible in their application and may be applicable to works of literature written in all places and ages.

Although evaluation is the goal of literary study, description is the means by which the goal is reached. Without evaluation and appreciation, however, the description of idea, form, and style is really beside the point; it becomes a peripheral issue, a vacuum. Too often a good student will avoid making any judgments or commitments at all, although he may beautifully describe, say, the prosody of a poem. Quite frequently, too, he feels comfortable as he goes about his discussion, because description, in contrast to evaluation, is "safe"; it does not require him to "go out on a limb." Evaluation frequently requires taking a debatable position, which others might degrade. No one likes to be exposed, even by someone else's assertion that an equally valid alternative exists.

Despite the obvious dangers and difficulties of evaluation you must take positions on the works you read. Not to do so is to avoid the most vital pattern in your educational development. You yourself must learn to decide what is good and not always to rely on your instructor to tell you. If you lose yourself in pure description, or if you merely take the safe way by following someone else's judgment, you are not doing the best for yourself. You need to develop your intellectual courage. Certainly during much of your career as a student you can get by with the simple statement, "This work is a great one," because most of the works you read are literary classics. But the perfunctory comment "This is great" is not enough, for you should always try to discover just what are the grounds for judgment. Your study of the classics should certainly be more than perfunctory. You should always attempt to learn what is good in good works, so that you will have grounds for evaluating and appreciating works that are not yet accepted as classics—recent works, or works by relatively unknown authors, or lesser works by well-known authors. Remember, you will not always be taking literature courses, and when you are on your own you will want to know how to judge for yourself.

You may sometimes find that works commonly adjudged to be good do not seem good to you. If such is the case, try to live with the work for a time. If you have ever played in a band or orchestra, or sung in a chorus, you surely have found some musical compositions distasteful when you first read them through. But as you reapproached the composition day after day, and worked on it and learned it, you probably discovered that you became fond of the work and that you finally became convinced of its value. This process confirms the statement that you will learn to understand and to like a good work of art when you have the opportunity to do so. If, however, you find that despite prolonged exposure to the work, you still do not concur in the general favorable judgment, be as certain as you can that your reaction is based on rational and logically defensible grounds.

You should realize too that your ability to judge will be increased as you learn about more and more fine works. You must read and learn as much as you can, for in this way you will be establishing the qualities of good literature firmly in your mind, and, naturally, as these qualities become clearer to you, you will be able to evaluate with greater ease. Now, you have the task of evaluating a single work for your theme. This single assignment should have a definite bearing on your judgment in future years, because careful effort now will permanently improve your critical faculties. Your instructor does not expect you to judge like a great critic, but he does expect that you bring to bear on your work all the ideas about good literature that you have acquired.

Rationale of Evaluation

There is no precise answer to the problem of how to justify an evaluation, and you would be misled if you were told that there is. Consequently evaluation is the most abstract, philosophical, and difficult writing you will do about literature, just as it is the most necessary. We must recognize that standards of taste, social mores, and even morals differ from society to society and age to age; nonetheless, some works of art have been adjudged good or even great by generation after generation, whereas others have been consigned to that vast dustbin "of historical interest only." The student therefore asks, "By what standards may a work be judged a good or great work?" and, "How do I make this judgment by myself?"

Task of Evaluation

In your theme you must ask: "Is the work I have read good, fair, or bad?" or, "Is it beautiful or not?" You must answer this question on artistic, not ideological grounds. In other words, you might say that a political speech does a good job of rousing the populace to vote a certain way, and as a result that it is a good—and here you probably mean *effective*—speech. But in claiming that it is a great work of art you would have to judge it on artistic grounds, not on political ones; you would in addition have to determine whether it was important not only for the moment but for all moments. As very few speeches transcend their era, most speeches are not great works of art.

In admiring a work, then, you must consider whether you have been misled by an excellence that is really minor. An atrocious piece of literature might exhibit a superb control over form, for example, and you might suppose it to be good. But if other considerations caused you to withhold your total assent from the work, this supposition would be foolish. In short, you must consider everything about the work you evaluate and not be diverted from your object by surface beauties.

Standards for Evaluation

There are many standards to help you evaluate a literary work. Some of the major ones are described below, and many have been suggested in earlier chapters. The terms involved are used and defined here in the senses to which they are usually restricted by people talking about literature. To the philosopher, the aesthetician, the student of semantics, the words are probably charged with other meanings, and a treatment of those meanings would necessitate a whole philosophical treatise. It should be emphasized, however, that one cannot think intelligently or seriously about literature without using these terms, and it is to help you interpret these words as they are generally used in regard to literature that they are included here.

TRUTH

Although *truth* or *truthful* is used in speaking of literature to mean *realism* or *realistic* (e.g., does Flaubert give a truthful picture of Emma Bovary's society?), its meaning here is restricted carefully. To speak of the truth is to imply generality and universality. Let us take a concrete illustration.

Sophocles' *Antigone* is a play that has survived the passage of 2,400 years. It concerns a society (the Greek city-state with a ruling monarch) that no longer exists; it deals with a religious belief (that the souls of the unburied dead never find rest) that passed from currency centuries ago; it involves an idea (of a curse following an entire family) accepted now only by the least educated members of our society. Wherein, then, lies the appeal, the truth, of *Antigone,* which makes it as much alive for our age as it was for the Greeks of more than 2,000 years ago?

The answer is at least partly in the permanence of the human problem that Antigone faces: "How do I reconcile my duty to obey the state with my duty to obey my conscience? And if the two conflict, which do I follow?" This dilemma, and the suffering inevitable for any man caught in it, regardless of which choice he makes, is one that men have probably faced since the beginning of time; while men and states exist, this conflict between laws and conscience will endure—and so will the great statement of that problem given in *Antigone*. In short, the play embodies, lives in terms of, and comments on, one of the great *truths* of human life. It measures up, then, to one standard we use in deciding whether a work of art is good or bad, great or mediocre. But other criteria must also be considered.

AFFIRMATIVENESS

Affirmativeness means here that human beings are worth caring about and writing about, no matter how debased the condition in which they live or how totally they abuse their state. All art should be affirmative. Although many works apparently say "no" to life, most say "yes," and a good argument can be made that the "no" works indirectly present a "yes." Thus, if a character like Macbeth or Hurstwood falls to the depths of misfortune, despair, and death, the author must demonstrate that there is a loss of some sort worth lamenting. Human worth is here affirmed even as a major character loses it. If a character like Mirabel in

Congreve's play *The Way of the World* is happy and in good estate at the end of the work, the author must show that his character's qualities have justified his good fortune. Life is again affirmed. If an unworthy character is fortunate at the end, like Joe Gowland in A. J. Cronin's *The Stars Look Down,* the author still affirms human worth by suggesting a world in which such worth may become triumphant. In short, the author may portray the use and abuse of life, the love and the hate, the heights and the depths, but his vision is always that life is valuable and worthy of respect and dignity. The best works are those that make this affirmation forcefully, without being platitudinous or didactic.

"THE JOINT FORCE AND FULL RESULT OF ALL"

The above quotation is from Pope's *Essay on Criticism,* in which most of what can be said about evaluation is said. Pope insisted that a critic should not judge a work simply by its parts but should judge the *whole,* the entirety of the work. You can profit from Pope's wisdom. You should carefully consider the total effect of the work, both as an artistic form and as a cause of impressions and emotions in yourself. Your total impression is important. James Joyce used the concepts "whatness" and "radiance" in describing the totality of a work; that is, when a work seems to be entirely itself, the force of its totality impresses the reader in a moment of revelation, or radiance. Although this sort of experience is almost mystical, and consequently impossible to describe, you must search your reactions after reading a work and see if you have been impressed with a sense of totality. Bear in mind that a great work may be imperfect —there may be flaws in style and organization; characters may be imperfectly drawn—but if the sum total of the work is impressive, the flaws assume minor importance. In other words, even if the author can be attacked on technical matters, the total effect of his work may overshadow the adverse criticism. Thomas Hardy and Theodore Dreiser are two authors in point; their language can frequently be shown to be at fault, but a reading of their best works reveals them to be superior novelists.

You should see, then, that one cannot judge a work as good or bad by referring to only one element within it. An interesting plot, a carefully handled structure, a touching love story, a valid moral—none of these attributes alone can justify a total judgment of "good." One can say, for example, that Dickens' *Oliver Twist* has an extremely ingenious plot and that it arouses our emotions effectively. But to evaluate the novel fully one must take into consideration several questions. Foremost among them are these: How does the character of Oliver withstand modern knowledge of child development? Could a child subjected from birth to the brutal experiences that Oliver endures develop into the person that Dickens presents? These considerations should make you realize that you cannot make a final judgment on the work as a whole without taking all its important aspects into account.

Another important phase of the "joint force and full result of all" is the way in which you become involved as you read. Most of what you read, if it has merit, will cause you to become emotionally involved with the characters and actions. You have perhaps observed that characters in some works seem real to you or that incidents are described so vividly that you feel as though you had witnessed them. In these cases you were experiencing the pleasure of involvement. The problem here is whether your pleasure was fleeting and momentary ("just kicks"), or whether it has assumed more permanence (whether it resulted from a passage that is permanently, or spiritually, satisfying).

Your question in evaluating a work, therefore, is whether your involvement was justifiable. A work that is sentimental or melodramatic may involve you in the plights of the heroes and heroines, but when you finish it you may feel let down or betrayed, because your emotions have been expended in an obviously artificial situation. Many operatic plots suffer from this defect; considered alone they should be condemned, but no one would judge them independently of the music, because music is the ultimate cause of emotional involvement in opera.

Closely integrated with the idea of involvement is the Aristotelian theory of *purgation* or *catharsis* in tragedy. How do you regard the character of Macbeth when he kills Duncan, or of Othello when he strangles Desdemona? Shakespeare causes you to become involved with both heroes, and when they perform evil deeds your own conscience cries out for them to stop. The result, when the play is over, is a "purgation" of your emotions; that is, if you experience these plays well, you will also have experienced an emotional "drain," which has been caused by your involvement with character and action. You can see that the use to which a writer puts your involvement is important in your judgment of his works.

VITALITY

It may seem strange to ask if a work seems "alive" or not, but this question is valid. A good work of literature has a life of its own and can be compared to a human being. You know that your friends are always changing and growing, and that you learn more and more about them as your friendship progresses. A work of literature can grow in the sense that your repeated experience with it will produce insights that you did not have in your previous readings. A classic example of such a work is *Huckleberry Finn,* known to children as an exciting and funny story of adventure but known to adults as a profound story about the growth of a human soul. Another example is *Gulliver's Travels,* in which critics for two centuries have been finding new insights and beauties. It is naturally difficult for you to predict the future, but if you have based your present opinion on reasonable grounds and have determined that the work is good, you may conclude that within the work there will be "food for future years." In short, you may conclude that the work is vital.

BEAUTY

This word is another chameleon. Whole books have been devoted to an attempt to define *beauty,* and the branch of philosophy named aesthetics is concerned entirely with determining what is beautiful. Briefly, however, beauty is closely allied with unity, symmetry, harmony, and proportion. To discover the relationship of parts to whole—their logical and chronological and associational functions within the work—is to perceive beauty in a work.

In the eighteenth century there was an idea that "variety within order" constituted beauty; the extent to which Pope's couplets vary within the pattern of the neoclassic couplet is an illustration of the eighteenth-century ideal. The Romantic and post-Romantic periods held that beauty could be found only through greater freedom. This belief in freedom has produced such characteristics of modern literature as originality for its own sake, experimentation in verse and prose forms, freedom of syntax, stream-of-consciousness narration, and personal diction. Despite the apparent change of emphasis, however, the concepts of unity and proportion are still valid and applicable. Studies of style, structure, point of view, tone, and imagery are therefore all means to the goal of determining whether works are beautiful. Any one of these studies is an avenue toward evaluation. Remember, however, that an excellence in any one of them does not make a work excellent. Frequently critics use such terms as "facile" and "surface excellence" to describe what they judge to be technically correct but artistically imperfect works.

YOUR PREFERENCES

Although personal likes and dislikes are the least valid criteria for judgment, they are not to be excluded. They are the principal guides to what you read, but they are valueless when purely whimsical—without any basis in thought or knowledge. They become more valuable as they reflect mature thoughts based on knowledge. The more knowledge behind a preference, the more reliable it is, because the preference then stems not from a vacuum but from a deeply ingrained basis of comparison. The word of a well-educated adult on the value of a work is naturally more reliable than that of a child. Once you realize that your personal likes become more valuable as you learn more and grow, then these likes become more useful in evaluating literature.

In writing, you should carefully distinguish between evaluating a work and merely liking or disliking it. You will readily admit that you might dislike works that everyone maintains are good; similarly, you may like some works that you would admit were worthless. You have heard people say "Everyone to his taste," or "I know what I like," and thus justify their preferences on unreasonable grounds. There is much truth, of course, in the argument that "personal taste is king," because preference definitely plays a part in evaluation and appreciation. But if you are to become a literate, disciplined reader, you will realize that pure subjectivism is inadequate. Evaluation must be based on solid grounds, grounds on which most human beings, despite personality differences, can agree.

In your theme you do not need to emphasize your likes and dislikes as a separate point, but instead your discussion should permit you to make your feelings clear by implication. The only exception occurs if you are asserting your like despite faults, or your dislike despite excellences.

Organizing Your Theme

In your theme you will attempt to answer the question of whether the work you have studied is good or not. If so, why? If not, why not? The grounds for your evaluation must be artistic. Although some works may be good pieces of political argument, or successfully controversial, your business is to judge them as works of art.

INTRODUCTION

In the introduction you should briefly describe your evaluation, which will be your central idea, and you should describe the points by which you expect to demonstrate your idea. As the grounds for evaluation are many, you should also mention briefly those grounds that you are not going to discuss in the body of your theme.

BODY

In the body you will attempt to demonstrate the grounds for your evaluation. Your principal points will be the excellences or deficiencies of the work you are evaluating. Such excellencies might be qualities of style, idea, structure, character portrayal, logic, point of view, and so on. Your discussion will analyze the probability, truth, force, or power with which the work embodies these excellences.

Avoid the descent into synopsis or analysis for its own sake. If you are showing the excellence or deficiency of a character portrayal, you must necessarily bring in a description of the character, but remember that your discussion of the character is to be pointed toward *evaluation*, not *description*, of the work as a whole. Therefore you must select details for discussion that will illustrate whether the work is good or bad. Similarly, suppose you are evaluating a sonnet of Shakespeare and mention that the imagery is superb. At this point you might introduce some of the imagery, but your purpose is not to analyze imagery as such; it should be used only for illustration. If you remember, as a cardinal rule, to keep your thematic purpose foremost, you should have little difficulty in making your discussion relate to your central idea.

CONCLUSION

The conclusion should be a statement on the total result of the work you are evaluating. Your concern here is with total impressions. This part of evaluation should underline your central idea.

SAMPLE THEME

A People's Dream: An Evaluation of Black Elk Speaks [1]

Those who read *Black Elk Speaks* might recall the excitement of discovery that Keats felt when he first read Chapman's translation of Homer. The book is authenticity itself, a unique and powerful record of responses and recollections of an Oglala Sioux warrior and visionary, Black Elk. The period described is that between about 1867 and 1890, when the westward expansion produced the defeat and finally the humiliation of the Indian nations that had roamed the western prairies freely before that time. In 1931, Black Elk, then a man of 68, related his story to his son, who translated it into English to be transcribed by John G. Neihardt. Despite the fact that the account—is it autobiography, history, meditation, rev-

---

[1] All quotations and parenthetical page numbers refer to *Black Elk Speaks: Being the Life Story of a Holy Man of the Oglala Sioux, as told through John Neihardt (Flaming Rainbow), Illustrated by Standing Bear* (New York: Pocket Books, 1972).

elation, or all four?—is thus a translation and a transcription, its authenticity is self-evident everywhere; its uniqueness and power are manifest in the expression of values and in Black Elk's simple, direct eloquence.

As an historic account, *Black Elk Speaks* presents a view of history that is a truthful antidote to the typical view of the "Indian Wars" that the western movie has promoted (recent exceptions being films like *Little Big Man*). As Black Elk saw it, the *Wasichu's* (white man's) thirst for gold and for land produced violence, conquest, and broken promises. The military defeats by the U.S. Army turned Indian against Indian, and resulted in impoverishment, flight, and death by starvation or massacre. With their buffalo and their ponies gone, the Indians had little choice but move onto reservations. Though the victor has always made "right," it has rarely been little more than half right, and the direct, personal account of Black Elk provides a truthful restorative.

The work is also an account of Black Elk's inner vision of truth. Feeling that he had a unique role to play in the betterment of his Sioux nation, he apparently thought that the descriptions of his visions, the most important being his great revelation at the age of nine, were of principal value in his narration. He was a man with mystic powers and could use them to effect cures and to predict the future. Although a sophisticated reader might easily dismiss this aspect of the work as superstition, to deny the authenticity of Black Elk's descriptions of his powers would be tantamount to denying the authenticity of works such as *Kubla Khan, The Pilgrim's Progress,* and the Book of Revelation, to name only a few.

While the authenticity of Black Elk's visions is admittedly controversial, there can be no controversy about the power and wisdom of his values. Principally he expresses belief in valor and endurance and respect for life and for the land. Almost a thesis in his account is his claim that the Indians were living on their own land and desired only to be left alone, in a cooperative harmony between "two legs" (human beings) and "four legs" (the other animals). With such a value, it is natural that he would look with horror at the slaughter of the buffalo herds—a deliberate policy, incidentally, that the American government carried out in order to render the Indians helpless:

> . . . I can remember when the bison were so many that they could not be counted, but more and more Wasichus came to kill them until there were only heaps of bones scattered where they used to be. The Wasichus did not kill them to eat; they killed them for the metal that makes them crazy [gold], and they took only the hides to sell. Sometimes they did not even take the hides, only the tongues; and I have heard that fire-boats came down the Missouri River loaded with dried

bison tongues. You can see that the men who did this were crazy. Sometimes they did not even take the tongues; they just killed and killed because they liked to do that. When we hunted bison, we killed only what we needed. And when there was nothing left but heaps of bones, the Wasichus came and gathered up even the bones and sold them (p. 181).

It is difficult to see how anyone with a grain of respect for life could see the slaughter in any other way, and yet, through such actions, the west was "won." But perhaps the gentler values of Black Elk, who provided shelter for a family of porcupines on a freezing night (p. 130) and who described his attitudes with such directness, may eventually become prominent.

It is, finally, Black Elk's straightforward, direct eloquence that is the best, most convincing aspect of the book. Everything that one might require from a great writer is here: conciseness, accuracy, strong feeling, irony, humor, pathos, use of images, vividness. Nothing is done to excess; Black Elk is a lover of detail, but just the right amount, and he did not engage in his emotions to the point of sentimentality. For example, his description of the dead after the senseless slaughter at Wounded Knee (Dec. 29, 1890) displays controlled bitterness and pathos:

> It was a good winter day when all this happened. The sun was shining. But after the soldiers marched away from their dirty work, a heavy snow began to fall. The wind came up in the night. There was a big blizzard, and it grew very cold. The snow drifted deep in the crooked gulch, and it was one long grave of butchered women and children and babies, who had never done any harm and were only trying to run away (p. 223).

One might quote many other examples from the book to show Black Elk's mastery. Especially unforgettable are his description of the power of a circle (pp. 164 f.) and his lament over the loss of his people's dream (p. 230).

An evaluation of *Black Elk Speaks* would not be complete without an emphasis on its power to evoke an almost overwhelming sorrow and regret over the loss that it describes. Today people are finding much value in a pluralistic culture, and as a result the values represented by Black Elk seem more worthy than ever of being followed and cherished. It is painful, almost too painful for words, to read in Black Elk's narrative just how the civilization that held these values was snuffed out. Truly, a book that so successfully provokes these thoughts is worthy of being enshrined in one's heart. *Black Elk Speaks* demonstrates that there is a whole tradition that has been ignored in our histories of literature.

THE REVIEW

CHAPTER 17
A theme reviewing a work of literature—the *review*—is a general essay on the quality of a literary work. It may also be thought of as a "critique," a "critical review," or simply an "essay." It is a free form, for in a review virtually everything is relevant—subject matter, technique, social and intellectual background, biographical facts, relationship to other works by the same author or by different authors, historical importance, and everything else. Because your aim in writing a review should be to judge generally the author's performance, the theme closest in purpose to the review is the theme of evaluation (Chapter 16). The review is different, however, because of its general nature, and in this respect is like the report (Chapter 2). In the review, evaluation is only one of the aims, for there may be other elements of the work under surveillance that should be mentioned, special difficulties that you want to explain and special features that you want to note.

Since the review is so free, it is also a challenge to the skills you have developed thus far as a discipline reader. Much of your college experience to date has been assimilation—acquiring information and applying certain skills. Because many of your assignments have been relatively limited, your tasks have been mainly doing and not so much deciding what to do. But with a review, you are left much to your own devices; you must decide not only what to say, but what to write about. Freedom of choice —this goal should be your constant aim, and it is important for you to realize that your experience is equipping you to know more and more what to do with this freedom. You should be able to put together, to synthesize, the knowledge you are acquiring; you should not only know how to answer questions, but you should also be able to decide what questions should be asked.

Because the review is the form that gives you the greatest opportunity to exercise your ability to choose, it is perhaps the most individual kind of writing about literature. As you become more skilled, the reviews you write might become more and more personal, in the sense that your choice of topics for discussion and the material you bring to these topics will become unique. This accumulation of insight and applied facts is the cause of the interest that literary criticism can provide. Indeed, many reviewers have gained such familiarity with so much literature, and such sureness of critical perception, that their reviews have become important works worthy of independent study. Sometimes these reviewers use the work under consideration primarily as a launching pad from which they go into their own orbits. Hence, such reviews might be important personal meditations or philosophical or political discourses.

Because the review is the most personal as well as general theme about literature, and also because of a close tie with the commercial side of literature and other forms of entertainment, it is also one of the most common forms of critical writing. Most of the professional writing about literature in America today is reviewing. Newspapers, magazines, and even radio and television feature reviews. Performances of plays, musical compositions, art works, scholarly performances, scientific works, and of course works of imaginative literature are all subject to review.

The review may be thought of as the "first wave" of criticism, with other, more deeply considered criticism to follow later. One immediate problem of the review is therefore to keep it from becoming too hasty, too superficial. Alexander Pope was probably considering this problem when he wrote the following couplet about the frequency of reviews and the stupidity of some of the reviewers (in the passage, substitute "works of art" for "verse," and "reviews" for "prose"):

> A *Fool* might once *himself* alone expose,
> Now *One* in *Verse* makes many more in *Prose.*
>
> —*Essay on Criticism,* I.7,8

Of all the types of themes described in this book, the review is the one that you are most likely to be called on to write in your later, post-college careers, either by formal publications or by publications issued by professional groups or churches and clubs. You should certainly know what a good review is and should be able to write one on request. It is good to bear in mind that a good review is the product of the fusion of three elements: the attitudes and knowledge of the reviewer, the notable features of the work to be reviewed, and the audience for whom the review is written.

The Audience and Your Selection
of Material

If literature in fact attempts to reach human beings in their capacity as human beings, as Wordsworth said, then the review is the one type of critical writing that attempts to reach the broadest possible human audience. As many other academic and scientific disciplines become more refined, they also become less available to human beings, until finally specialists talk only to specialists about special problems. Whereas there is certainly a place for specialized writing about literature—and some of these later chapters have indicated how literary discussions can become technical—the student should remember that critical writing should always aim at a general, literate audience. The public that supports literature should benefit from the knowledge and best opinion of persons highly educated in literary studies. Although a product of technical methods, literary study should be used for cultivating public taste. The situation of the review, then, is one of the most important facing the critic. The aim should be to improve taste, to create a demand for excellence, and to approve the good and disapprove the bad.

The audience you are attempting to reach in your review is to be regarded as a group of equals who are generally about as well read and about as expert as you are. You may assume that these readers have not read the work you are reviewing, but you should also assume that they might read it or are about to start reading it. You should therefore act as an alert and perceptive commentator. You are, as it were, describing a course you have traversed for the benefit of those about to go the same course. If there are any points of interest or obstacles or detours, you should describe them. Your aim, however, is not to tell your reader so much as to make him feel that he now does not need to read the work himself. You should by no means "talk down" to him just because he is unfamiliar with the work to be reviewed, but there is no need for too technical a discussion. You should let the reader into the work a little, to tell him what he may expect to find. You should whet his curiosity, arouse his enthusiasm, make him feel that the work is indeed worthy of his spending his time in reading it himself.

The job of reaching your reader is indeed delicate, for you must strike the right note exactly; you must necessarily include a description of the events or principal ideas in the work, but you must not attempt to make your description exhaustive. Do not, for example, describe the final chapter of a book that has a surprise ending, as you would in a report. If the author draws a number of important conclusions, do not describe every one; concentrate only on one or two, leaving the rest to your reader to discover for himself. If your subject is a book of poems, do not discuss every poem, but concentrate only on those that seem important or typical.

Perhaps the best frame of mind you can muster before you begin to write is this: imagine that you are preparing your reader to read the work himself; imagine that you are providing him with parachute and rip cord, protective clothing, and the airplane ride, but that he himself must make the jump.

Organizing Your Theme

Your review should contain the following things, formed into a thematic structure.

INTRODUCTION

In this section you should place the work in perspective. In what period was it written? What is the nationality of the author (if he is of another nationality)? What kind of background knowledge is needed for an understanding of the work, or what kind, and how much, is supplied by the author (i.e., a knowledge of oil drilling, of conditions in the old West, etc.)? To what genre does the work belong? What general issues need explaining before you begin your discussion of the work? Although most frequently you will be asked to review a play or novel, it is good to bear in mind that you may also be reviewing techniques of acting and staging a play. If you are reviewing a new edition of an old work, you may be judging the relevance of the past to the present and also the scholarly helps provided by the editor (if you have a scholarly edition to review). Try always to show that your work has relevance to the present group of readers. Be sure to include your central idea and thesis sentence.

BODY

In the body of your theme you should try to arouse your reader's interest in the work you are reviewing or else to discourage him from reading the work if the work itself dictates this conclusion. Beyond providing the introductory information, your principal objective is to describe the strengths and weaknesses of the work. To write such a description you must call into play just about everything you have learned about analyzing literature for ideas, form, and style. In a sense, the review can be as specific as you wish to make it, for the greatest part of the body should be given to analysis. In this analysis, you may bring out your own strengths and interests as a critical reader. It may be, for example, that you have discovered in your literary studies that you have become proficient in discussing structure. If we suppose that you have observed a tightly knit structure in the work you are reviewing, you might choose to discuss that element in the body of your review, and thereby you would be appealing to your reader's response to artistic excellence. Similarly you may have enjoyed talking about imagery in poetry, and in reviewing a book of poems you might choose that for discussion. You should always recognize, however, that your discussion should be of limited extent. There is no need for a detailed, word-by-word analysis. It is not a theme of structure that you want, or one on imagery, but a review emphasizing these elements.

In certain instances or special cases you might also call into play certain disciplines that have interested you thus far in your college career. Your study of sociology, for example, may have led you to feel competent in handling ideas connected with that subject. Hence, in your review of a novel you might bring your sociological awareness to bear on the work. A discussion of *Studs Lonigan* or *The Autobiography of Malcolm X* would benefit from such an approach. Or you may have developed an interest in psychology, and may feel especially interested in treating the characters in a work according to your understanding of psychological problems.

Whatever your personal interests and specialties, however, the best guide for the subject matter of the body is the work itself, which may very well force you to make certain considerations. Obvious characteristics may necessitate the form of your discussion. In the sample theme, for example, the unusual features of the characters and the dialogue in Pinter's play *The Homecoming* literally shape the form of the review. The sample theme therefore touches on aspects of *character analysis* (Chapter 3) and *style* (Chapter 14), even though it is by no means a complete essay on either of these topics. Many readers of literature would probably also choose in a review to emphasize the characters and dialogue, but many might choose to discuss the bizarre humor, or the connection with existential philosophy, and so on.

In a type of review stemming from discussions of the work itself, the reviewer is less interested in pointing out features in the work reviewed than he is in presenting his own train of thought prompted by his reading of the work. A review of this type is not so much a review as it is a personal essay, which may take the form of (1) a consideration of the implications of the work, going beyond them into a more far-reaching discussion, or (2) a discussion stemming from dispute or disagreement with the conclusions or implications of the book. In this second type, the writer chooses to work from what he considers to be the flaws or shortcomings in the work being reviewed; in the first type, he considers the work as a thesis that he chooses to develop in his own way.

CONCLUSION

Your conclusion should be an attempt at evaluation of the work, certainly not as extensive as that in a theme of evaluation but at least an outline of your responses and a suggestion to your reader of how he might respond, granted that you have shown that your interests coincide approximately with his. If the body of your review has emphasized evaluation, you should close your essay with a simple résumé of your points. If you are ever asked to review a work in, say, no more than 150 words, the greatest part of the review, about 130 words, should be devoted to evaluation.

Hints

1. Whereas the discussion so far has emphasized the general audience—and this should be your aim—there are many situations in which reviewing may be done for specialized audiences. Reviews, and the organization of them, must be tailored according to the audience. To test this fact, try the following exercise. Suppose that you are going to write two reviews of the same work for two magazines designed to reach (a) a group of engineers, and (b) a religious group. It is to be assumed that these publications are aimed at persons in these groups not generally, in their capacities as human beings, but specifically, in their capacities as engineers or as followers of a faith. Therefore, would your reviews be the same for each group, or would one emphasize practical aspects of the work and the other religious aspects? To go on, suppose also that you are writing for groups interested in problems of (a) rural America, (b) the urban poor, (c) young adult courtship, (d) national politics, (e) international relations, (f) satire, (g) literary style, or (h) humor. You see that in each case (granted that the work you are reviewing would be relevant to all these groups) the materials you select for discussion would necessarily be dictated by the group you try to reach.

2. Perhaps the greatest problem in writing a review is that of preserving a thematic structure. The form itself poses this difficulty because of the general nature of the reviewing task. Therefore you must be especially cautious to state your central idea clearly somewhere in the first paragraph and keep returning to it throughout your review.

3. Most reviewing assignments will be about recent works of literature. Remember that your task is to apply standards of good literature to the work in front of you, with the general notion of determining how well the work stands up.

4. The techniques of writing a review may be applied to assignments in other courses. In a political science course, for example, you may be asked to write reviews of three books. Your aim in writing the reviews would be to assess the worth of the books as contributions to the study of political science. The same is true for books on philosophy, psychology, sociology, history, and so on.

The Homecoming *and the Articulation of Silence: The Sound of One Hand Clapping* [1]

The Homecoming is in the tradition of the theater of the absurd. To some readers, this fact may suggest grotesque characters, maimed in body and soul, who reside in garbage cans and do very little or who live in never-never lands and do very little as they wait for other characters who never appear. It may also suggest that the inarticulateness of the characters and the static action may at play's end create muteness and puzzlement in the audience. To a great extent, *The Homecoming* (1965) by the British dramatist Harold Pinter, shares these forbidding characteristics, but the play is also good theater; in fact, it is fascinating theater. It compels by virtue of its very inaction, and it reveals provocative insights into modern life. To gain these insights, however, the student of literature must devote himself to understanding Pinter's characters and his unusual techniques and conventions, for once these are studied, the play becomes richly suggestive and powerful.

The most dominating and pervasive character in the play is Max, a seventy-year-old ex-butcher, whose drab London home serves as the setting. Max is given no surname, an absence, like so many other absences in the play, that is part of Pinter's method to suggest the rootlessness—the aimlessness and facelessness—of modern man. The namelessness both intrigues and alienates the reader, for at the same time that he comes to know the characters intimately, he is aware of how little he knows about them and how much more he would like to know. But Pinter nevertheless presents many intimate and fascinating details: Living with Max are two of his sons, Lenny and Joey, and his sixty-three-year-old brother, Sam. Lenny is a sadist and apparently a pimp. Joey does demolition work during the day and is attempting a career as a professional boxer at night. Sam is a chauffeur and also, apparently, a sodomist (at least,

1 Harold Pinter, *The Homecoming* (New York: Grove Press, 1965 and 1966).

Max thinks he is a sodomist). The play receives its name because Teddy, Max's lethargic eldest son, who has become a professor of philosophy in America and has been away for six years, returns home with his wife Ruth, a pensive woman who formerly worked as a photographer's model.

One may expect no lessons in polite social behavior from such a set of characters. Gracious they are not. All the veneer of civilization is stripped away from them. It is almost as though Pinter has created the bare human consciousness, the stream of thoughts and reflections that are suppressed in ordinary human relationships, although they are nevertheless present. Here there are no artificial enthusiasms, no etiquette, where no kindness is; or, where there is a conventionally polite or meaningless comment, it is inappropriate, and it merely underlies the unconventionality of the situation. Thus, when Teddy unexpectedly returns home and is seen by Lenny, there is no warm greeting, no laughter, no inquiry into the past six years of separation, no merriment, no cordiality; there are only two minimally courteous but hollow "hullo's." Similarly, Teddy walks calmly away from his wife without a word of goodbye or reproach. Does the author suggest that human beings would behave thus if they did not feel compelled to follow the conventions of polite society? Is there a discrepancy between wishes and action, and if the two were fused, would human beings be like the characters in *The Homecoming?* If so, Pinter is presenting a revealing although not a happy truth about life.

The key to understanding the characters, in fact, and the cause for their appeal despite their shortcomings as fully rounded human beings, is that Pinter has made their behavior almost solely a function of their thoughts. He has taken a simple human incident, and has apparently asked this question about it: "What would happen under these circumstances if all the characters behaved exactly as they felt?" *The Homecoming* is his answer. The reader could easily envisage another set of matching incidents going on simultaneously, in which all the social graces would be causing the characters to behave conventionally. Much of the theatrical effectiveness of *The Homecoming* results from this unspoken but nevertheless real contrast between the stage action and the conventional action that might be expected under the same conditions.

One might pursue this avenue of speculation, for in the realm of suggestion and fantasy the play is a rich fabric of "could be's" and "might be's." The characters contribute to the richness of the play in many ways, one of these being their names. At the outset, we learn that Max is now old though once powerful, and that his brother "Uncle Sam," is tired after chauffering people around all day. Could this be taken as Pinter's suggestion that the roles of England and America as world powers are nearing their end? Similarly, there is temptation to inquire into the meaning of the Biblical names. The dead Jessie was Max's wife and mother of his sons. Biblically, Jesse was the grandson of Ruth and the father of King David, from whose line the Messiah was to derive. Samuel (Sam) was influential in selecting David as king. According to some views, Joseph (Joey) was the father of Jesus, but according to others, he was no more than the husband of Mary (in this play, Joey gets no "gravy"; if this fact is intended as a Biblical allusion, what bizarre humor!). All these relations are of course mixed up in *The Homecoming,* and the names, except for Jessie, are common enough (and Teddy and Lenny are nonBiblical names). Because of the discussion between Lenny and Teddy, however, and also because of the general spiritual drift of Pinter's characters, the names may very well be a means of enforcing the assertion that people in the twentieth century have lost their certainty. The heroes of Biblical times are a far cry from the antiheroes of today; the world is minimal, everywhere minimal.

The play's action is similarly minimal. It would be difficult to maintain that there is any action at all, as that word is usually understood, except for the brief violence at the end of the first act. The action in the second, concluding act involves not so much action as the development of an incredible scheme, hatched by the younger sons and the father, that involves Ruth. The most surprising action, which is the play's climax—if it has one—consists simply in Teddy's consenting to the scheme and his consequent departure. In short, the action is absurd.

This apparent senselessness or absurdity is also characteristic of other aspects of the play, the most obvious of which is Pinter's dialogue. The speech is sparse and laconic, interspersed with occasional rhapsodic outbursts as various characters become emotionally stimulated. Frequently the dialogue contains apparently illogical and irrelevant changes of subject, and in this regard it is perhaps more naturalistic than what appears in most other plays. Also realistic, in the sense of lifelike even though not "literary," are the many pauses that break up the speeches. These pauses are carefully written into the directions and on the stage would certainly produce a slow-moving, monolithic pace. The pauses also underline the essential solitude of most of the characters. As a particular character speaks, and hears no response, he waits a moment, then goes on, but the effect is to show that the other characters, instead of forming a responsive audience, really are part of an indifferent and self-occupied universe. Once again, the dialogue suggests, what would people say if they spoke as they really felt?

Out of such characteristics of *The Homecoming* one may find the same suggestiveness, ambiguity, and beauty of traditional literature. Symbolically, here are people living without illusions, with their ties to tradition cut; they have no reverence, as Lenny says, for the unknown, no faith. Knowledge and philosophy have filtered into irrelevant and snobbish channels, as with Teddy, and present no chance for nourishing the dessicated plants of life. The significant pauses in the speeches dramatize the conflict between man, on the one hand, and nothingness, on the other. In the world of Max and his sullen sons, there is little if anything to fill up the void—a family group with no real internal loyalty but much hostility. Through these characters and their strange dialogue and behavior, Pinter suggests that many families are such in name only, and that many homes are no more than places where people live together. To come home to such a place is not to receive warmth or love or strength with which to face the world.

In fact, *The Homecoming* is very much like a sporting event in which the team one supports is losing, except that in the play there is no winner. We see no victors dashing down the field in glory, only characters in a perpetual pose, like the retreating Teddy, walking away from an increasing series of defeats. Certainly one cannot leave such a play in a mood of great cheer, but one must recognize that Pinter has created a world that is consistent with an important interpretation of modern life. There are many other diversionary pursuits that may provide the happy endings we enjoy witnessing, but Pinter's play is not one of these. As drama, *The Homecoming* successfully creates conflict, tension, and emotional release. As philosophy, it creates the perplexity that a great segment of humanity is feeling today. One cannot expect more from the theater.

The Theme on
FILM

CHAPTER
18

"Film" has today become the respected word for "movies" and motion pictures. It is a highly specialized kind of drama, utilizing, like drama, the techniques of dialogue, monologue, and action. Like drama also, it employs spectacle and pantomime. Unlike drama it embodies many additional techniques that are peculiarly a result of the technology of photography, editing, film development, and sound. If you are planning to write about film, many of your considerations may be purely literary. Structure, tone, ideas, imagery, style, historical period—all these may be considered in a theme on film as readily as in a theme on a play, novel, poem, or short story. In addition, the techniques of film are so specialized—so much of an extension of what you normally see on a printed page—that a discussion of film requires more technical awareness than is normally needed by the disciplined reader. Although there are many techniques, however, it is possible to carry on an intelligent discussion without an extensive use of terminology.

Film and Other Literary Forms

Film may be likened to a dramatic production. A typical production is a realization on stage of a dramatic text. The producer and director, together with actors, artists, scene designers, costume-makers, carpenters, choreographers, and lighting technicians, attempt to bring a dramatic text to life. Though occasionally a stage production may employ brief sections of film, slides, and tape recordings for special effects (e.g., the witches in *Macbeth,* the ghost in *Hamlet*), the stage itself limits the freedom of the production. Aside from budget, the makers of film have few such limitations. In this respect film is like the novel or the story, in which the absence of any restrictions beside the writer's imagination permits the inclusion of any detail whatever, from the description of a chase to the re-enactment of a scene in the Napoleonic wars. In reading, when you attempt to visualize a scene, you are using your imagination. When you look at a film, the film-maker has in effect provided you with a ready-made imagination. Is there to be a scene on a desert island? The film-maker has gone on location to such an island, and in his film he presents the island itself, complete with beach, sand dunes, palm trees, native huts, and authentic natives-turned-actors. He leaves little to your imagination. Is there to be a scene on a distant planet? Obviously the film-maker cannot go on location there, but he will have imagined such a scene, and will have created a working location for it in the studio; with lighting, props, and costumes he will have shown you all the conditions likely to be found on that planet. Film, in short, enables a dramatic production to achieve something approaching the complete freedom that one finds in novels and stories.

Film is also uniquely its own medium. The director of a film presents you with something that is complete and inseparable, unlike the director of a play. The play director gives you his own interpretation of particular scenes and speeches. You are to take these as one person's interpretation, and to judge them accordingly. The film-maker, however, presents you with a completed package: acting, dialogue, action, and visual and audial effects are all together and must be interpreted together. There is no separate part. For this reason, famous film-makers like D. W. Griffith, Ingmar Bergman, and Alfred Hitchcock are always considered as the originators of their films. They may not have written the dialogue, but their own contributions as directors in control of production are so vast that they are virtually the creators. The director of a play does not have this same autonomy.

Film and Art

To the degree that film is confined to a screen, it may visually be compared with the art of the painter or the still photographer. There is a whole language of visual art. Paintings and photographs have compositional balance. One object may appear in relationship to another as a background forces the eye upon a visual center of attention. A color used in one part of a painting may be balanced with the same color, or its complement, in another part of the painting. The use of certain de-

tails, say the inclusion of the entrance of a cave, or the interior of a
house, or a shield, or a spear, may have particularly symbolic significance.
Paintings may become allegorical by including certain mythical figures,
or machines or computers in the background of the painting. Particular
effects may be achieved with the use of the textures of the paint. Sometimes the paint may be put on flat with a brush, while at other times it
may be put on thickly with a knife in order to create a raised, textured
surface. The techniques and effects are virtually endless, as the history
of art since the Renaissance will show.

The still photographer has many of the same resources as the
painter, except that he cannot create quite the same textures with his
camera and his developer that the painter can with his paint. Basically
the photographer transfers an image of reality to a finished print or slide.
But he does have freedom of focus with his lenses, and can throw one
object into focus while putting others out. He also has the freedom to
select camera speeds, and can either stop an action at 1/1,000 of a second,
or let it remain blurred at 1/25 of a second. With the exacting control of
developers, he can create many monochromatic, polychromatic, blurred,
textured surfaces, and with techniques such as these he truly has a great
deal of interpretive freedom in handling the initial photographic reality
that is the basis of his art.

The film-maker is able to utilize almost all the resources of the
still photographer, and most of those of the painter. Artistically, the
most confining aspect of film is the rectangular screen, but aside from that
film is quite free. With a basis in a dramatic text called a "script" or
"film-script," it employs words and their effects, but it also employs the
language of art and especially the particular verisimilitude and effectiveness of moving pictures. In discussing a film, then, you should see that
film communicates not just by words, but also by use of its unique and
various techniques. You can treat the ideas, the problems, the symbolism
in a film, but while treating them you should recognize that the visual
presentation is inseparable from the medium of film itself.

Techniques

There are many techniques of film, and a full description and documentation of them could, and has, become extensive.[1] In preparing to write a
theme about film, however, you should try to familiarize yourself with

---

[1] See, for example, Rudolph Arnheim, *Film as Art* (Berkeley: University of Cali-
fornia Press, 1969), Daniel Talbot, ed., *Film: An Anthology* (Berkeley: University of
California Press, 1969), and Louis D. Giannetti, *Understanding Movies* (Englewood
Cliffs, N.J.: Prentice-Hall, Inc., 1972).

those aspects of technique that have an immediate bearing on your responses to the film and your interpretations of it. Since film is both visual and audial, we will begin with the visual.

VISUAL

Primarily camera technique permits great freedom in presenting scenes. If you are seeing a stage production of a play, your distance from the actors is fixed by your seat in the theater. In a film, on the other hand, the visual viewpoint is constantly shifting. The film may begin with a distant shot of the actors—a "longshot"—much like the sight you might have on a stage. But then you might be given a closeup of various actors, and sometimes closeups, in intimate scenes, of various parts of their bodies. The camera may zoom in or out to present you with a sudden closeup or panorama. Usually an actor speaking will be the subject of a closeup, but the camera may also show closeups of other actors who are reacting to the first actor's statements. You must decide on the effects of closeups and longshots yourself, but it should be plain that the frequent use of either—or of middle-distance photographs—is a means by which film directors specifically convey meaning.

In the latter part of Mike Nichols' *The Graduate,* for example, there are numerous longshot scenes showing the main character against broad backgrounds of houses and streets. The effect is that the hero ultimately feels rebellion against the larger world that is trying to force him into a "mold." By contrast, in *Faces,* directed by John Cassavetes, emphasis is constantly placed on closeups of the various actors. The effect is to draw attention to the internal, psychological agony experienced by many of the characters.

The camera may also be moved rapidly, or slowly, from character to character, or from character to some natural or man-made object. In this way a film may show a series of reactions to an event. It may also show visually the attitude of a particular character or it may represent a visual commentary on his actions. If a young couple is in love, as an example, the camera may shift from the couple to flowers, trees, and water, thus associating their love visually with objects of beauty and growth. Should the flowers be wilted, and the trees be without leaves, and the water brackish, the visual commentary might well be that the love is doomed and hopeless. Because characters are constantly seen in settings, real or symbolic, you should always be aware that the cinematic manipulation of setting is even more a part of the statement of the film than it might be in a story, in which even an alert reader may often lose awareness of such relationships.

The camera may also be used to create effects that no other medium can convey. Slow motion, for example, can focus concentration on a certain aspect of a person's character. A girl running in slow motion happily through a meadow enables the viewer to concentrate on the possible joy conveyed by the slow rhythms of her body and the patterns of her dress and her hair. In Sydney Pollacks' *They Shoot Horses, Don't They?*, a sequence early in the film shows a horse with a broken leg being shot. This sequence is done in slow motion, a fact that has great significance at the end of the film when a young man with a slow-moving mind cooperates with a depressed young girl as she commits suicide. It is clear that the shooting of the horse occurred when the young man was a child, and that the scene somehow has influenced him to pull the trigger when the girl asks him to. The slow-motion technique of both shootings is designed to show how they are linked in the young man's befuddled mind.

There are many other techniques of camera use and of later editing that also have a bearing on action and character. The focus may be made sharp at one point, but fuzzy at another. Moving a speaking character out of focus may suggest that his listeners are beginning to disregard him. The use of sharp or fuzzy focus may also visually show that a character has seen things exactly or inexactly. In an action sequence, the camera may follow the moving character, a technique that is called "tracking." It is possible to track from a car or truck, which may follow the movement of running human beings or horses, or the movement of cars. A cameraman on foot may be the tracker, or the camera may shoot movement from a helicopter or an airplane. Movement may also be captured by a fixed camera that follows a character from one point to another in a panoramic view. Then, too, the camera may be held fixed and the moving character may simply walk, run, or ride across the screen. If he is moving in a car, the car may become blurred. For special comic effects, the film may be reversed in order to emphasize the illogicality of the actions being filmed. Reversing, of course, is a result of the developing, editing, and cutting process, which is a means by which film-makers can create many other visual effects, such as *fading* or *dissolving* from one scene to another, or superimposing one scene upon another simultaneously.

The process of editing deserves special consideration, for it is the soul of the film-maker's art. A typical film is made up of many separate sequences, all put together during editing sessions. In one scene a character may be seen boarding a plane. Then there may be a scene showing the plane taking off, then flying. Then may follow a scene landing, followed by the character getting off the plane. The entire action may conclude with several different views of the character riding in a taxi to a specific destination. In the film, the whole sequence may take no more than half a minute, yet the entire episode may consist of perhaps a dozen separate views from the camera. It is editing that puts everything together. The camera records many views; the director selects from among these in creating a film.

LIGHT, SHADOW, COLOR

As in the theater, the film-maker utilizes light, shadow, and color as a means of communication. Characters filmed in a bright light are presumably being examined fully, whereas characters in shadow or darkness may be hiding some of their motives. The use of flashing light might show a changeable, mercurial, and perhaps sinister character or situation. In color, the use of greenish-tinted light may suggest ghoulish motivations. Colors of course have much the same meaning that they have in any other artistic medium. Always, colors are carefully arranged. Like the stage director, the film-maker will arrange the blocking of his characters and scenery to create a pleasing arrangement and complementing of colors. Should he throw the colors out of arrangement, however, he may be using the clashing colors to suggest a disharmony in the mind of one or several of his characters. He may also employ light for similar effects. A scene in sunshine, which brings out all the colors, and the same scene in rain and clouds or in twilight, all of which mute the colors, create different moods.

PANTOMIME AND ACTION

In film there are often many periods in which action takes place with no dialogue. The camera may show a man reacting to a situation, or a boy running through a woods, or a couple walking in a park. The scene may run on for several minutes, with all the footage being devoted to movement. Such wordless action is essentially *pantomime* rather than drama. To some degree, all actors employ pantomime by gesture and facial expression. In a dramatic production, pantomime is featured mainly as "business," and many dramas call often for pageantry and swordplay. The unspoken devices of the stage are soon exhausted, however (unless the production happens to be ballet or actual panotmime), and any production must soon return to spoken dialogue. But in film there is great potentiality for rhapsodical focus on movement. In addition, musical accompaniments can be so pleasantly interwoven with the action that dramatic statement can be rendered effectively without the use of the spoken word (see, for example, the Swedish film *Elvira Madigan*, directed by Bo Widerberg, in which many wordless scenes are beautifully augmented with music by Mozart).

The strength of film has always been the portrayal of direct action, forecefully and realistically photographed and presented in sequence. Love affairs, chases, trick effects, fights, ambushes, movement of all sorts —all these make an immediate appeal to the viewer's sense of reality. Without the chase, for example, films would probably not have created the following they now have. Actions of love and violence are immediately stimulating, not as they would be in life, but stimulating enough to create a public demand for more and more. Obviously one of the things you should look for in film is the effectiveness of the portrayal of the action: What is the relationship of the action to the theme of the film? Does the action have any bearing on the characters, or does it seem to have departed from character into an indulgence in action for its own sake? Is the action particularly realistic? Does the camera stay at a distance, showing the persons as relatively small in a vast natural or artificial world? Do closeups show smiles, frowns, eagerness, or anxiety? Is any attempt made to render temperature by action, say cold by a character's stamping his feet, or warmth by the character's removing a coat or shirt? Does the action show any changing of mood, from sadness to happiness, or from indecision to decision? What particular aspects of the action point toward these changes?

Closely related to the portrayal of action is the way in which the film shows the human body. We have already spoken of the closeup as a technique for rendering certain aspects of the drama. Other methods, too, can be employed. A photograph showing an actor in complete proportion may be emphasizing the normality of that person, or it may show the views toward humanity of the film-maker. But perhaps at times the film may create certain distortions. The "fisheye" lens creates such a distortion, usually of the center of a face, that often shows a character's view of another character, or to show the film-maker's thoughts about a character. Sometimes the view creates bodily distortions, emphasizing certain limbs, or other parts of the body. Focusing on a scolding mouth or a suspicious eye may create such distortions. If distortion is used, it invites interpretation: perhaps the film-maker is attempting to show that certain human beings, even when supposedly normal, bear weaknesses and even psychological disturbances.

ACTION AND THOUGHT

A film, like a drama, is presented in the dramatic point of view. Accordingly the film-maker, like the dramatist, is confined to what can be heard of conversations and speeches, and to what can be seen of action. All rendering of characters must be made through this dramatic, externalized point of view. If you cannot hear it or see it, you cannot put it on film. Even so, there are freedoms in the medium of film that are not a part of drama. If the film-maker wants to show introspection, for example, he can do so in a variety of ways. Shakespeare employed the soliloquy as his means of showing introspection. The film-maker also uses soliloquy or monologue, but can put it in the sound track while presenting a closeup of the thinking character. Thus the suggestion is that the speech is an actual duplication of inward mental activity. In Sir Laurence Olivier's film *Hamlet,* for example, the soliloquies are produced in this way.

Film may conveniently show thought through action. A thought represented by monologue may be interrupted by a scene, occurring simultaneously, influencing that thought. Also, a thought may be merged with a "flashback" in order to show actions and speeches that may have had a part in shaping the thought. Film may create dream sequences to show a character's aspirations, and it may employ the *montage* technique in order to show rapid mental motion, moving from one scene without comment to another, and to still others.

MONTAGE

The technique of montage is perhaps the unique property of films, for it permits great rapidity of scene changes, and therefore permits great freedom of expression through association. Montage is to film as imagery is to literature; it is one of the most important cinematic techniques. It is different from a movement of the camera from one scene to another, for it is exclusively a result of editing. One scene at the start of Charlie Chaplin's *Modern Times,* for example, shows a large group of men rushing along a stairway on the way to their factory jobs. Immediately following this scene is a view of a large herd of sheep. The camera by itself could not create such a shift, but the editing process makes it simple. The obvious conclusion is that the men are being herded and dehumanized by their involvement in modern, mechanized industry. A similar effect is created at the opening of the 1971 Australian film *Walkabout.* A man is shown going to his job at the office; montage is then used to show a scene of a simple brick wall. The association suggests that the man has reached a psychological impasse; he is figuratively up against a wall, and does not know where to turn. This montage prepares the viewer for the man's suicide and attempted murder of his two children early in the film. At the end of the same film, the man's daughter is shown in her home, and the same brick wall is shown again immediately following the scene. An impasse similar to that of her father, suggests this association through montage, has occurred in her life. When viewing a film in which montage is used, be prepared to draw conclusions like the following:

"Scene two of the montage sequence is like Scene one," or "Scene two, or one, has been influenced by Scene one, or two," or "Scene two is a visual commentary on Scene one." Whenever you see montage used, rest assured that the director is asking you to make interpretations like these.

SOUND

The first business of the sound track in a film is naturally to include the spoken dialogue. But there are many other effects that become a part of the sound track. Music of various sorts is selected to suit the mood of the film. Special sound effects are used to augment the action; the sound of a blow, for example, will be enhanced electronically in order to cause an impact on the viewer's ears that is similar to the force of the blow itself. If a character is engaged in introspection, muted strings may create a mellow sound to complement his mood. But if he is verging on a psychosis, the sound may become percussive and cacophonous. At times the sound may be played through a mechanical apparatus of some sort in order to create weird or ghostly effects. Often a character's words will be echoed rapidly and sickeningly in order to show his dismay or anguish. In a word, sound is a vital part of film. Once you leave the theater, or the television set if you have been watching the late show, it is difficult to remember all aspects of sound, say a certain melody that serves as mood or background to the action, but you should make the effort to observe some of the various uses to which the sound is put.

Preparing Your Theme

Obviously the first requirement is to see a film. It is wise to see it twice or more if you can, because it is reasonable to assume that your discussion will take on value the more thoroughly you know the material. It is difficult to take notes in a darkened theater, but you should make an immediate effort, after leaving, to take notes on the various aspects of the film that impressed you. Be especially concerned to write down the names of the director and the principal actresses and actors. Try to make your notes as complete as you can, for when you write your theme you will not be able to verify details and to make illustrative quotations as you can when you are writing about a work that you can check and re-check. If any particular speeches were worth quoting from the movie, you should try to remember the general circumstances of the quotation, and also, if possible, any key words. Try to recall uses of costume and color, or (if the film was in black and white) particularly impressive uses of light and shade. An effort of memory will be required in writing a theme on film.

Organizing Your Theme

INTRODUCTION

Here you should state your central idea and thesis sentence as usual. You should also include background information necessary for understanding what you will bring out in the body of your theme. It is appropriate to include here the names of the director, or director-producer, and the actresses and actors worthy in your judgment of particular mention.

BODY

The most difficult choice that you will face in writing about film is deciding on a topic. There is much, and much that is non-literary. If you have no other instructions, you might conveniently decide on subjects like those described in other chapters of this book—e.g., characterization, ideas, structure, problems. Remember, however, to widen your discussion of such topics to a consideration of the techniques of film as well as to the dialogue.

Then, too, you may choose to confine your attention strictly to special cinematographic techniques, stressing their relationship to the theme of the film, their appropriateness, and their quality. If you have never paid particular attention to techniques of film or to photography, or if you have never worked a home-movie camera, you might find some difficulties here. But if you concentrate on certain scenes, you may be able to recall enough to describe some of the techniques, particularly if you have helped yourself with good notes.

In judging a film you might also choose to emphasize the quality of the acting. How well did the actors adapt to the medium of film? How convincing were their performances? Did they portray emotions convincingly? Did they possess good or poor control over their facial expressions? Did their appearance lend anything to your understanding of the characters they portrayed? How well did they control bodily motion? Were they graceful? Awkward? Did it seem that the actors were genuinely creating their roles, or just reading through the parts?

Or you may wish to write a general review, bringing in all these various aspects that go into the total package that is the film. If you write a review, consult Chapter 17 for ideas on how to proceed.

CONCLUSION

You might best conclude by evaluating the effectiveness of the cinematographic form to the story and to the idea. Were all the devices of film used in the best possible way? Was anything particularly overdone? Was anything underplayed? Was the film good, bad, or indifferent to a point, and then did it change? Why? How? The development of answers to questions like these will be appropriate in the conclusion of your theme.

SAMPLE THEME

Ingmar Bergman's **Virgin Spring:**
An Affirmation of Complexity

Virgin Spring, a black-and-white film in Swedish with English sub-titles, is directed by Ingmar Bergman and written by Ulla Isaksson. It is a complex but affirmative rendering of an old Scandinavian folk tale. It first appeared in 1960, and has been shown many times since by various film societies and clubs. It is well acted, with particularly strong performances by Max von Sydow as the father, Töre, and by Birgitta Pettersson as the daughter, Karin. The fabric of the film is woven of violence, horror, revenge, and mystery; against this background, however, there emerges a pattern of purpose and affirmation. On the surface the story of the film is simple enough. In medieval times a young girl is permitted to ride alone to the church to deliver candles, but on her way she is murdered by three herdsmen. The three men take her garments and ask shelter for the night at her home, where they try to sell the clothes to her parents. The father concludes that the three men have murdered his daughter, and he murders them in revenge. Going to recover his daughter's body, the father vows to build a church on the spot where she fell. When the body is removed, a spring of water gushes forth from the point where her head lay. While the film could thus be regarded as an inspiring miracle play, designed to confirm religious faith, the impact of the characterization and cinematic techniques is that any faith, or any commitment whatsoever, is a difficult and sometimes self-contradictory struggle.

The characterization brings out the complexity. The servant girl, for example, is ostensibly a malcontent, a dark-haired figure of evil committed to Odin the god of battles and death. She is to be contrasted with the fair-haired Karin, the daughter, who is a figure of goodness and purity. But the servant girl is not seen so simplistically, for she is shown as a menial whose freedom is restricted and whose potential beauty is useless. Desiring fine clothes and servants herself, she has nothing. Her approaching motherhood will not be accompanied by marriage. Her resentment, and her worship of the mysterious Odin, which presumably brings down disaster on the family she serves, are therefore not unmitigated evil but understandable responses to an undesirable condition. Her placing the frog in the bread loaf is not an act of evil, despite its consequences, but rather an extreme act of spitefulness, frustration, and disgust. Such complexity marks Bergman's uniquely modern handling of an old story.

The same complexity may be seen in Karin, the daughter. She is the sacrificial victim, and her ultimate rape and death arouse the horror and indignation that one feels at seeing purposeless violence. But at her home, before she goes on her journey, she is shown with some of the haughtiness and spitefulness that characterize a spoiled person. She is vain, and she wheedles herself into favorable positions with her parents. Fussy, she will not go on the trip to church until her dress is just right. This is not to say that she is bad, but rather that she is human, not a figure of unqualified virtue, but one of human and therefore frail capacities. Perhaps this complexity lends even more pity to her destruction than if she had been shown as a simple figure on a tapestry.

The most complex characterization is that of the father, Herr Töre. It is Töre's lot to wreak vengeance on the three crazed herdsmen, and to make vows to build the church where his daughter was killed. Töre does not go easily to either task, however, for he performs a ritualistic cleansing before attacking the three men, and his regret and horror after his deed are made apparent. Similarly, his prayers alongside his daughter's corpse indicate his bewilderment, frustration, and incomprehension. His previous quiet, almost inarticulate manner is thus shown as covering greater, almost philosophic capabilities. He is a man thrust into situations that he cannot control or comprehend, and he tries to make his way as best he can. Of particular interest is his declaration of inability to understand God's ways. In view of this declaration his decision to build the church may be seen as a human commitment, a compromise solution, rather than an ordinary memorial act of devotion.

While these characterizations are important in illustrating the complexity of Bergman's treatment of the tale, the film's major strength is in the direction and in the filming. It was clearly Bergman's intention to dramatize through photography the complex, ambiguous, mysterious forces that swirl around the centers of human motivation. In what is in effect the epigraph of the film, for example, Bergman photographs the servant girl from above as she calls on Odin to assist her. This downward view conditions our subsequent attitudes toward the girl. When she meets the gnomic man in the woods, however, even she demonstrates uneasiness at the grotesque, distorted forces portrayed by the man. The same kind of mad force is suggested in the actions of the three herdsmen when they first see Karin riding through the woods. Their attitudes are captured on film by an increasingly irrational and depraved set of actions, augmented by the closeups of the bizarre mute herdsman when he tries to speak. Even so, their violence is restrained until the frog is discovered in the bread. Here the forces that were enveloping the servant girl are unleashed on the herdsmen, for the appearance of the frog triggers their incomprehending violence on the girl.

Such forces can be suppressed only by much greater, if equally vague, forces, and it is here that Bergman gains the utmost from camera and light. Clearly his views of Karin riding along the shore of the lake show beauty and innocence, but inability to control evil. Karin is clothed in light, and her horse is white. The lake is clear, and the scene is one of beauty. By contrast, when Bergman focuses the camera on Töre before the vengeance scene, he portrays a more complex and powerful set of forces. First, Töre is at the gate when the three herdsmen approach; he is in darkness and appears as a stolid, guardian-like figure. Later, Bergman shows him tearing up a young tree in preparation for his ritualistic bath and switching. Bergman in this scene captures a sense that Töre gathers strength directly from the earth. The scene is portrayed as a union of man, earth, and sky, in a vague, ghastly light, as though the forces conducing to rightness are equally as vast, as vague, and as ambiguous as those leading to evil.

In the face of this ambiguity, the virgin spring itself is to be seen as an affirmation of the difficulty and mystery of life. Bergman emphasizes the beauty of the gushing water in both sight and sound. It would be easy to accept this water as a new birth, a sign that horror and sacrifice are over. But it seems more reasonable, in view of the main actions of the film, to see the spring as a sign that there is value in making an effort to overcome hostile forces. The spring, like the tree, gives strength, and both come from the earth, which is shown throughout by Bergman as hill, vale, mud, and shore. As a symbol, the spring cannot guarantee that hostile forces can ever be eliminated, or that horror and violence can be stopped. The future will hold many re-enactments of just such situations as Karin encounters on her innocent journey. But if persons like Töre make the commitment and the effort, evil at least will not prevail.

It is clear that Bergman has done well with a good script. At first one might wonder at the extent of Karin's preparations before her journey, but as the tale unfolds it may be seen that this preparation serves (1) to establish involvement with her character, and (2) to show her clothing, which later on becomes convincing evidence that the three herdsmen have murdered her. Similarly, the extensive movement of the three herdsmen when they first see Karin, which may seem unnecessary, creates an impression of their sinister irrationality. Logically, there is nothing done to excess, nor is there anything wanting in the film. In just about every technical matter from acting to photography and to editing, *Virgin Spring* is a major achievement in the art of the film.

Taking Examinations on
LITERATURE

APPENDIX
A
Taking an examination on literature is not difficult if you prepare in the right way. Preparing means (1) studying the material assigned, studying the comments made in class by your instructor and by fellow students in discussion, and studying your own thoughts; (2) anticipating the questions by writing some of your own on the material to be tested and by writing practice answers to these questions; and (3) understanding the precise function of the test in your education.

You should realize that the test is not designed to plague you or to hold down your grade. The grade you receive is in fact a reflection of your achievement in the course at the time the test is given. You have been admitted to a recognized institution of higher learning; therefore you may assume that you have the ability to do superior, satisfactory, or at least passing work. If your grades are low, the chances are good that you can improve them by studying in a coherent and systematic way. For many students, adequate preparation can make the difference between staying in school or leaving. Those students who can easily do satisfactory work might do superior work if they improved their method of preparation. From whatever level you begin, you can improve your achievement by improving your method of study.

Remember that your instructor prefers to see evidence of your improvement; he is anxious to read good examinations and would like to have them all excellent. Assuming that you write literate English, your instructor has two major concerns in evaluating your test: (1) to see the extent of your command over the subject material of the course ("How good is your retention?"), and (2) to see how well you are thinking and responding to the material ("How well are you educating yourself").

Although you must never minimize the importance of factual command, the writing that reflects your understanding of these facts will be of prime significance in determining your grade. To phrase this idea another way: command over facts is important, and without it your mind cannot respond properly; but once the facts are remembered, your mental sharpness assumes prominence. Ultimately, any good test is designed to elicit the extent of your understanding at that given moment, in the belief that challenging your understanding is important to the growth of your mind. There should be no cavalier disregard of factual knowledge; without a factual basis your answers, and your mind, will amount to little.

Preparation

With these thoughts, your problem is how to prepare yourself best to have a knowledgeable and ready mind at examination time. If you simply cram facts into your head for the examination in hopes that you will be able to adjust to whatever questions are asked, you will likely flounder, and your examination will result in a boring chore for your instructor and an unsatisfactory grade for you.

Above all, keep in mind that your preparation should begin not on the night before the exam but as soon as the course begins. When each assignment is given, you should complete it by the date due, for you will understand your instructor's lecture and the classroom discussion only if you know the material being discussed. Then, about a week before the exam, you should review each assignment, preferably re-reading each assignment completely. With this preparation completed, your study on the night before the exam will be fruitful, for it might be viewed as a climax of preparation, not the entire preparation itself.

Go over your notes, and as you do so, refer constantly to passages from the text that were mentioned and studied in class by your instructor. A good idea is to memorize as many significant phrases from the passages as possible; then when you are writing your exam your knowledge of a small quotation from the text shows your instructor that you have a good knowledge of the material. As you study, it is good to think not only about main ideas but also about technical matters, such as organization and style. Any time you have a reference in your notes (or in your memory) to technical problems, observe or recall carefully what your instructor said about them, and about their relationship to ideas. Technique is always related to ideas, and if you show understanding of both, your exam is likely to be successful.

Your final preparation should consist of more than re-reading your notes and re-examining key passages from the text. It should also contain writing and thinking, and here your ability to plan and practice your own questions and answers will be of great assistance. Make up some questions; perhaps you might rephrase a sentence from your notes into a question. Here is a brief fragment from some classroom notes on the subject of Dryden's *Absalom and Achitophel:* "A political poem—unintelligible unless one knows the politics of the time." Your sample question from this fragment might be: "Why is *Absalom and Achitophel* unintelligible without an understanding of the politics of the time?" Then you could spend fifteen or twenty minutes answering this question. Or you might look over a key passage from the text, decide what its subject is, and ask questions like "What does X say about _____ subject?" and "What is the effect of _____ in _____?" Spend as much time as possible in this way, making practice questions and answers on ideas and also on technique.

Let us try an example. Suppose you are reading Browning's "My Last Duchess." You might ask yourself this practice question about it: "Why did the Duke give orders to have his former wife killed?" Then you would begin writing an answer. About midway through you would realize that the question is difficult and ambiguous: *why* applies either to the reasons given by the Duke or to the conclusions you yourself have made. You might, as a result, recast the question into two: (1) "What reasons does the Duke reveal for having given the orders to kill his wife?" and (2) "What, in your opinion, are the reasons for which the Duke gave these orders?" You could then write a satisfactory answer to either one of these questions separately or could also make them two parts of the original question. From problems like these you would gain experience not only in asking, answering, and organizing questions, but in knowing that the phrasing of questions is important.

Your questions may, of course, be of all types. You might study the organization of a work carefully and then ask yourself about that organization. Or you might become interested in a certain character and wish to practice on a question asking for an analysis of that character. Time spent in this way can never be wasted, for as you carry on your practice *you are in fact studying with great care.* In addition, this practice will surely make the examination less of a surprise to you than it would be otherwise. The less you are surprised, the better will be your performance. Possibly you could even anticipate the questions your instructor might ask.

Sometimes another view can augment your own understanding of the material to be tested. If you find it possible to study with a fellow student, both of you can benefit from discussing what was said in class. In view of the necessity for steady preparation throughout a course, keep in mind that regular conversations (over coffee or some other beverage to your taste) well in advance of the examination are a good idea.

Questions

There are two types of questions that you will find on any examination about literature. Keep them in mind as you prepare. The first type is *factual,* or *mainly objective,* and the second is *general, comprehensive, broad,* or *mainly subjective.* In a literature course, however, very few questions are purely objective, except possibly for multiple-choice questions.

FACTUAL QUESTIONS

MULTIPLE-CHOICE QUESTIONS. These are the most purely factual questions. You are familiar with them from college entrance exams and also, perhaps, from other courses. In a literature course, your instructor will most likely reserve them for short quizzes, usually on days when an assignment is due, to assure himself that you are keeping up with the reading. Multiple choice, of course, can test your knowledge of facts, and it also can test your ingenuity in perceiving subtleties of phrasing in certain choices. Multiple choice on a literature exam, however, is rare.

IDENTIFICATION QUESTIONS. These questions are decidedly of more interest. They test not only your factual knowledge but also your ability to relate this knowledge to your understanding of the work assigned. This type of question will frequently be used as a check on the depth and scope of your reading. In fact, an entire exam could be composed of only identification questions, each demanding, perhaps, five minutes to write.

What might you be asked to identify? Typical examples are:

A Character, for example, Maria in Joyce's short story "Clay." You would try to indicate her position, background, her importance in the story, and especially her significance in Joyce's design. You should always emphasize the second part, for it shows your understanding.

Incidents, which may be described as follows: "A woman refuses to go on tour with a traveling show" (assuming that either *Sister Carrie* by Dreiser or *The Big Money* by Dos Passos is being tested). After you locate the incident, try to demonstrate its *significance* in the story's main design.

Things. Your instructor may ask you to identify, say, an "overcoat" (Gogol's "Overcoat"), or "spunk water" (*Tom Sawyer*), or some other significant object.

Quotations. Theoretically, you should remember enough of the text to identify a passage taken from it, or at least to make an informed guess. Generally, you should try to locate the quotation, if you remember it, or else to describe the probable location, and to show the ways in which the quotation is typical of the work you have read, with regard to both content and style. You can often salvage much from a momentary lapse of memory by writing a reasoned and careful explanation of your guess, even if the guess is incorrect.

TECHNICAL AND ANALYTICAL QUESTIONS AND PROBLEMS.   In a scale of ascending importance, the third and most difficult type of factual question is on those matters with which this book has been concerned: technique, analysis, and problems. On your test you might be asked to discuss the *structure, tone, point of view,* or *principal idea* of a work; you might be asked about a *specific problem;* you might be asked to analyze a poem that may or may not be duplicated for your benefit (if it is not duplicated, woe to the student who has not read his assignments well). Questions like these are difficult, because they usually assume that you have a fairly technical knowledge of some important terms, while they also ask you to examine the text quite rigidly within the limitations imposed by the terms.

Obviously, technical questions will occur more frequently in advanced courses than in elementary ones, and the questions will become more subtle as the courses become more advanced. Instructors of elementary courses may frequently use main-idea or special-problem questions but will probably not use many of the others unless they specifically state their intentions to do so in advance, or unless technical terms have been studied in class.

Questions of this type are fairly long, perhaps with from fifteen to twenty-five minutes allowed for each. If you have two or more of these questions to write, try to space your time sensibly; do not devote eighty per cent of your time to one question, and only twenty per cent to the rest.

BASIS OF JUDGING FACTUAL QUESTIONS

In all factual questions, literate English being assumed, your instructor is testing (1) your factual command, and (2) your quickness in relating a part to the whole. Thus, suppose that you are identifying the incident "A woman refuses to go on tour with a traveling show." You would identify Sister Carrie as the woman, and say that she is advised by her friend, Lola, to stay in New York (where the big opportunity is) and not to go on tour, where nobody important will see her. You would also try to show that the incident occurs when Carrie is just a minor dancer, during her early years in show business. But, you should, more importantly, show that her decision leaves her in New York, where a new opportunity develops, quickly enabling Carrie to become a star. You should conclude by saying that the incident prepares the way for all Carrie's later successes and shows how far she has advanced above Hurstwood's deteriorating state, monetarily speaking. The incident can therefore be seen as one of the most significant in the entire novel.

Your answers should all take this general pattern. Always try to show the *significance* of the things you are identifying. *Significance* of course works in many directions, but in a short identification question you should always try to refer to (1) major events in the book, (2) major ideas, (3) the structure of the work, and (4) in a quotation, the style. Time is short; therefore you must be selective, but if you can set your mind toward producing answers along these lines, you will probably approach what your instructor expects.

Here are three answers that were written to an identification question. The students were asked to identify "The thing which was not," from the fourth voyage of Swift's *Gulliver's Travels*.

Answer 1. This quotation serves as an example of a typical saying in the language of the Houyhnhnms. It means that the thing was false. It shows their roundabout method of saying things.

Answer 2. This quotation is found in Chapter IV of "A Voyage to the Country of the Houyhnhnms." Gulliver is told this said quotation by his Master, one of the Houyhnhnms (a horse). It is brought out when the two of them are discussing their own customs and culture, and Gulliver is telling his Master how he sailed over to this country. The Master finds it hard to believe. He tells Gulliver that lying is altogether foreign to the culture of the Houyhnhnms. He says speech is for the purpose of being understood and he cannot comprehend lying and is unfamiliar with doubt. He goes on to say that if someone says "the thing which was not" the whole end of speech is defeated. I think what the Master has said to Gulliver clearly illustrates Swift's thought that man should use language as a means to communicate truth or otherwise its purpose is defeated. We can also see Swift's thought that this very beautiful concept of language and its use is not taken up by man. This degrades mankind.

Answer 3. The thing which was not, a variation on "*is* not," is used throughout the fourth voyage of *Gulliver* by the Houyhnhnm Master as a term for lying—telling a thing contrary to fact. The term is interesting because it shows a completely reasonable reaction (represented by that of the Houyhnhnm Master) toward a lie, with all the subtle variations on the word we have in English. By whatever term we use, a lie is *a thing which is not* (except in the mind of the person who tells it) and destroys the chief end of speech—truthful communication. The term is therefore an integral part of Swift's attack in *Gulliver* on the misuse of reason. A lie misleads the reason, and thereby destroys all the processes of reason (e.g., logic, science, law) by supplying it with nonexistent things. Because our civilization depends on the reasonable pursuit of truth, a lie about anything is thus actually an attack on civilization itself. Swift's Houhynhnms have this value, then, that they provide us with a reasonable basis for judging elements in our own life, and hopefully, for improving them where reason can improve them.

The first answer is not satisfactory, since it is inaccurate in sentences 1 and 3, and does not indicate much thought about the meaning of the quotation. The second answer is satisfactory; despite faults of style, it shows knowledge of the conditions under which the quotation is delivered, and also indicates some understanding of the general meaning of the quotation. The third answer is superior, for it relates the quotation to Swift's satiric purposes in *Gulliver's Travels* and also shows how lying actually becomes a perversion of language and reason. The distinguishing mark of the third answer is that it shows *thorough* understanding.

One thing is clear from these sample answers: *really superior answers cannot be written if your thinking originates entirely at the time you are faced with the question;* the more thinking and practicing you do before the exam, the better your answers will be. Obviously the writer of the third answer was not caught unprepared. You should reduce surprise on an exam to an absolute minimum.

The more extended factual questions pose, in addition to the problem of showing knowledge of facts and understanding significance, the necessity for more thoroughly developed organization. Remember that here your knowledge of essay writing is important, for the quality of your composition will inevitably determine a part, or perhaps a major share, of your instructor's evaluation of your answers.

It is therefore best to take several minutes to gather your thoughts together before you begin to write, because a ten-minute planned answer is preferable to a twenty-five minute unplanned answer. Surprising as this idea may seem, you do not need to write down every possible fact on each particular question. Of greater significance is the use to which you put the facts you know and the organization of your answer. When the questions are before you, use a sheet of scratch paper to jot down the facts you remember and your ideas about them in relation to the question. Then put them together, phrase a thesis sentence, and use your facts to illustrate or prove your thesis.

It is always necessary, particularly when you are dealing with "problem" questions, to work key phrases from the original questions into your thesis sentence. Let us suppose that you are given the question: "What are some reasons for which Dick Diver loses his professional abilities and consequently drifts into oblivion?" (Fitzgerald's *Tender is the Night*). Your answer might begin in the following way: "Dick Diver loses his professional abilities for many reasons. Fitzgerald suggests that many of his energies are taken up by Nicole, but I believe that a more comprehensive reason is the paralysis of his self-esteem resulting from his superficial life among the international set. . . ." Presumably, your answer would then proceed to discuss the view you attribute to Fitzgerald and then your own. Notice that your first sentence clearly states the aims and limits of the answer, so that your answer will be completely self-contained. Whatever your method, however, do not simply start writing without reference to the question, for if your first sentence does not describe the answer to follow, your instructor will probably feel that he is reading your answer in a vacuum, and your grade will be affected accordingly. Your best approach to tests is to regard each answer as a small essay, demanding good writing, thinking, and organizing.

For comparison, here are two paragraphs from a twenty-five minute question on Fitzgerald's story "The Rich Boy." The question was: "What do Anson's two love affairs contribute to your understanding of his character?" Both paragraphs are about Anson's first love affair, with Paula Legendre:

1

The Paula affair helps understand Anson. Paula best understood him through their relationship. Anson was searching for stability and security in life; he felt he could achieve these with Paula. This was shown through the following idea: if only he could be with Paula he would be happy. Paula saw him as a mixture of solidity and self-indulgence and cynicism. She deeply loved him, but it was impossible for him to form a lasting relationship with her. The reason for this was his drinking, and his code of superiority. This was shown in the fact that he felt hopeless despair before his pride and his self-knowledge. His superiority can be further observed through his physical and emotional relationship with Paula. His entire relationship with Paula was based on his feelings that emotion was sufficient, and why should he commit himself? Her marriage greatly affected Anson; it made a cynic out of him. His attitude toward women influenced his relationship with Dolly, too.

2

To show that Anson has a dual nature, Fitzgerald develops the Paula Legendre episode at great length. Paula represents everything that Anson's reliable side needs: conservatism, equality of social and economic position, earnestness of purpose, and love. Presumably, the lengthy, low conversations between the two are presented to illustrate the positive, substantial character of Anson. But Fitzgerald is also illustrating the weakness of Anson's character—a weakness that he brings out by the relationship with Paula. As a result of a lifelong position of unchallenged wealth and status, without any real responsibility, Anson has developed into a man of shallow and superficial emotions, even though he *knows*, consciously, what mature emotions are. Thus, he cannot face the responsibility of marriage with Paula: he gets drunk and embarrasses her; he delays proposing marriage at the logical moment in the magic of love and moonlight, and therefore he lets Paula's mood vanish forever into the night. When Paula, who despite her wealth is more stable than Anson, marries another man, Anson's serious side is deeply disturbed, but his superficial side is made happy. Unfortunately, this division has made him a perpetual child, unable to cope with adult life. These same characteristics are also enforced by Fitzgerald in the affair with Dolly Karger.

It is easy to see that Column 2 is superior to Column 1. If Column 1 were judged as part of an outside-class theme, it would be a failure, but as part of a test it would probably receive a passing grade. Column 2 is clearer; it develops its point well and uses evidence more accurately to illustrate its point.

GENERAL, OR COMPREHENSIVE QUESTIONS

Many students are fond of the *general, comprehensive, broad,* or *freewheeling* question, which they like to regard as *subjective,* giving them the opportunity to demonstrate their mental proficiency. These students prefer the general question to the specific question, which, they feel, forces them to remember mere, picayunish details. The reason for their preference is fairly easy to assess, for frequently students may interpret a question so broadly that they ignore the obviously intended implications of the question and devote themselves to answering some other question that was never really in the instructor's mind. Then, in later discussions with their instructor, they defend their "interpretations" and plead for higher marks. Defending a poor performance in this way is deplorable and sometimes deceitful, not to speak of its damaging effect on the purpose of education. For these reasons, many instructors avoid broad questions—and the resulting problems—entirely.

Despite abuses, however, there is a definite place for general questions, particularly on final examinations, when your instructor is interested in testing your general or "total" comprehension of the course material. You have much freedom of choice in deciding what to write, but you must constantly bear in mind that your instructor is looking for intelligence and knowledge in what you choose to say.

Considerable time is usually allowed for answering a comprehensive question, perhaps forty-five minutes or more, depending on the scope and depth that your instructor expects. He may phrase the question in a number of ways:

1. A direct question asking about philosophy, underlying attitudes, "schools" of literature or literary movements, main ideas, characteristics of style, backgrounds, and so on. Here are some typical questions in this catgory: "Define and characterize Metaphysical poetry," or "Discuss the influences of science on literature in the Restoration," or "Describe the dramatic prose of the Jacobean dramatists."

2. A "comment" question, usually based on an extensive quotation, borrowed from a critic or written by your instructor for the occasion, about a broad class of writers, or about a literary movement, or the like. Your instructor may ask you to treat this question broadly (taking in

many writers) or he may ask you to apply the quotation to a specific writer.

3. A "suppose" question, such as "Suppose Rosalind were in Desdemona's place; what would she do when Othello accused her of infidelity?" or "What would Pope say about Joyce's *Ulysses*?"

BASIS OF JUDGING GENERAL, OR COMPREHENSIVE QUESTIONS

In dealing with a broad, general question you are in fact dealing with an unstructured situation, and you yourself must supply not only an *answer* but—almost more important—must also create a *structure* within which your answer can have meaning. You might say that you make up your own question, which will be derived from the original, broadly expressed question. If you were asked to "Consider Shakespeare's thoughts about the ideal monarch," for example, you would do well to structure the question by narrowing its limits. A possible narrowing might be put as follows: "Shakespeare dramatizes thoughts about the ideal monarch by setting up a contrast between, on one side, monarchs who fail either by alienating their close supporters or by becoming tyrannical, and, on the other side, monarchs who succeed by securing faithful supporters and by creating confidence in themselves." With this sort of focus, you would be able to proceed point by point, introducing supporting data as you went. Without such a structure, you would experience difficulty.

As a general rule, the best method to adopt in answering a comprehensive question is that of comparison-contrast. The reason is that it is very easy in dealing with, say, a general question on Yeats, Eliot, and Auden to write *three* separate essays (on [1] Yeats, [2] Eliot, and [3] Auden) rather than one. Thus, you should force yourself to consider a topic like "The Treatment of Alienation," or "The Attempt to Find Truth," and then to treat such a topic point by point rather than author by author. If you were answering the question posed on Shakespeare's thoughts about the ideal monarch, you might try to show the failures of Richard II and Richard III against the successes of Henry IV and Henry V. It would also be relevant to introduce, by way of comparison and contrast, references to Antony, and even to King Lear or to Prospero (from *The Tempest*), or to others. By moving from point to point, you would bring in these references as they are germane to your topic. But if you treated each figure separately, your comprehensive answer would become diffuse and ineffective. For further ideas on this method, see Chapter 9, on comparison and contrast.

In judging your response to a general question, your instructor is interested in seeing: (1) how intelligently you select material, (2) how well you organize your material, (3) how adequate and intelligent are the generalizations you make about the material, and (4) how relevant are the facts you select for illustration.

Bear in mind that in comprehensive questions, though you are ostensibly free, the freedom you have been extended has been that of creating your own structure. The underlying idea of the comprehensive, general question is that you, personally, possess special knowledge and insights that cannot be discovered by more factual questions. You must therefore try to formulate your own responses to the material and to introduce evidence that reflects your own particular insights and command of information.

Parting Advice

Whenever you take an exam, use your common sense about answering questions. Answer the questions asked, and not some others, for your instructor is interested in seeing how well you follow directions and observe the wording of the questions. If the question begins "Why does . . ." be sure to explain *why* the subject indeed *does;* do not just describe *what* is *done.* If you are asked to describe the organization of a literary work, be sure to describe the *organization.* Remember that a principal cause of low grades on exams is that many students do nothing but write a synopsis, without ever answering the questions asked. Look at the questions carefully, and answer them, trying always to deal with the issues in them. In this way, you can insure success on your exam.

A Note on

DOCUMENTATION

APPENDIX B It is not the intention here to present a complete discussion of documentation but only as much as is necessary for a typical theme about literature. You will find complete discussions in most writing handbooks and guidebooks to research, and in the *MLA Style Sheet,* Second Edition. Whenever you have questions about documentation, always ask your instructor.

In any writing not derived purely from your own mind, you must document your facts. In writing about literature, you must base your conclusions on material in particular literary works and must document this material. If you ever refer to secondary sources, as in themes about genre or about a literary work as it reflects its historical period, you must be especially careful to document your facts (see Chapters 8 and 15). To document properly you must use illustrative material in your discussion and mention the sources for this material either in your discussion or in footnotes to it.

Illustrative Quotations

When you wish to make fairly extensive quotations in a theme, you should leave three blank lines between your own discourse and the quotation, single-space the quotation, and make a special indention for it. The following example is a fragment from a theme about John Gay's *Trivia,* an early eighteenth-century poem. Here is the physical layout of the writer's discussion and the quotation:

In the poem Gay shows his familiarity with the practices of the many hoodlums and bullies of his time. According to him, many Londoners lived in dread. We may presume that they did not dare to walk the streets at night for fear of being mugged by a gang of toughs:

> Now is the time that rakes their revels keep;
> Kindlers of riot, enemies of sleep.
> His scattered pence the flying Nicker flings,
> And with the copper shower the casement rings.
> Who has not heard the Scourer's midnight fame?
> Who has not trembled at the Mohock's name? (lines 321–326)

If I thought Mohocks and Scourers would come after me to rob me and beat me, I would not venture out myself.

The same layout applies when you are quoting prose passages. In quoting lines of poetry, you must always remember to quote them as lines. Do not run them together. When you center the quotations as in the example, you do not need quotation marks.

If you wish to use shorter quotations, incorporate them directly into your discussion, as parts of your sentences set off by quotation marks. If you quote consecutive lines of poetry, indicate the conclusion of each line with a bar or slash (/) and begin each new line with a capital letter. Show omissions by three periods (. . .), but if your quotation is short, do not surround it with the periods. Look at the absurdity of using the three periods in a sentence like this one: "Keats asserts that '. . . a thing of beauty . . .' always gives joy." Indicate words of your own within the quotations by enclosing them in square brackets ([ ]). Here is another fragment to exemplify these practices:

> In his poem, Gay deplores the miseries of the city at night. If a person must go out, he discovers that "Where a dim gleam the paly [i.e., dim] lanthorn throws / O'er the mid pavement, heapy rubbish grows" (335–336). If a person is unlucky enough to go out riding in a coach, he may find himself "In the wide gulf" where "the shattered coach o'erthrown / Sinks with the . . . steeds" (342–343).

Always reproduce your source exactly. Because most freshman anthologies and texts modernize the spelling and punctuation in works that are old, the problem may never arise. But if you use an unmodernized text, as in many advanced courses, duplicate everything exactly as you find it. Suppose that in a seventeenth-century work you encounter the word *divers* with the meaning of the modern *diverse*. If you modernize the spelling (*divers* in this sense is now archaic), you change the accent and thereby affect the rhythm of the passage you have been reading. In prose, this change would perhaps be immaterial, but in poetry it would definitely be unfortunate. Similarly, if you start changing spelling, you should theoretically change punctuation. Or suppose you encounter a word that is no longer used; should you replace the original with a modern word with the same meaning? In other words, when do you stop modernizing and start changing your text? You are better off to leave it exactly as you find it.

Formal Documentation

It is essential that you grant recognition to any source from which you have derived factual or interpretive information. If you fail to grant recognition, you run the risk of being challenged for representing as your own the results of other people's work. To indicate the source of all derived material, you must, formally, use footnotes at the bottom of your page or else at the end of your theme, or, informally, embody some form of recognition in the body of your paper. Although the care necessary for noting book names and page numbers often annoys many students, you should realize that footnotes and informal references exist not to cause you trouble but to help your reader. First, your reader may want to consult your source in order to assure himself that you have not misstated any facts. Second, he may dispute your conclusions and wish to see your source in order to arrive at his own conclusions. Third, he may become so interested in one of your points that he might wish to read more about it for his own pleasure or edification. For these reasons, you must show the source of all material that you use.

If you are using many sources in a research report, it is wise to document your paper formally. The procedures discussed here will be sufficient for most papers requiring formal documentation. For especially difficult problems, consult the *MLA Style Sheet,* Second Edition, or the section on documentation in your writing handbook.

The first time you make a quotation from a source, or refer to the source, you should write a footnote, which should contain the following information in this order:

FOR A BOOK

1. The author's name, first name or initials first.
2. The name of the story or poem, in quotation marks.
3. The name of the book, underlined.
4. The edition, if it is indicated (e.g., "Fourth edition").
5. The name or names of the editor or editors, if any. Abbreviate *editor* as *ed., editors* as *eds.*
6. Within parentheses:
   (a) The city of publication, followed by a colon. Do not include the

state or country unless the city might be confused with another (e.g., Cambridge, Mass.) or unless the city is unlikely to be known by any but natives in its particular area (e.g., Larchmont, N.Y.; Emmaeus, Pa.).

(b) The publisher. This information is frequently not given, but it is wise to include it.[1]

(c) The year of publication.

7. The page number or numbers. For books commonly reprinted (like *Gulliver's Travels*) and for well-known long poems (like *Paradise Lost*) you should include chapter or part numbers or line numbers, because many readers might locate your source in a different edition.

FOR A MAGAZINE ARTICLE

1. The author, first name or initials first.

2. The title of the article, in quotation marks.

3. The name of the magazine, underlined.

4. The volume number, in Roman numerals.

5. The year of publication, within parentheses.

6. The page number or numbers.

Note: To prepare for subsequent footnotes, write a statement at the end of the first footnote that you will henceforth use a shortened reference to the source, such as the author's last name, or the title of the work, or some abbreviation, according to your preference.

SAMPLE FOOTNOTES

[1] Joseph Conrad, *The Rescue: A Romance of the Shallows* (New York: Doubleday & Co., Inc., 1960), p. 103. Hereafter cited as *The Rescue*.

[2] George Milburn, "The Apostate," *An Approach to Literature*, 3rd ed., Cleanth Brooks, John Thibaut Purser, and Robert Penn Warren, eds. (New York: Appleton-Century-Crofts, Inc., 1952), p. 74. Hereafter cited as "The Apostate."

[3] Carlisle Moore, "Conrad and the Novel as Ordeal," *Philological Quarterly*, XLII (1963), 59. [Notice that when you give a volume number, you do not put a *p.* before the page number.] Hereafter cited as *Moore*.

[4] *Moore*, p. 61.

[5] *The Rescue*, p. 171.

[6] "The Apostate," p. 76.

[1] If faced with a choice, some editors prefer citing the publisher rather than the city of publication. For identification purposes, this citation is more accurate, but as yet it has not come into general use. Ask your instructor about his preferences, and be guided by his advice.

As a general principle, you may exclude from your footnote any material that you have incorporated into the body of your paper. For example, suppose that in your theme you have mentioned the name of your book and the author. Then you should include only that material that pertains to publication. The principle is that you do not need to repeat in a footnote anything that has already been expressed in your theme itself. Look at this example:

> In *Charles Macklin: An Actor's Life,* William W. Appleton points out that Macklin had been "reinstated at Drury Lane" by December 19, 1744, and that he was playing his stellar role of Shylock.[7]
>
> [7] (Cambridge, Mass.: Harvard University Press, 1961), p. 72.

Informal Documentation

Sentiment today among many editors and most persons who pay printing bills is that writers should incorporate as much reference material as possible within the text of a paper. If you are using many sources, the use of footnotes avoids much ambiguity, but even so you should make a point of including the names of authors, articles, and books into the body of your theme, as in the example based on Appleton's reference to Macklin.

When you are writing a theme based on only one work of literature, as is the case for most of your themes, it is possible to use only one footnote and then to rely on a completely informal system. The principle of informal documentation is to incorporate as much documentation as possible into your discussion, in order to avoid the bother of footnoting.

In your first footnote, indicate that all later references to the source will be indicated in parentheses:

[1] Lucian, *True History and Lucius or the Ass,* Paul Turner, trans. (Bloomington: Indiana University Press, 1958), p. 49. All parenthetical page numbers refer to this edition.

The next time you refer to the source, do the following:

1. If you are making an idented quotation, indicate the page number, line number, or chapter number, preceded by a dash, immediately below the quotation, as follows:

   > Nobody grows old there, for they all stay the age they were when they first arrived, and it never gets dark. On the other hand, it never gets really light either, and they live in a sort of perpetual twilight, such as we have just before sunrise.
   >
   > —p. 39

2. If you are incorporating a quotation into your own discussion, do the following:

(a) If your sentence ends with the quotation, put the reference in parentheses immediately following the quotation marks and immediately before the period concluding your sentence:

> Sidney uses the example that "the Romaine lawes allowed no person to be carried to the warres but hee that was in the Souldiers role" (p. 189).

(b) If the quotation ends near the conclusion of your sentence, put the reference in parentheses at the end of your sentence before the period:

> William Webbe states that poetry originated in the needs for "eyther exhortations to vertue, dehortations from vices, or the prayses of some laudable thing"; that is, in public needs (p. 248).

(c) If the quotation ends far away from the end of your sentence, put the reference in parentheses immediately following the quotation mark but before your own mark of punctuation:

> If we accept as a truth Thomas Lodge's statement, "Chaucer in pleasant vein can rebuke sin vncontrold" (p. 69), then satire and comedy are the most effective modes of moral persuasion in literature.

Here is a final admonition: in all cases, consult your instructor about the procedures he wishes you to follow. He is your final authority.

A Perspective on
RESEARCH THEMES

APPENDIX Research, as distinguished from pure criticism, refers to
using primary and secondary sources for assistance in solving a literary problem. That is, in criticising a work, pure and simple, you consult only the work in front of you, while in doing research on the work, you consult not only the work but many other works that were written about it or that may shed light on it. Typical research tasks are to find out more about the historical period in which a work was written, or about prevailing climates of opinions of the times, or about what modern (or earlier) critics have said about the work. It is obvious that a certain amount of research is always necessary in any critical job, or in any theme about a literary work. Looking up words in a dictionary, for example, is only a minimal job of research, which may be supplemented by reading introductions, critical articles, encyclopedias, biographies, critical studies, histories, and the like. There is, in fact, a point at which criticism and research merge.

It is necessary that you put the job of doing research in perspective. In general, students and scholars do research in order to uncover some of the accumulated "lore" of our civilization. This lore—the knowledge that presently exists—may be compared to a large cone that is constantly being filled. At the beginnings of mankind's existence, there was little knowledge of anything, and the cone was absolutely at the bottom, at its narrowest point. As civilization progressed, more and more knowledge appeared, and the cone thus began to fill. Each time a new piece of information or a new conclusion was recorded, a little more knowledge or lore was in effect poured into the cone, which accordingly became slightly fuller and wider. Though at present our cone of knowledge is quite full, it appears to be capable of infinite growth; at least, no one is able to say at the moment that a time will ever come when every fact available in the universe will be known, so that the cone, for our purposes, is constantly filling, never filled. Knowledge keeps piling up and new disciplines keep developing. As the volume increases it becomes more and more difficult for one person to accumulate anything more than a small portion of the entirety. Indeed, historians generally agree that the last person to know virtually everything about every existing discipline was Aristotle—2,400 years ago.

If you grant, as everyone does, that you cannot learn everything, you can make a positive start by recognizing that research can provide two things: (1) a systematic understanding of a portion of the knowledge filling the cone, and (2) an understanding of, and ability to handle, the methods by which you might someday be able to make your own contributions to the filling of the cone. The principal goal of education is to help you to attain a state where you are prepared to make your own contributions. Research is a key method of reaching this goal.

Thus far we have been speaking broadly about the relevance of research to any discipline. The chemist, the anthropologist, the ecologist, the marine biologist—all employ research. Our problem here, however, is literary research. As has been said, a critical paper on a primary source (e.g., "Tone in *The Invisible Man*") without any external aids is one kind of research. In the sense usually applied in literature courses, however, research is the systematic study of library sources in order to illuminate a literary topic.

Selecting a Topic

Frequently your instructor will present you with a specific topic for your research paper. If he does you will have no problem about deciding on a topic and can go directly ahead with your research work and writing. If you have only a general research assignment, however, your first problem is to select a topic. Before you embark on that task, you should have at least a general notion of the kind of research paper you would find most congenial. The various types are as follows:

1. A paper on a particular work, say "The Character of Strether in James's *The Ambassadors*," or "Kurtz as a type of antihero in Conrad's *Heart of Darkness*," or tone, ideas, form, problems, and the like, in some work. A research paper on a single work is essentially similar to a theme on the same work. The only difference is that the research paper takes into account more views and facts than those you are likely to have without the research. This type of paper is particularly attractive if you are studying a novelist or a playwright, whose works are usually quite long.

2. A paper on an idea, or some facet of style, imagery, tone, or humor of a particular author, tracing the origins and development of the topic through a number of different works by the author. An example might be "The Idea of the True Self as Developed by Frost in His Poetry Before 1920." This type of paper is particularly suitable if you are writing on a poet whose works are mainly short, though a topic like "Shakespeare's idea of the relationships between men and women as dramatized in *The Winter's Tale, All's Well That Ends Well, A Midsummer Night's Dream,* and *As You Like It*" would also prove workable.

3. A paper based on comparison and contrast. There are two types here.

(a) A paper on an idea or some artistic quality common to two or more different authors. With such a topic you would carry out a process of writing similar to any paper in which you intend to make a comparison. Your intention might simply be to show points of similarity or contrast, or it might also be to show that one author's work may be read as a criticism of another's. A typical subject of such a paper might be "The 'hollow-man' theme in Eliot, Auden, and Dreiser," or "Goldsmith's *She Stoops to Conquer* as a response to selected sentimental dramas of the eighteenth century."

(b) A paper concentrating on opposing critical views of a particular work or body of works. Sometimes much is to be gained from an examination of differing critical opinions, say "The Conflict over *Lolita*," "The Controversy over Book IV of *Gulliver's Travels*," or "Pro and Con over Roth's *Portnoy's Complaint*." Such a study would attempt to determine the critical climate of opinion and taste to which a work did or did not appeal, and it might also aim at conclusions about whether the work was in the advance or rear guard of its time.

4. A paper showing the influence of an idea, an author, a philosophy, a political situation, or an artistic movement on specific works of an author or authors. This type of paper is like the assignment on a literary work as it reflects its historical period (Chapter 15), except that here you emphasize the background more than the work. A paper on influences can be fairly cut-and-dried (e.g., "The influence of Italian army customs and operations on the details in Hemingway's *A Farewell to Arms*"), or else it can be more abstract and psychological (e.g., "The influence of the World War I psyche on the narrator in *A Farewell to Arms*"). Before you select such a topic be sure to ask your instructor whether he believes in influences and would accept a paper on such a topic.

5. A paper on the origins of a particular work or type of work. One

avenue of research for such a paper might be to examine an author's biography to discover the germination and development of a work (e.g., "*Heart of Darkness* as an outgrowth of Conrad's experience in the Belgian Congo"). Another way of discovering origins might be to relate a work to a particular type or tradition (e.g., "*Hamlet* as revenge tragedy," or "*Mourning Becomes Electra* and its origins in the story of Agamemnon").

After you have considered these types it may be that an idea of what to write may come to you easily. Perhaps in the course you are taking you have particularly liked one author, or several authors. If so, then you might start to think along the lines of types 1, 2, and 3 right away. If you are interested in influences or in types, then the latter two kinds may suit you better.

If you have decided on no topic after re-reading the works you have liked, however, then you should carry your search for a topic into your school library. Look up your author or authors in the card catalogue. Usually the works written by the authors are included first, and then works written about the authors are second. It is in the secondary cards where you should look, for it should be your first goal to call out a relatively recent book-length critical study published by a university press. Use your judgment here: if you see a title indicating that the book is a general one dealing with the author's major works, and not just one work, then you should take that book out. Once you have it, study those chapters relevant to your base work (e.g., *Heart of Darkness* or "Youth" in a book about Joseph Conrad). Most writers of critical studies describe their purpose and plan in their introductions or first chapters. So read the first part of the book. If there is no separate chapter on the base work, use the index and go to the relevant pages. Reading in this way should soon supply you with sufficient knowledge about the issues and ideas raised by the base work to enable you to select a topic you will wish to study further. Once you have made your decision, you are ready to go ahead and gather a working bibliography.

Setting Up a Bibliography

The best way to gather a working bibliography of books and articles is to begin with major critical studies of the writer or writers. Again, go to the card catalogue and call out books that have been published by university presses. These books will usually contain selective bibliographies. Be particularly careful to read the chapters on your base work or works, and to look for the footnotes. Quite often you can circumvent many blind alleys of research if you record the names of books and articles listed in footnotes. Then refer to the bibliographies included at the ends of the books, and cull out any likely looking titles. Now, look at the dates of publication of the critical books you have been using. Let us suppose that you have been looking at three, published in 1951, 1963, and 1969. The chances are that the bibliography in a book published in 1969 will be fairly complete up through about 1966, for the writer will usually have completed his manuscript about three—or sometimes four—years before the book actually was published. What you should do then is to aim at gathering a bibliography of works published since 1966 or 1965. You may assume that writers of critical works will have done the selecting for you of the most relevant works published before that time. If you are working on an advanced paper in a graduate course, however, you should be more thorough: re-check bibliographies for possible sources that the critics might have missed. If you are going forward with a thesis, check everything in sight, because a bibliography for a thesis should aim at exhaustiveness.

THE MLA INTERNATIONAL BIBLIOGRAPHY

Fortunately for students doing literary research, the Modern Language Association of America has been providing a virtually complete bibliography of literary studies for years, not just in English and American literatures, but in the literatures of most modern foreign languages. The Association started achieving completeness in the late 1950's, and by 1969 had reached such an advanced state that it divided the bibliography into four parts. The first volume of the *1969 MLA International Bibliography* (published in 1970) is devoted to "General, English, American, Medieval and Neo-Latin, and Celtic Literatures," and it contains 9,109 entries. All four volumes are bound together in library editions, just as the earlier bibliographies were bound separately for reference-room use. Most university and college libraries have a set of these bibliographies readily available on open shelves or tables. There are, of course, many other bibliographies that are useful for students doing research, many more than can be mentioned here meaningfully. As an entry into the vast field of bibliography on English studies, you might consult Donald F. Bond, compiler, *A Reference Guide to English Studies* [A Revision of the *Bibliographical Guide to English Studies* by Tom Peete Cross] (Chicago: University of Chicago Press [Phoenix Books], 1962). This work lists a total of 1,230 separate studies and bibliographies on which further research may be based. Section VII lists 100 "Periodical Publications Containing Reviews and Bibliographies." There is more here than can be readily imagined. For most purposes, however, the *MLA International Bibliography* is more than adequate. Remember that as you progress in your reading, the footnotes and bibliographies in the works you consult also will constitute an unfolding bibliography.

The *MLA International Bibliography* is organized for your convenience. If your author is Richard Wright, for example, look him up under "American Literature V. Twentieth Century," the relevant listing for all twentieth-century American writers. If your author is Shakespeare, refer to "English Literature VI. Renaissance and Elizabethan." So many books and articles appear each year on Shakespeare that the bibliography lists the separate plays alphabetically under the Shakespeare entry. Depending on your topic, of course, you will find most of the bibliography you need under the author's last name. Journal references are abbreviated, but a lengthy list explaining abbreviations appears at the beginning of the volume. Using the MLA bibliographies, you should begin with the most recent one and then go backward to your stopping point. Be sure to get the complete information, especially volume numbers and years of publication, for each article and book you wish to consult.

If your research carries you into a great number of primary sources, then you should rely on *The Cambridge Bibliography of English Literature,* in five volumes. The *CBEL* is selective for secondary sources, but is invaluable as a general guide to the canon and the various editions of individual authors' works. If you want to see a first edition of poems by the eighteenth-century poet Christopher Smart, for example, the *CBEL* will describe the edition, and it also will describe an acceptable or standard modern edition of the poems if you want the best reading edition.

You are now ready to consult your sources and to take notes.

Taking Notes and Paraphrasing Material

There are many ways of taking notes, but the consensus is that the best method is to use note cards. If you have never used cards before, you might profit from consulting any one of a number of handbooks and special workbooks on research. Robert M. Gorrell and Charlton Laird present a lucid and methodical explanation of taking notes on cards in their *Modern English Handbook,* 5th ed. (Englewood Cliffs: Prentice-Hall, Inc., 1972), pp. 86–96, and any handbook that you have used will contain a similar discussion. The principal virtue of using cards is that cards may be classified, numbered, renumbered, shuffled, used in different contexts, thrown away, and arranged in a useful order when you actually start writing your research paper. If some other system is more in line with your own feelings, however, and you are willing to sacrifice the flexibility and freedom of cards, so be it.

As you take notes, be sure always to get the sources and pages for every entry, no matter how short. Record only one thing on each card—one quotation, one paraphrase, one observation—never two or more. You lose flexibility if you put two things on a single card.

A major problem in taking notes, a problem that can cause grief later on in writing, is to distinguish copied material from your own words. Here you must be super-cautious. Always—*always*—put quotation marks around *every direct quotation you copy verbatim from a source.* Make the quotation marks immediately, before you forget, so that you will always know that the words of your notes within quotation marks are the words of another writer.

Often, as you take a note, you may use some of your own words, and some of the words from your source. In cases like this it is even more important to be cautious. Put quotation marks around *every word* that you take directly from the source, even if you find yourself literally with a note that resembles a picket fence. At a later time, when you begin writing your paper, your memory of what is yours and not yours will become dim, and if you use another's words in your own paper, but do not grant recognition, you lay yourself open to the charge of plagiarism. It is better to be fussy about quotation marks.

PARAPHRASING

The best principle in taking extensive notes is to aim at re-phrasing or paraphrasing the sources. A paraphrase is a re-statement of resource material using your own words. A paraphrase can never quite duplicate the source, and some people maintain that paraphrasing even at best is misleading. When you are doing research, however, you are responsible for getting down ideas and facts that you find, and therefore you must work on paraphrasing.

The biggest problem in paraphrasing is genuinely to put the ideas into words that are independent of the source. Often it is difficult to find any better words than those in the original. If you have already discovered this difficulty, do not be surprised. The writer of the original unquestionably put things in the best way he could. Improving on the original, or just stating the same ideas and facts as in the original, is therefore not easy. Your sole aim should be to make a short transcription of the substance of the original. Retain the ideas as faithfully as possible, and if you cannot avoid using some of the words in your source, or if your own words are in identical order with the original, be sure to use quotation marks and also to observe that your order coincides with that of the original.

To see the problems of paraphrase, let us look at a paragraph of original criticism, and then see how a student doing research might take notes on it. The paragraph is by Professor Maynard Mack, from an essay entitled "The World of Hamlet," originally published in *The Yale Review*, XLI (1952), and reprinted in *Twentieth Century Interpretations of Hamlet*, David Bevington, ed. (Englewood Cliffs: Prentice-Hall, Inc., 1968), p. 57:

> The powerful sense of mortality in *Hamlet* is conveyed to us, I think, in three ways. First, there is the play's emphasis on human weakness, the instability of human purpose, the subjection of humanity to fortune—all that we might call the aspect of failure in man. Hamlet opens this theme in Act I, when he describes how from that single blemish, perhaps not even the victim's fault, a man's whole character may take corruption. Claudius dwells on it again, to an extent that goes far beyond the needs of the occasion, while engaged in seducing Laertes to step behind the arras of a seemer's world and dispose of Hamlet by a trick. Time qualifies everything, Claudius says, including love, including purpose. As for love—it has a "plurisy" in it and dies of its own too much. As for purpose—"That we would do, We should do when we would, for this 'would' changes, And hath abatements and delays as many As there are tongues, are hands, are accidents; And then this 'should' is like a spendthrift's sigh, That hurts by easing." The player-king, in his long speeches to his queen in the play within the play, sets the matter in a still darker light. She means these protestations of undying love, he knows, but our purposes depend on our memory, and our memory fades fast. Or else, he suggests, we propose something to ourselves in a condition of strong feeling, but then the feeling goes, and with it the resolve. Or else our fortunes change, he adds, and with these our loves: "The great man down, you mark his favorite flies." The subjection of human aims to fortune is a reiterated theme in *Hamlet*, as subsequently in *Lear*. Fortune is the harlot goddess in whose secret parts men like Rosencrantz and Guildenstern live and thrive; the strumpet who threw down Troy and Hecuba and Priam; the outrageous foe whose slings and arrows a man of principle must suffer or seek release in suicide. Horatio suffers them with composure: he is one of the blessed few "Whose blood and judgment are so well co-mingled That they are not a pipe for fortune's finger To sound what stop she please." For Hamlet the task is of a greater difficulty.

It is obvious that no note can do full justice to such a well-substantiated paragraph of criticism. There are subleties and shades, and a mingling of discourse with interpretive and appreciative reminiscences and quotations from the play, that cannot be duplicated briefly, and which will be lost when put into other words. But if you wish to take notes at all you must make arbitrary decisions about what to transcribe. If you want mainly the topic of such a paragraph, the following type of note might be sufficient:

> *Hamlet* shows a mood of "mortality" in three ways. The first is an emphasis on human incapacity and "weakness." Corruption, forgetfulness, loss of enthusiasm, bad luck, misery—all these suit the mood of approaching death (Mack, p. 57).

This note is brief, concentrating on material in the early part of the paragraph rather than the middle and end. For such a short note, it is reasonable to paraphrase the *first* part of a paragraph of criticism, for it is there that the writer most often states his topic idea. Observe also that the note contains a sentence in which the note-taker has tried to describe in general terms the details substantiating the topic.

Let us suppose that you wish to take a fuller note, in anticipation of including in your paper not just the topic of the paragraph, but also some of the supporting detail. Such a note might look like this:

> Mack cites "three ways" in which a "powerful sense of mortality" is shown in *Hamlet*. The first is the showing of man's "weakness," "instability," and helplessness before fate. In support, Mack refers to Hamlet's early speech on a single fault leading to corruption, also to Claudius's speech (in the scene persuading Laertes to trick Hamlet). The player-king also talks about his queen's forgetfulness and therefore inconstancy by default. As slaves to fortune, Rosencrantz and Guildenstern are examples. Horatio is not a slave, however. Hamlet's case is by far the worst of all (Mack, p. 57).

When the time comes to write a paper, it would be appropriate to use any part of a note like this one. The note-taker's phraseology is almost completely his own, and the few quotations are given quotation marks. As long as the original writer is given proper credit for ideas used, and *the page number of the original is cited,* the note-taker could make almost any use he chose of the material in the notes.

With only a little practice, you should be able to paraphrase original criticism. Always keep in mind the objective of getting ideas into your own words, no matter how great the temptation to quote the original directly. Once again, and again, always be careful to use quotation marks when you retain original wording.

As you read the items in your bibliography, continue to take notes, and do not understimate the value of making your own commentaries as you go. The best time to get your original ideas down on paper is precisely the moment when they occur to you as a result of your reading. Often you may notice a detail that the critic has missed, or you may see the hint of an idea that the critic does not develop. When such lucky chances occur, you should create your own note. Label it clearly as your own, and you may find that you are well on the way toward a major idea in your final theme.

Planning Your Theme and Using Your Research

When you have finished taking notes on your reading, you are ready to go ahead with the job of planning and beginning your paper. Remember that research is a technique, and that the use of research does not necessarily imply that all research papers must be long. Research may be applied in a short critical paper as well as in a longer one. The length of your theme is usually a requirement of the assignment. Naturally, a short paper would require you to bring in fewer results of research than a longer paper.

The common problem in preparing and writing a research theme is to determine your own dependence on the sources. Should you base your theme entirely on the sources, or should you attempt to interpret them or argue with them? How many of your own ideas should you include in your theme? To what extent should you include interpretations of the base text that originally was the concern of the criticism and commentary you have read? These are the major questions that might occur to you as you plan your theme.

In fact, the research that you have done does not, or should not, alter the form of the theme you write. The principal difference between what you write without the aid of extensive research and what you write with this aid is (1) the ideas and facts you use from others, and (2) the ideas that others have caused you to have. There should theoretically be no difference in the type of theme you finally write. Thus, you should still write a theme like the analysis of a specific problem, the study of an idea, the treatment of point of view, imagery, structure, and so on, even though you are adding information from other sources to your theme. The real problem in writing a research theme is that you must integrate your results into a coherent theme that is somehow still uniquely your own. In a word, most problems in research themes are problems in composition.

There are accordingly a number of methods of employing research as you write. In most themes you will probably find that you may use them all. The one goal you should keep in front of you, however, is that the pattern of research should be to work from the *known* to the *unknown*. Remember the image of the cone. The research you have done is your examination of what already is known—already in the cone—and the pattern of your use of this research is to arrive at conclusions that have not already existed—to add your own ideas to the cone. This is not to say that as a student you should expect your research work to create any new directions immediately, but it is to say that the *pattern* of your education should always point toward creativity and originality. This pattern is vital.

Here are some ways of incorporating research into a theme:

1. *Providing conclusions and factual information from others.* The first use of research, and the most common, is to indicate what others have said by way of providing conclusions and/or factual information about a work or problem. It goes almost without saying that nobody can draw conclusions unless there is a factual basis for them. Facts cannot be

imagined (though they often are), but must be discovered. For this reason you will constantly find yourself quoting primary and secondary sources for information to support your conclusions. Here is a fragment of material showing how research can bring information into a paper. The subject is Henry James's view of reality in his novel *The Ambassadors:*

> To a considerable degree in *The Ambassadors,* James writes out of a conviction that reality is psychological and internal, not objective and external. One commentator on the book has found in it a philosophical conviction which he traces to John Locke and the British empiricists, to whom "man's basic entity . . . was a mental substance . . . [and in] the mental substance alone a knowable reality." [1] In *The Ambassadors* James, by making Lambert Strether's mind and emotions the medium through which the world is seen, dramatizes just such a position. Form and content then complement one another perfectly, and their interaction creates a philosophical position which has properly been termed by one critic, Tony Tanner, "epistemological scepticism." [2] Tanner, one of the most perceptive critics on James, has observed that epistemology was one of James's primary interests. In Tanner's view, James was constantly facing the question not only of how human beings perceive the "endless flow of sensations" surrounding them "from the world," but also of how they *"should"* look at the world.[3]

The major problem in using research in this way—as a supply of information and interpretation and as substantiation for argument—is that the writer too easily passes the responsibility for his own thinking onto the shoulders of his sources. If you look at things from your instructor's point of view momentarily, how can he judge your work if all you do is to describe what others have said? You would then be like a master of ceremonies, introducing various performers who then do their acts. If in writing a research paper you see yourself mainly as a master of ceremonies, then you are really not performing yourself. Yet it is only on the basis of your own performance that you can be judged. Clearly, *you must always attempt to create your own thoughts and observations, even when doing research.*

    2. *Using research as a springboard into argument or agreement with a critic.* A second use of research—and a most important one—is that of examining what one or several critics or commentators have said in order (a) to dispute with them, or (b) to agree with them. This use forces you to be argumentative, and in this way you place the responsibility for thinking squarely where it belongs—on your own shoulders. As you create arguments, you are also fulfilling that pattern of originality that should be your educational goal. You may not be filling the cone, but you are

[1] John Henry Raleigh, "Henry James: The Poetics of Empiricism," *PMLA,* LXVI (1951), 111. Hereafter cited as "Raleigh."

[2] Tony Tanner, *The Reign of Wonder: Naivety and Reality in American Literature* (New York: Harper and Row, 1967), p. 288. Hereafter cited as *Tanner.*

[3] *Tanner,* p. 267.

doing what is necessary for filling it eventually. Beethoven had to learn scales and harmony before he became a composer. To the degree that you build upon the works of critics and commentators in order to show through your conclusions that they were right or wrong, you are fashioning your thoughts in patterns that make a contribution to knowledge.

An example showing the use of research as a springboard into argument follows. The example is about the character of Strether, the narrator in James's *The Ambassadors*. The argument in the example is one opposing the details first brought out, but the example would be equally valid if the argument were to be in agreement. If a writer wrote in agreement, however, he would presumably have to add to the arguments presented in the section laying out the details. If one argues in disagreement, he can concentrate on rebutting arguments, and furnishing details in support. In the following example, the material representing the writer's attempt to be original by disputing an established critical opinion will be italicized:

> Opinion is strong that Strether is to be taken with unreserved acceptance. To some critics he possesses "the soul" of an artist, to use Leon Edel's words.[1] Since James admired art and the aesthetically responsive, proponents of this view assume that he admired Strether too. To others the argument for viewing Strether as having positive "meaning function" within the novel lies on James's conviction that the growth of consciousness is also a growth toward "beatitude." [2] Dorothea Brook, in her book *The Ordeal of Consciousness in Henry James,* speaks in religious terms of the "redemptive" quality of suffering when the sufferer has the "supreme gift of consciousness—specifically self-consciousnes." [3] When Strether takes leave of Europe in the final pages of the book, a solid body of criticism has it that he has undergone a virtual apotheosis. Jay Martin, for example, claims that Strether has made a "divine ascension into a state beyond good and evil." [4]
>
> *But it is difficult to believe that James, in a mature novel like* The Ambassadors, *created major characters who were without fault. He was too relentlessly honest, too perceptive, and too concerned with the morally grey areas of life to see character so simplistically. It does not seem reasonable to separate the positive nature of Strether's perceptions from the negative actions which he takes as a result of these perceptions. Above all, it is the Strether of the book with whom we must deal, not the ideas toward art or morals which James may have expressed elsewhere. That James surrounds Strether so completely with ironies and comic circumstances makes the position untenable that Strether is a risen hero.*

This passage is no more than a fragment, but it is possible to see in it a desirable turn of mind. The writer is pushing beyond the frontier of

[1] Henry James, *The Ambassadors,* Leon Edel, ed. (Boston: Houghton Mifflin Co., 1960), p. vii.

[2] John Henry Raleigh, "Henry James: The Poetics of Empiricism," *PMLA,* LXVI (1951), 109.

[3] (Cambridge, Eng.: Cambridge University Press, 1962), pp. 16, 22.

[4] *Harvest of Change: American Literature 1865–1914* (Englewood Cliffs: Prentice-Hall, Inc., 1967), p. 356.

established views. Presumably he would continue the line of dispute he is taking, and would draw on the original text for evidence that he would use to support his position. It might well be that the position taken—as the position that you may take—may be open to dispute itself, but that does not really matter. What does matter is the pattern of pushing outward toward something new.

3. *Using research in order to discover a new area of discussion.*   The third use of research, and one closely related to the second, is to discover and show what others have not yet done. Once you can show that a vacuum exists, then it follows that you can fill it. If you have studied a great number of sources, and have observed that none of these deals with a particular insight or interpretation that you have unearthed on your own, or if no critic deals with a major point of comparison that you have raised independently, it seems clear that you have staked out an original area for yourself. It is by such means that a great deal of scholarship is originated. Luckily, it frequently happens to many students that in reading a number of critics, such new ideas present themselves. Perhaps you have had the experience yourself of uncovering an idea, and then crossing your fingers as you read further sources in the hope that the next book or article will not contain your idea. If no one has announced or developed your idea, the area was clear, and you could move in and build on it.

Many writers have done just that. If you examine much critical work, you will notice that writers often begin their studies with a rapid review of existing scholarship on their topic—and this method is true of all disciplines, not only of literary studies. The writer usually conducts this review as part of a strategy to show that his topic is going to be original and new. A sample of this technique is the following, a section from a paper that treats the subject of Kurtz, a major figure in Joseph Conrad's tale *Heart of Darkness:*

> There is near unanimity among the critics that Kurtz represents the good man gone sour. T. S. Eliot in "The Hollow Men" quotes Conrad's phrase "Mistah Kurtz—he dead," as his epigraph, showing his belief that Kurtz is symbolic of the twentieth-century hollow man. Lilian Feder describes Marlow's voyage to recover Kurtz as having parallels with Aeneas's descent into the underworld as described in Book VI of Virgil's *Aeneid*.[1] Along similar lines, William L. Godshalk describes Kurtz as a "diabolical Christ" figure.[2] Both Douglas Hewett [3] and Albert J. Guerard [4] deal with the principle of evil represented by Kurtz. Frederick R. Karl describes Kurtz as a "god devil" [5] and claims that "the story is about the loss of responsible heart." It would probably be difficult to find a critic who did not deal with some aspect of the evil represented by Kurtz.

[1] "Marlow's Descent Into Hell," *Nineteenth-Century Fiction,* IX (1955), 280–92.
[2] "Kurtz as Diabolical Christ," *Discourse,* XII (1969), 100–07.
[3] Conrad: *A Reassessment,* 2nd ed. (Chester Springs, Penna.: Dufour, 1969).
[4] *Conrad the Novelist* (Cambridge, Mass.: Harvard University Press, 1958).
[5] *A Reader's Guide to Joseph Conrad* (New York: Noonday Press, 1960), p. 138.

> *None of the critics, however, treats the idea that Kurtz is a type derived from a long line of antiheroes who represent the reverse side of an optimistic coin. When the framers of the U.S. Constitution created our system of representative government, they were optimistic, but when they created the electoral college as a direct check on the popular vote, they must have been thinking that at the heart of people even in the new world there lurked the same darkness that possessed Kurtz. It is this same awareness that one can see in Swift's Yahoos and in Browning's satiric portrait of the Bishop in "The Bishop Orders His Tomb at St. Praxed's Church." It is worth exploring the parallels that Kurtz has with the Yahoos and with Browning's Bishop, together with other satirical portraits by Browning.*

While you are likely to use this technique frequently at the beginning of your paper, and at the beginnings of various sections of a long research paper, it is equally useful anywhere as you progress in your various points. Here is a short fragment from the middle of an argument, on the same topic, Kurtz:

> One may then see that Kurtz is shown surrounded by darkness, unrelieved by some of the light that Browning casts on the character of his Bishop. The point to make about the darkness is that it is *always* operative in human beings, nor is it ever absent. Some of the studies on Kurtz do not sufficiently recognize the permanence of the darkness. They fail to emphasize that Kurtz is to be seen as a typical human being, not a freak. The darkness seems to be accidental to them: they claim that Kurtz has sunk into an abyss "darker than savagery itself," in the words of Wilfred S. Dowden,[1] or else they speak of Kurtz's "corruption and disintegration," as does J. I. M. Stewart.[2] The assumption here is that Kurtz is different because he has fallen away from civilization, but in truth the critics have failed to make an important point. The only element distinguishing Kurtz from anyone else is that he has had the opportunity to indulge himself without fear of reprisal. In a position of power like that of St. Praxed's Bishop, he too—and so too, perhaps, alas, all of us—would burn the church in order to disguise his thefts. The darkness is always around us; the Yahoo is always a part of us.

Concluding Advice

Whenever you write a research theme, remember that research is a means to an end. The object of securing facts and opinions from other writers is to secure your own mind as you go ahead to construct your own views of the world. By studying literary and social historians and literary critics, you can learn their methods along with the things that they can teach you. When you write, you should apply their methods for your

---

[1] *Joseph Conrad: The Imaged Style* (Nashville: Vanderbilt University Press, 1970), p. 72.
[2] *Joseph Conrad* (New York: Dodd, Mead & Co., 1968), p. 77.

own purposes. Abandon now the notion that a research paper is to be only a recitation of what others have said. Acquire the notion that the research paper is an occasion for launching yourself into the pattern of human learning. In a way, you might look at your entire education as an experience in research. The goal is not just to acquire, but to build. If you are to be successful, you must see yourself as preparing for a future in which you will be supplying the facts and interpretations upon which others may build; you will have the responsibility of applying known facts and principles to problems for which as yet there are no solutions.

Index